Expectations and the
Structure of Share Prices

A National Bureau
of Economic Research
Monograph

Expectations and the Structure of Share Prices

John G. Cragg and
Burton G. Malkiel

The University of Chicago Press

Chicago and London

JOHN G. CRAGG is professor of economics and head of the Department of Economics at the University of British Columbia. BURTON G. MALKIEL is dean of the Yale School of Organization and Management and the William S. Beinecke Professor of Management Studies and professor of economics at Yale University.

The University of Chicago Press, Chicago 60637
The University of Chicago Press, Ltd., London

Library of Congress Cataloging in Publication Data

Cragg, J. G.
   Expectations and the structure of share prices.

   (A National Bureau of Economic Research monograph)
   Bibliography: p.
   Includes index.
   1. Stock—Prices—Mathematical models. 2. Corporate profits—Forecasting—Mathematical models. 3. Capital assets pricing model. I. Malkiel, Burton Gordon. II. Title. III. Series.
   HG4636.C7 1982   332.63′222′0724   82-8388
   ISBN 0-226-11668-9   AACR2

Relation of the Directors to the
Work and Publications of the
National Bureau of Economic Research

1. The object of the National Bureau of Economic Research is to ascertain and to present to the public important economic facts and their interpretation in a scientific and impartial manner. The Board of Directors is charged with the reponsibility of ensuring that the work of the National Bureau is carried on in strict conformity with this object.

2. The President of the National Bureau shall submit to the Board of Directors, or to its Executive Committee, for their formal adoption all specific proposals for research to be instituted.

3. No research report shall be published by the National Bureau until the President has sent each member of the Board a notice that a manuscript is recommended for publication and that in the President's opinion it is suitable for publication in accordance with the principles of the National Bureau. Such notification will include an abstract or summary of the manuscript's content and a response form for use by those Directors who desire a copy of the manuscript for review. Each manuscript shall contain a summary drawing attention to the nature and treatment of the problem studied, the character of the data and their utilization in the report, and the main conclusions reached.

4. For each manuscript so submitted, a special committee of the Directors (including Directors Emeriti) shall be appointed by majority agreement of the President and Vice Presidents (or by the Executive Committee in case of inability to decide on the part of the President and Vice Presidents), consisting of three Directors selected as nearly as may be one from each general division of the Board. The names of the special manuscript committee shall be stated to each Director when notice of the proposed publication is submitted to him. It shall be the duty of each member of the special manuscript committee to read the manuscript. If each member of the manuscript committee signifies his approval within thirty days of the transmittal of the manuscript, the report may be published. If at the end of that period any member of the manuscript committee withholds his approval, the President shall then notify each member of the Board, requesting approval or disapproval of publication, and thirty days additional shall be granted for this purpose. The manuscript shall then not be published unless at least a majority of the entire Board who shall have voted on the proposal within the time fixed for the receipt of votes shall have approved.

5. No manuscript may be published, though approved by each member of the special manuscript committee, until forty-five days have elapsed from the transmittal of the report in manuscript form. The interval is allowed for the receipt of any memorandum of dissent or reservation, together with a brief statement of his reasons, that any member may wish to express; and such memorandum of dissent or reservation shall be published with the manuscript if he so desires. Publication does not, however, imply that each member of the Board has read the manuscript, or that either members of the Board in general or the special committee have passed on its validity in every detail.

6. Publications of the National Bureau issued for informational purposes concerning the work of the Bureau and its staff, or issued to inform the public of activities of Bureau staff, and volumes issued as a result of various conferences involving the National Bureau shall contain a specific disclaimer noting that such publication has not passed through the normal review procedures required in this resolution. The Executive Committee of the Board is charged with review of all such publications from time to time to ensure that they do not take on the character of formal research reports of the National Bureau, requiring formal Board approval.

7. Unless otherwise determined by the Board or exempted by the terms of paragraph 6, a copy of this resolution shall be printed in each National Bureau publication.

(Resolution adopted October 25, 1926, as revised through September 30, 1974)

Contents

Preface

This monograph investigates a number of interrelated questions about the formation of expectations and the pricing of capital assets. Central to the empirical work is a unique body of expectations data collected over the decade of the 1960s. The book first describes the data and then examines a number of questions regarding the consensus, accuracy, and completeness of the forecasts as well as the underlying process that appears to generate the forecasts. The book then turns to the development of a restatement of financial-asset valuation theory and goes on to use the expectations data we have collected to test the model. We find that our data permit far more satisfactory tests of valuation models than have been possible before and that they help provide important insights into the structure of security prices. Because we believe that these data will be helpful to other researchers, we have published the data themselves in as much detail as our respondents would permit.

More than a decade has passed since the data were originally collected, and so they may not represent the most up-to-date practices. There are, however, important advantages to our having waited a considerable period before publishing our results. First, one of the questions we ask concerns the accuracy of the forecast data and it is necessary to wait a considerable period in order to compare realizations with long-run forecasts. Indeed, in a preliminary article dealing with just the first two years of our data, we were not able to provide proper tests of accuracy because the forecast period had not yet elapsed (see Cragg and Malkiel 1968).

There is a second advantage in a delay, in that the data were collected during a period when the capital-asset pricing model and other, more recent valuation models were not generally known in the financial community. Hence the data were clearly not influenced by now popular notions concerning how assets are actually valued in the market. In this sense, the data can be considered uncontaminated and should provide fair tests of alternative valuation models.

A major data-gathering effort such as the one reflected in this study requires considerable financial support, and we have been enormously aided by several institutions. A vital contribution was made by the Institute for Quantitative Research in Finance. That institute was the original sponsor of this study and not only provided important financial help but also aided in the recruitment of a large number of the institutional investors which cooperated in the study. Princeton University's Financial Research Center—which in turn has been generously aided by the Merrill Foundation, the John Weinberg Foundation, and the Princeton University Class of 1950—provided invaluable support during the course of the study. Finally, the book was supported in part by the Debt-Equity Project, which is sponsored by a grant to the National Bureau of Economic Research by the American Council of Life Insurance. The National Bureau of Economic Research not only provided funds during the final stages of the study but also, through its seminars and meetings and through the dissemination of its working papers, provided important assistance to us in completing the manuscript.

It would simply be impossible to thank individually all of the people who offered suggestions and help during the course of this study. We should, however, make special note of the individuals who read the final manuscript and offered extremely valuable comments. We record our deepest debt of gratitude to G. C. Archibald, Philip Dybvig, Benjamin Friedman, Stewart Myers, and Richard Quandt. They all made important substantive contributions but are, of course, blameless for any errors that may remain.

A study such as this which involves considerable computer work could not have been done without the help of many research assistants. We would like to thank Tom Chung, Deborah Holman, Darryl Pressley, James Rauch, William Silbey, and especially Stephen Williams for invaluable support.

Particular thanks are due to Elvira Krespach, our principal computer programmer over the course of the study. We also were helped by several people in producing the final manuscript. We are grateful to Constance Dixon, Phyllis Durepos, Maryse Ellis, Murriel Hawley, Louise Olson, Helen Talar, and especially Barbara Hickey, who oversaw the production work and typed much of the final draft.

John G. Cragg
Burton G. Malkiel

1   Nature and Sources of Data

This study involves a number of interrelated topics concerned with the formation of expectations and with the pricing of capital assets. Our objective is to develop and test realistic models of common stock prices and returns based on expectations held by participants in the market. In order to provide tests of security-price models that are more satisfactory than those previously published, we have collected a unique body of expectations data over the decade of the 1960s.[1] These data are also of interest in their own right and worthy of detailed study. After a brief outline of the plan of the book and an indication of the study's major findings, this chapter describes these data.

1.1 Outline of the Study

Our first major area of research interest is the expectations data themselves, which are discussed in the present chapter.

Among the issues we will be considering in chapter 2, the following sorts of questions are indicative of our focus: •

1. What is the extent of consensus among forecasters? Do the data suggest that models of capital-asset pricing based on homogeneous expectations are likely to provide a valid description of reality?

2. How accurate are the forecasts? A variety of tests will be used comparing the accuracy of the forecasts with a number of predictions derived from historical data.

---

1. Some partial results using a portion of the data from the first two years of the sample were published in Cragg and Malkiel (1968) and Malkiel and Cragg (1970). Most of the tests reported in this study are new, however.

3. Are the forecasts consistent with the rational-expectations hypothesis?

4. Is there information in the forecasts that is not reflected in market prices and that might be profitably exploited?

5. To what extent do the forecasts seem to arise from the forecasters' first predicting a few key variables (such as national income) and then estimating the effect of these variables on each company?

To summarize some of the major findings of chapter 2, we found that a common-factor model seemed consistent with the data. For most years, at least two factors are indicated, and we interpret this finding as suggesting that the forecasts do rest on certain economic variables such as real growth, inflation, etc. Despite the apparent applicability of the common-factor model, however, we did find considerable lack of consensus in the forecasts. Forecast accuracy can be described as poor. While the forecasts were superior to extrapolations from past observations (which were of essentially no use at all), we found no information in the forecasts that was not already impounded in market prices. Finally, our investigation of the rationality of the forecasts produced mixed results. While certain narrow implications of the rational-expectations hypothesis could be rejected, we could not reject the broader implications of the hypothesis; i.e., there was no evidence of readily available information that was not contained in the forecasts and no information in the forecasts that was not contained in market prices.

The next major focus of the study is on developing a restatement of capital-asset pricing theory so that we can use the expectations data we have collected to test the model. Chapter 3 is devoted to the development of that model and to problems of its empirical implementation using our data.

Following the seminal contributions of Markowitz (1959) and Tobin (1958) in formulating a model for portfolio selection, a considerable body of theory has developed concerning the pricing of capital assets in organized securities markets. Some of the most important early contributions were made by Sharpe (1964), Lintner (1965), and Mossin (1966). The main feature of the theory is that the values of all securities are determined simultaneously. In this general-equilibrium framework, using a mean-variance approach, a very simple structure of capital-asset prices is derived in which the expected returns of individual securities are a simple linear function of the security's systematic or nondiversifiable risk (usually called the security's beta).

The original capital-asset pricing model has now been widely questioned on the basis of empirical evidence and a large number of modified theories has been proposed. While the evidence points to a reasonably linear long-run relationship between risk and return, where risk is taken to be a security's nondiversifiable risk, actual and theoretical relationships do not correspond, with the measured relationship being much flatter than the theoretical relationship. Moreover, the risk-return relationships over different time periods have been erratic and the estimates of the so-called riskless market rate of return seem unrealistic. Finally, estimated betas are quite sensitive to the index against which they are measured and some researchers have doubted whether the tests supporting the theory are statistically valid. Thus serious questions have been raised about the actual relationship between risk and return as well as about the underlying theory generating the relationship.

Since the theory does not appear fully supported by the data, it is legitimate to look closely at the assumptions of the underlying model. The critical assumptions upon which the capital-asset pricing model rests include the absence of transaction costs, identical beliefs among investors about the distribution of future returns, the ability to borrow or sell short at going market rates, and the existence of a risk-free security. Not only are these assumptions unrealistic, but some of them are in fact contradicted by expectations data we have collected from security analysts that imply considerable differences of opinion regarding future returns. Thus, in order to arrive at a theoretical structure suitable for empirical testing, it is necessary to alter the capital-asset pricing model to account for a variety of market imperfections.

Our approach is to develop a diversification model of security valuation using the return generation process suggested by Ross (1976, 1977). We need not rely on all the assumptions of the traditional capital-asset pricing model but rather on the common observation that many portfolios containing the securities of major corporations can be considered to be widely diversified. Within the assumed return generation process, this observation yields the same kind of valuation formula as the Ross arbitrage pricing model, though on somewhat different grounds. Specifically, investors can be assumed to regard the covariances of the various returns as stemming from their linear dependence on a limited number of random factors. These "factors" might represent the stock market as a whole, the level of economic activity as represented by national income, interest rates, inflation, and so on. In addition to considering models of security returns, we examine some valuation models that are explicitly formulated with respect to security prices.

Chapter 4 presents an empirical analysis of the various models of security prices and returns. To our knowledge, there has been only limited empirical testing of asset pricing models that has employed proper expectations measures. The availability of a continuous set of anticipations data permits the substitution of *ex ante* for *ex post* measures of rates of return. We are aware of one other major study, that by Friend,

Westerfield, and Granito (1978), that has used anticipations data in tests of asset pricing models, but this study was done only for four time periods and only for the simple capital-asset pricing model (CAPM).

In performing our tests, we use the expectations data we have collected to generate a series of expected returns during the 1960s for a large cross section of companies. We then test the simple CAPM as well as a variety of multifactor models. Not only the expected returns data but also the risk proxies represent expectational measures. A major strength of our empirical tests is that we are able to generate both *ex ante* risk and *ex ante* return measures directly from our data.

We conclude that the security returns implied by our expectations data are related to "systematic" risk elements appropriately defined. Particularly important are risk measures derived from the expectations data we have collected. We also find that security prices can be explained far better by our expectational measures than with historical data. Moreover, a multifactor model of security returns seems more satisfactory than the simple CAPM. It seems clear that risk should not be considered a one-dimensional variable as became popular after the initial development of the CAPM. We find moreover that valuation relationships are not stable over time and that different systematic risk influences vary in importance over time. For example, early in the 1960s inflation and interest-rate risk played little role in security valuations, yet later in the decade they played a far more important role than the traditional risk measure based on the simple CAPM. Finally, we find that the expectations data together with the estimated valuation relationships cannot be used to isolate "undervalued" or "overvalued" securities. There is evidence that our expectations data are fully impounded in current prices, leaving no opportunity for earning excess returns. In the final analysis, then, our study confirms the existence of efficient markets.

One of the most intriguing of our findings concerns a new risk proxy that appears to be particularly useful in explaining both expected returns for securities and actual stock prices. We found that the best single risk measure available for each company was the extent to which different forecasters were not in agreement about that company's future growth. It is possible to interpret this measure as representing specific risk, in which case the finding might be taken to be inconsistent with recent models of security valuation including our own. On the other hand, our risk variable may indirectly measure the sensitivity of different securities to underlying common factors and thus serve as a most effective proxy for a variety of *systematic* risks. At the very least, our results suggest that risk undoubtedly has dimensions not fully captured by the covariances with market indexes or by other variables that have dominated recent work on valuation. They also suggest that the variance of analysts' forecasts may represent the most effective risk proxy available.

1.2 The Participating Security Analysts and the Company Sample

The major task of professional security analysts is to forecast the future earnings and dividends of the companies they study. These forecasts are of particular interest because in them it is possible to observe divergence of opinion among different individuals dealing with the same quantities. But expectations regarding earnings (and dividend) growth are not the only important variables that they must calculate. Current accounting conventions are so far from uniform that estimates of precisely what a firm may have earned in a prior accounting period may also be considered to be an expectational variable.

The data used in this study were collected from nineteen investment firms. The participants were recruited through requests to three organizations. The first was a group of firms which used computers for financial analysis and met periodically to discuss mutual problems. The second was the New York Society of Financial Analysts. The third was the Institute for Quantitative Research in Finance, an organization of investment firms formed to encourage the development of quantitative techniques in finance.[2] From these groups, twenty-five firms agreed initially to participate in the study.

Unfortunately, not all volunteers were able to supply data useful to this study, either because the actual supplying of data would have been too burdensome (the data being kept for internal records in a form that made their extraction difficult) or because the data supplied were not comparable to other data being used by us (usually because the expectations were formulated at different dates). Because one of our main objectives was to examine differences and similarities in predictions of the same quantities, such data were not used in the present study. As a result the expectations data from only nineteen of these firms were finally used. Even among these nineteen firms there was far from complete overlap either in the corporations for which the predictions were available or in the particular type of expectations data that they were able to provide.[3] Moreover, only one firm supplied both long- and short-term growth rates for the same years.[4] Typically, the firms published (or made available) for their clients either long- or short-term growth rates but not both. Thus we can consider that, in effect, we have two samples, one of long-term, the other of short-term forecasts.

Of the nineteen participating firms, five were large money-center banks heavily involved in trust management, five were mutual-fund

---

2. This same organization provided financial support to the authors during the data-gathering phase.

3. We are deeply grateful to the participating firms, which wish to remain anonymous.

4. Two additional firms supplied both long- and short-term growth rates but not in the same years.

management companies responsible for the portfolio selections of several mutual funds, five were brokerage houses involved in servicing institutional clients as well as the general public, two were investment advisory firms, and two were pension-fund managers.

We would not argue that these estimates necessarily give an accurate picture of general market expectations. It would, however, seem reasonable to suggest that they are representative of opinions of some of the largest professional investment institutions and that they may not be wholly unrepresentative of more general expectations. Since investors consult professional investment institutions in forming their own expectations, individuals' expectations may be strongly influenced—and so reflect—those of their advisers. That several of our participating firms find it worthwhile to publish these projections and provide them to their customers provides prima facie evidence that a certain segment of the market places some reliance on such information in forming its own expectations. Also, insofar as other security analysts and investors follow the same sorts of procedures as those used by our sample analysts in forming expectations, general investors' expectations would resemble those of the analysts. Consequently, these predictions may well serve as acceptable proxies for general expectations and surely seem worthy of detailed analysis.

It should be noted that security analysts are not limited to published data in forming their expectations. They frequently visit the companies they study and discuss the corporations' prospects with their executives. These discussions cover such matters as the accounting conventions of the firms, their current and planned capital expenditures, their marketing programs, their projections, etc. As a result these analysts are usually able to form opinions about the quality of corporate management and these opinions often strongly influence their forecasts.

The basic company sample consisted of the 175 companies listed in the Appendix. Data were collected from 1961 through 1969, though the data were very sparse in the last years, especially 1969. As noted above, data were not always available for each company for each of the years covered. As we shall see below, this hindered us in doing some of the empirical tests we would have liked to have done.

The sample of 175 companies was not selected at random but rather on the basis of data availability. The companies covered by the data we have collected represent only a small fraction of those whose shares are traded on organized securities markets. Furthermore, it was not the case that all forecasters supplied data for the same set of companies; instead, there was considerable variation in which companies any particular forecaster covered. This varied coverage reflected the practices of the financial firms involved. Our procedure was to obtain the forecasts that the firms had already made rather than to solicit forecasts for a specific list of companies. We then selected our sample to cover only those companies for which there was overlap in the predictions made. For a company to be included in the sample at least three securities firms had to furnish expectations estimates in each of two years. We lost a few companies from our original sample through subsequent merger, which made it impossible to track the accuracy of the predictions made.

These aspects of the data gethering raise questions about the possibility of sample-selection biases arising from our use of an availability sample. There is no doubt a bias toward large companies. Most firms did tend to make forecasts for the large-capitalization companies in which investment interest is centered. This is especially so since the clients of the advisers and brokers in the sample were typically institutional investors, which tend to specialize in larger firms. Our sample does therefore represent most of the trading volume on organized exchanges and most of the total capitalization of listed shares even though it contains only a small fraction of the total listed companies.

Whether there are other biases is less clear, or what their nature might be. It is not the case that the predictions were formed to support "buy" recommendations or that they represent only those predictions which give rise to such recommendations. We understand that all companies for which detailed forecasts were made were included in our data. But just what criteria were used for selecting the companies to be investigated by a particular firm is not entirely obvious. Primarily, we suspect that it represents past interest especially as expressed in prior inclusion in institutional and individual portfolios, and it is not apparent how this would bias the sample except for the size bias already noted.

One might worry that our forecasts do not really represent the expectations on which the values of securities actually depend. Instead, they may only reflect a paper trail created to give the illusion of responsible action which in fact has quite other bases. This possibility cannot be ruled out a priori, but two points should be made. First, much of the empirical work is designed to investigate whether our data do represent the expectations on which valuation depends. Second, it would be strange if firms expended considerable resources to lay a paper trail without also trying to obtain the most useful and relevant information to be had for the cost.

It is possibly worth noting that the pattern of data availability should be considered a substantive finding of our studies. Even among professional security managers, equally precise and well-formed expectations are not made for every company. Different investment firms often had clearly formed opinions about different companies. This is an aspect of expectations in securities markets that has as yet received virtually no theoretical attention.

As noted above, the sample of the short-term forecasters was essentially a different sample from the long-term one, with only one overlapping predictor. We were, however, able to use the same 175 companies included in the long-term sample. Thus we again find the same large-company bias in the short-term sample. But we did have some additional short-term forecasts available for a maximum of 85 companies. These forecasts were used in our study of the accuracy of the short-term predictions (where we used a 260-company sample) but not in the later valuation work.

1.3 The Data Collected

1.3.1 Normalized Earnings

It is well known that the market does not necessarily capitalize the reported earnings for a firm during the preceding year. Instead, it is likely that investors employ some concept of normal earnings for each firm. Consider, for example, the hypothetical case of a firm that has been earning $5 per share for a number of years. Suppose that during one year, as a result of damage caused by a severe hurricane, earnings decline to $3 per share, the $2 difference being a nonrecurring loss. Will the market capitalize the $3 per share earnings? It is more likely that investors will recognize that this is a temporary dip in earnings. In evaluating the stock, they will tend to apply an appropriate price-earnings multiple to the amount they consider represents the normal earning power of the company and not to the actual earnings figure. This belief about the appropriate figure receives support from the fact that one of the first jobs of a security analyst is to adjust the firm's accounting earnings to arrive at an indication of true earning power (see Graham et al. 1962, chapter 34).

The problem of evaluating earnings is particularly acute for cyclical companies. The market does not apply a constant multiplier to cyclically varying earnings. Earnings multiples tend to fall as earnings rise, and rise as earnings fall, because of the cyclical path of the earnings. Thus the price-earnings ratios that are relevant for valuation may be the ratios of prices to normalized rather than reported earnings. These normalized earnings are estimated to be the earnings that would occur at a normal level of economic activity if the company were experiencing normal operations—that is, operations not affected by such nonrecurring items as strikes, natural disasters, and so forth.

There is an additional problem in using published accounting earnings figures as the basis of a valuation study. Reported earnings depend on a number of variable accounting procedures and management decisions in such areas as depreciation and inventory policy. Consequently, the use of reported earnings figures would not be likely to put companies on a comparable basis. Thus one of the most important reasons for using normalized earnings figures is to ensure that the same accounting conventions are applied to all companies. Particular care was taken to ensure that those which furnished normalized earnings adopted uniform conventions with respect to consolidation of subsidiaries and accounting for depreciation and investment tax credits. For example, the convention applied to the normalized utility earnings figures used in the current study is that all earnings were adjusted (by the analysts) to a "flow through" basis. Thus, for example, all tax savings resulting from the investment tax credit were allowed to "flow through" directly to corporate earnings. Similar conventions had to be adopted with respect to such factors as the earnings of nonconsolidated subsidiaries—particularly foreign ones—the treatment of some nonrecurring items, and so forth. We then took the average of the normalized earnings figure $(\overline{NE})$ to be the relevant earnings variable for valuation.

1.3.2 Expected Growth Rates

Two types of expected growth rates were furnished, short-term (for the following year) and long-term. The long-term growth rates were estimated by nine securities firms.[5] Each long-term growth-rate figure was reported as an average annual rate of growth expected to occur in the next five years. At first thought, such a rate of growth depends on what earnings are expected to be in five years' time and on the base-year earnings figures. However, this dependence need not be very great if the growth rate is regarded more as a parameter of the process determining earnings than as an arithmetic quantity linking the current level of earnings to the expected future level. Discussion with the suppliers of the data indicated that all firms were attempting to predict the same future figure, the long-run average ("normalized") earnings level, abstracting from cyclical or special circumstances. The bases used were less clear. Some firms explicitly used their estimates of "normalized" earnings during the year in which the prediction was made. Others provided different figures as bases: in one case the firm estimated actual earnings; in another a prediction of earnings for the future two and trailing two quarters was used as a base. These differences in bases did not seem to be reflected in the growth rates, however, since attempts to adjust the rates for differences in base figures introduced rather than removed disparities among the predictions. In dealing with long-term growth, therefore, we use the growth rates as supplied by each participant and not some adjusted figures.

These growth rates were used individually in the study of forecast accuracy reported in chapter 2. They were averaged across predictors each year for use in the valuation studies reported in chapter 4. The

---

5. Not all nine firms provided growth-rate estimates for each of the companies in the sample during each of the years covered.

figures reported in the appendix of this chapter are averages of the available forecasts supplied by those of the nine predictors which did supply data for a particular company in a particular year. When we need to refer to individual long-term predictors, we use the numerals 1–9.

In addition to these expectations of long-term growth rates, we also collected estimates of the following year's earnings from eleven securities firms.[6] These earnings projections were converted into growth rates by dividing the estimates by present-year average "normalized" earnings estimates and subtracting unity.[7] As we discuss at more length in chapter 2, we found, somewhat to our surprise, that the implicit forecasts of short-term (one-year) growth were not highly correlated with the long-term anticipations and we were able to use both sets of data in some of the empirical valuation work presented in chapter 4. As in the case of the long-term expectations, the individual predictions were used in the study of forecast accuracy presented in chapter 3. Averages were used in the valuation work and are reported in the appendix to this chapter. We refer to predictors of short-term earnings growth by the letters $A–K$ to distinguish readily these forecasts from the long-term ones.

1.3.3 Estimates of Past Growth Rates

Two of the participating firms provided estimates of past growth rates as well as future predictions. The figures represented perceived growth over the past eight to ten years, the past four to five years, the past six years, and the last year. It may seem unnecessary to rely on security analysts for estimates of historic growth rates. However, the past growth of a company's earnings is not, in any meaningful sense, a well-defined concept. Earnings—being basically a small difference between two large quantities—can exhibit large year-to-year fluctuations. They also can be negative, which creates problems for most mechanical calculations. Indeed, no mechanical method for calculating past growth rates can be fully satisfactory.

To illustrate the difficulty which underlies such an approach, suppose we simply take as the expected growth rate the (compounded) per share earnings growth rate over the past five years. The base year may represent a cyclical trough or may have been a particularly poor year for other reasons. The resulting large growth rate could be completely misleading—cyclical companies could appear to be "rapid-growth" stocks at certain times. While this difficulty can be lessened by calculating the growth rate from a least-squares trend line fitted to the earnings or by increasing the number of years included in the calculations, these tech-

---

6. Three of these eleven firms also supplied long-term forecasts. However, in only one case did we have the same firm supplying *both* long- and short-term predictions in the same years.

7. The result of this calculation is the short-term growth forecast.

niques cannot eliminate the problem. Moreover, several technical difficulties could be enumerated which make the use of calculations of growth rates from historical data an inherently treacherous affair.

In addition, the accounting definition of earnings is not in exact conformity with the economically relevant concept of profits or return on investors' capital. For these reasons, calculated growth rates are sensitive to the particular method employed and the period chosen for the calculation. Consequently, such calculations may be a poor reflection of what growth is generally considered to have been, and may not be useful in assessing the past performance of corporations. Furthermore, it may be supposed that in assessing security analysts' predictions of growth, their own estimates of past growth are more likely to be relevant than objectively calculated rates. The extent of agreement among the two types of measures is among the subjects considered in the next chapter. The past growth rates we collected were used in our analysis, but we do not present the individual figures here since they are less important than the future growth forecasts.

1.3.4 Extent of Consensus among the Forecasters

While we are unable to publish the individual data, researchers may well find that the extent of consensus among our forecasters represents a promising expectational measure in valuation studies. As we shall show below, this variable was extremely useful in our own empirical work. Consequently, in the appendix we list the variance of the (long-term) forecasted growth rates. In calculating the variances of the predicted long-term growth rates, we divided by $N - 1$ observations (using the usual formula giving an unbiased estimate for independent quantities). As a consequence, in the last years of our survey when we very often had only two forecasters, there is a tendency to observe some very large numbers for the variances of the growth rates since the sampling error of the variance estimates can be expected to be large. While there would indeed seem to be a greater dispersion in the growth estimates later in the 1960s compared with the earlier part of the decade, a substantial part of the increase in the dispersion of the estimates of the variances of the predictors is the result of the smaller number of the predictions. The difficulties associated with having different numbers of predictions for separate companies and the small numbers of predictors made it seem unprofitable to use statistics such as the range or interquartile range to measure dispersion. No variances were reported for 1969 since in a very large number of instances we had only one predictor per company. Whenever only one predictor (or none) furnished a growth estimate, the variance was not calculated and a line of asterisks is given in the appendix. A zero variance represents perfect agreement among those which did supply a forecast.

1.3.5 Industrial Classification

All our participating firms also supplied an industrial classification. While other classifications are available, the concept of industry is not really precise enough to get a fixed, unquestionable assignment of corporations to industries. Particular problems are presented by conglomerate companies. Perceived industry may be more relevant than any other grouping in an investigation of anticipations. The classification we use represents a consensus about industry among our participants. Where disagreements occurred (as was often the case with conglomerates), the corporation was simply classified as "miscellaneous." The classification represented considerable aggregation by us over finer classifications, and only eight industries were distinguished. These were

1. electricals and electronics,
2. electric utilities,
3. metals,
4. oils,
5. drugs and specialty chemicals,
6. foods and stores,
7. "cyclical"—including companies such as automobile and steel manufacturers, and meat packers,
8. "miscellaneous."

The first column of the appendix tables gives the company's industrial classification.

1.4 Concluding Comments

This study utilizes a body of expectations data in order to shed light on the nature of expectations formation in the securities markets and to test theoretical propositions concerning the nature of capital-asset pricing. This chapter has described the expectations data that will be utilized and has indicated the method by which these data have been collected.

In view of the unique[8] nature of these data, the considerable effort involved in their collection, and the relevance of such data in many aspects of securities research, we have endeavored to gain permission from our survey participants to publish these data for use by other researchers. Unfortunately, we do not have permission to release the individual predictions. As we shall indicate in the next chapter, the over-all quality of these estimates as useful forecasters is generally rather poor and individual firms feared that their identity might be ascertained if

8. We know of no comparable data available during the 1960s. Some short-term forecasts were published and analyzed during the 1970s, however. In 1980, one firm began publishing long-term growth forecasts of a number of securities firms. The publication, called the *Institutional Brokerage Evaluation Service*, if continued, should begin to provide a wide variety of both short- and long-term forecasts.

the individual forecasts were made public. We do, however, have permission to publish the average predictions of our survey participants as well as the standard deviation of the forecasts, and these data are presented in the appendix below.

Appendix

This appendix contains data on the expectational variables used in the studies of valuation and forecast accuracy. Five variables are presented. The first is the ratio of price to normalized earnings ($P/\overline{NE}$) (table 1.A.1). The ratio for each firm was calculated by dividing end-of-year market price from the Standard & Poor's compustat tape by the average of the normalized-earnings estimates of two securities firms. The second variable is the average predicted future long-term growth rate ($\bar{g}_p$) (table 1.A.2). This variable represents the anticipated long-term (five-year) growth rate of earnings per share. The figures presented in the table are averages of up to nine predictors. Not all of the nine predictors, however, made forecasts for each company in each of the surveyed years.

The third variable, presented in table 1.A.3, is the analysts' predictions of short-term growth. The numbers in the table represent the ratios of the anticipated earnings per share for the next year divided by average normalized earnings less unity, $[(\tilde{E}_{t+1}/\overline{NE})-1]$. Thus the predictions are, in effect, the expected short-term growth rate. Estimates are based on the forecasts of eleven predictors, although—as in the case of the long-term growth rates—not all eleven predictors made forecasts for each of the companies in each of the years covered. None was available in 1969.

The fourth variable represented the dividend-payout ratio ($D/\overline{NE}$) (table 1.A.4). The ratio was calculated by dividing the indicated dividend rate per share as of the end of the year (as estimated by the predictor which furnished data in all years) by the average normalized earnings estimate (σ_p^2). The final variable shown is the variance of the long-term growth forecasts (table 1.A.5). In the calculation, division was made by $N - 1$, with N being the number of predictors. These figures are not calculated for 1969.

In the first column of each table, the sample companies are categorized by industry group. The classifications used represented a consensus about industrial affiliation among the survey participants. Where disagreements occurred among our respondents about the appropriate industrial classification, the corporation was classified as miscellaneous.

The sample of 175 companies was selected on the basis of data availability. Nine years of data are included, covering the years 1961 through 1969. Where data were not available for a particular company in a specific year, the cell has been filled with several asterisks.

Table 1.A.1 Ratio of Price to Normalized Earnings *(P/NE)*

Industry Code		1961	1962	1963
7	A.C.F. Industries, Inc.	*******	16.3230	22.9630
1	Addressograph-Multigraph (AM Corp.)	45.6170	22.9550	25.8150
8	Air Reduction Co. (B.O.C. Fin. Corp.)	17.7740	14.7620	15.4140
2	Allegheny Power System Inc.	*******	19.1180	18.8430
8	Allied Chemical Corp.	22.2500	17.7000	21.6830
3	Alcan Aluminum Ltd.	23.1250	14.6360	20.0000
3	Aluminum Company of America	28.6810	21.2140	26.4420
4	Amerada Pet. (Amerada Hess)	22.1780	20.2000	21.7580
5	American Cyanamid Co.	18.9670	19.3630	21.3840
2	American Electric Power Co.	26.7310	25.0000	27.2800
5	American Home Products Corp.	36.7440	22.8800	25.0000
8	Amer. Mach. & Foundry Co. (AMF Ind.)	26.0160	13.6670	13.9290
8	Amer. Nat. Gas Co. (Amer. Nat. Res.)	20.5000	19.1380	18.3330
3	Amer. Smelt. & Refin. (UV Ind.)	*******	12.6670	12.7760
8	American Telephone & Telegraph Co.	24.4170	20.3040	23.3050
8	American Tobacco (Amer. Brands, Inc.)	*******	11.4080	11.1760
3	Anaconda Co.	*******	8.9011	9.7396
3	Armco Steel Corp. (ARMCO Inc.)	12.9590	11.6570	14.6390
7	Armour & Co. (Esmark)	******	15.1740	15.7330
4	Atlantic Richfield Co.	10.9000	10.1840	11.6490
8	Atlas Chem. Ind. Inc. (Imperial Ch.)	18.3650	12.7660	18.4620
2	Baltimore Gas & Electric Co.	*******	20.3910	21.1540
1	Beckman Instruments, Inc.	46.6150	32.0080	24.3850
8	Beneficial Finance Co.	20.1960	19.2060	19.8700
3	Bethlehem Steel Corp.	14.6980	9.5417	11.1820
7	Boeing Co.	*******	9.0000	10.2500
6	Borden Inc.	24.6050	18.6290	19.9610
2	Boston Edison Co.	19.2240	20.1390	21.5380
5	Bristol-Myers Co.	37.3470	29.0160	30.0640
1	Burroughs Corp.	*******	16.5440	14.5380
8	C.I.T. Financial Corp. (RCA Corp.)	19.7920	17.6770	15.4950
6	Campbell Soup Co.	29.1300	22.1140	27.6190
7	Caterpillar Tractor Co.	17.7910	16.9890	20.8700
2	Central & Southwest Corp.	29.2660	25.4620	26.4290
2	Cincinnati Gas & Electric Co.	19.5740	18.8210	18.1820
4	Cities Service Co.	13.1850	12.3640	11.4220
2	Cleveland Electric Illuminating Co.	22.1490	18.9630	18.8730
6	Colgate Palmolive Co.	20.3770	14.6250	17.3680
2	Consolidated Edison Co.	20.0300	20.0600	18.7710
2	Consumers Power Co.	22.0200	20.4220	20.8620
4	Continental Oil Co. (CONOCO)	20.1820	16.6790	17.7940
6	Corn Products Co. (CPC Intl. Inc.)	31.4860	24.5180	26.8890
8	Crown Zellerback	18.8490	18.2000	20.4670
1	Cutler-Hammer Inc. (Eaton Corp.)	19.0620	14.1720	14.8050
2	Dayton Power & Light Co.	*******	20.8490	19.4920
2	Detroit Edison Co.	*******	21.8100	21.0480
8	Dow Chemical	28.6760	21.8140	25.7940
2	Duquesne Light Co.	19.6090	19.0150	18.6230

1964	1965	1966	1967	1968	1969
19.3900	16.8750	10.9000	11.3000	17.0000	10.7000
19.1750	22.2170	15.2000	31.6000	23.3000	16.9000
15.5040	17.8440	13.2000	12.5000	17.3000	*******
20.1790	17.8230	16.5000	12.2000	*******	*******
18.4370	16.5130	11.8000	13.3000	20.0000	11.4000
21.3890	18.6570	6.5000	5.2000	6.0000	11.3000
21.7700	25.5420	37.1000	35.2000	38.5000	14.8000
21.3140	16.3060	15.4000	16.2000	21.8000	10.9000
21.5620	21.6250	14.8000	14.7000	16.8000	13.3000
26.8940	24.3060	17.5000	16.4000	17.6000	12.5000
25.2400	27.7460	21.8000	26.4000	23.7000	27.2000
14.0380	15.7000	11.7000	*******	*******	*******
18.8270	18.2570	12.3000	10.9000	*******	*******
14.5960	14.8960	11.1000	10.9000	12.7000	*******
21.8400	18.0000	15.7000	13.2000	14.6000	11.3000
12.9900	13.0930	10.0000	*******	*******	*******
10.8850	13.6080	11.4000	7.8000	25.3000	8.2000
11.9440	14.6110	9.8000	9.8000	10.5000	10.5000
13.1870	*******	*******	*******	*******	*******
12.0790	13.3860	11.6000	10.8000	29.3000	18.5000
17.0000	14.2740	10.7000	*******	*******	*******
21.7860	20.4550	17.5000	13.1000	14.8000	10.7000
54.5280	27.1640	25.6000	32.6000	41.5000	33.6000
18.6940	16.5650	11.1000	9.4000	12.2000	10.2000
10.3310	14.2920	10.4000	9.4000	10.2000	9.3000
11.8750	14.9430	32.4000	18.2000	13.1000	28.0000
22.8420	19.1760	14.1000	15.9000	19.4000	11.0000
22.8490	18.8300	16.8000	13.9000	*******	*******
30.6670	33.9380	32.4000	37.0000	34.4000	28.8000
15.7810	26.6000	25.1000	35.6000	44.2000	36.9000
13.0290	11.8100	10.7000	11.0000	15.1000	10.4000
26.2710	21.5150	15.9000	17.5000	17.6000	18.5000
27.5000	21.8680	15.9000	18.7000	22.0000	16.9000
26.4940	23.1760	20.4000	18.8000	17.9000	14.5000
21.4040	18.5710	15.0000	13.5000	14.5000	10.4000
14.4550	12.5370	11.2000	10.4000	20.3000	9.3000
20.8550	19.5180	16.4000	12.9000	14.9000	10.7000
19.3630	15.4170	11.4000	17.6000	19.2000	16.1000
20.2090	16.9000	11.5000	11.9000	13.1000	10.2000
23.7910	21.2260	17.0000	14.3000	16.2000	10.6000
17.9410	14.8440	12.5000	12.3000	13.6000	8.3000
22.0200	20.9310	16.8000	15.8000	17.4000	12.8000
20.7340	16.0330	12.2000	13.9000	16.1000	13.2000
18.2020	20.2170	12.6000	18.5000	25.0000	16.8000
21.4520	18.9130	15.3000	12.9000	15.2000	10.9000
21.9700	19.6050	15.0000	11.8000	15.3000	10.2000
25.5000	22.5180	16.3000	19.3000	17.1000	15.5000
20.0000	17.2080	15.5000	13.6000	*******	*******

Table 1.A.1 (continued)

Industry Code		1961	1962	1963
8	Eastman Kodak Co.	34.5350	26.0780	29.6340
7	Ex-Cell-O Corp.	*******	12.9370	11.7320
6	Federated Dept Stores Inc.	25.0000	18.7500	23.1380
8	Firestone Tire & Rubber Co.	17.4270	14.7890	15.8420
2	Florida Power Corp.	32.5000	29.4170	27.3850
2	Florida Power & Light Co.	34.8850	28.3680	28.6270
6	Food Fair, Inc.	22.6430	12.7610	12.7690
7	Ford Motor Co.	14.5970	11.0740	11.8750
7	General Amer. Transp. Corp. (GATX)	26.1720	20.5840	20.5520
1	General Electric Co.	25.7260	21.6200	25.2540
6	General Foods Corp.	33.8160	25.1200	26.6300
6	General Mills Inc.	20.5300	17.3290	20.0640
7	General Motors Corp.	18.5370	15.6040	18.5000
7	General Portland Cement Co.	14.5620	10.5150	13.7310
2	General Public Utilities Corp.	20.8590	20.1410	18.8240
8	General Telephone & Electronics	28.2930	19.5650	24.8040
8	Goodrich (B.F.) Co.	18.9140	10.8540	13.6180
8	Goodyear Tire & Rubber Co.	18.9360	13.8830	17.6060
6	Grand Union Co. (Cavenham Ltd.)	20.6820	11.0710	13.4910
6	Great Atlantic & Pacific Tea Co.	22.2430	15.0480	14.8570
4	Gulf Oil Corp.	12.5760	11.9030	13.7230
2	Gulf States Utilities Co.	28.0360	22.0630	24.3080
6	Heinz (H. J.) Co.	23.4580	16.3840	17.0870
8	Hercules Inc.	35.0420	24.5590	22.5000
1	Hewlett Packard Co.	61.6670	37.9920	27.5180
1	Honeywell Inc.	33.6770	19.5660	35.2980
8	Household Finance Corp.	19.6080	16.7260	18.5200
2	Houston Ltg. & Pow. Co. (Hous. Inds.)	34.1110	29.6150	28.8330
2	Idaho Power Co.	25.3450	22.3730	21.5830
7	Ideal Cement (Ideal Basic Ind. Inc.)	*******	14.1800	15.9170
2	Illinois Power Co.	24.4140	22.5000	23.2860
7	Ingersoll-Rand Co.	19.5980	15.4650	18.7430
3	Inland Steel Co.	15.4440	11.9840	13.8280
1	International Business Machines	64.3330	36.2790	40.1580
7	International Harvester Co.	*******	12.8390	14.6340
3	Intl. Nickel Co. Canada (INCO)	28.9410	18.3820	20.3330
8	International Paper Co.	20.0680	14.1080	17.1330
1	Intl. Telephone & Telegraph Corp.	27.0350	18.3700	21.8810
7	Johns-Manville Corp.	18.2400	14.3330	16.2500
3	Jones & Laug. Steel Corp. (LTV Corp.)	*******	11.4070	13.4080
3	Kaiser Aluminum & Chemical Corp.	*******	20.5070	19.5890
6	Kellogg Co.	*******	21.2260	28.9830
3	Kennecott Copper Corp.	12.8460	10.8750	11.0960
8	Kimberly-Clark Corp.	22.3550	15.7300	19.6070
6	Kroger Co.	19.1940	15.4030	16.2860
8	Liggett & Myers (Liggett Group)	16.7690	9.3486	11.5230
5	Lilly Eli Co.	27.9030	25.1180	33.8190
1	Litton Industries, Inc.	51.9170	37.8170	33.3510

1964	1965	1966	1967	1968	1969
29.0050	36.1150	29.5000	33.1000	31.5000	28.8000
12.8120	16.0000	*******	*******	*******	*******
27.3810	21.6800	15.3000	18.8000	17.8000	16.8000
17.5490	16.3760	15.3000	13.3000	13.7000	12.7000
27.0710	24.4740	22.7000	19.2000	17.9000	16.7000
27.5910	26.3750	22.1000	20.8000	19.7000	16.6000
14.5000	13.2580	8.2000	10.7000	*******	*******
12.0830	11.0970	7.4000	9.8000	9.5000	9.6000
21.2500	22.2350	14.2000	15.0000	20.5000	12.6000
27.2260	30.2560	19.8000	21.3000	24.9000	20.5000
22.0890	21.1540	17.6000	16.3000	19.3000	10.7000
22.1260	21.1610	16.7000	16.2000	19.4000	16.7000
18.7320	16.5600	9.7000	13.7000	25.2000	13.3000
12.6470	10.4460	9.0000	13.0000	*******	*******
20.8900	18.6080	15.5000	13.3000	14.4000	10.4000
27.4550	25.5560	20.5000	17.5000	18.1000	12.8000
13.2760	12.4730	12.0000	12.6000	16.8000	11.0000
17.5730	17.4310	13.2000	14.2000	15.0000	13.2000
18.1360	13.5530	8.0000	11.1000	13.5000	10.6000
16.5840	14.9460	11.3000	12.7000	18.9000	12.0000
15.7050	14.1460	10.9000	12.7000	14.3000	9.8000
26.7140	26.5850	22.5000	20.0000	19.2000	14.2000
16.1470	14.1130	8.6000	12.0000	14.6000	12.8000
24.4000	19.3680	15.7000	15.5000	19.2000	14.8000
28.8220	38.6820	31.9000	45.0000	48.2000	43.8000
11.3380	26.8470	16.5000	35.2000	34.9000	28.4000
15.4580	17.0700	13.0000	11.1000	14.0000	11.9000
31.6670	26.0490	22.7000	20.9000	20.5000	16.0000
25.2380	19.6670	15.5000	13.6000	15.8000	12.4000
14.0980	13.0000	*******	*******	*******	*******
22.8850	20.4600	18.3000	14.8000	15.9000	12.1000
17.0000	18.6440	*******	*******	*******	*******
11.8920	12.5700	9.7000	9.7000	9.5000	8.3000
33.4290	33.6030	29.8000	45.5000	40.1000	36.5000
16.2630	15.0410	9.5000	10.9000	13.8000	11.6000
21.0000	20.5110	16.6000	19.5000	18.6000	18.7000
17.4670	15.3750	10.0000	13.5000	17.1000	15.4000
19.4260	19.1780	16.2000	21.1000	21.2000	17.9000
16.3360	14.1080	10.7000	13.8000	21.8000	13.6000
11.1520	12.5110	7.9000	8.6000	19.0000	*******
17.3190	19.5330	14.0000	14.0000	14.6000	14.1000
29.2420	21.2180	16.8000	17.9000	17.4000	15.2000
14.1540	16.2420	14.1000	10.0000	15.2000	8.2000
15.8620	14.3140	10.7000	13.3000	18.0000	16.3000
20.2000	14.6940	8.8000	16.0000	12.5000	*******
12.7910	11.2250	12.0000	*******	*******	*******
35.7970	35.6380	27.0000	28.1000	31.6000	36.1000
25.1640	38.2040	27.9000	36.2000	39.1000	16.4000

Table 1.A.1 (continued)

Industry Code		1961	1962	1963
7	Lockheed Aircraft Corp.	*******	13.4160	9.8276
2	Long Island Lighting Co.	24.8890	21.7370	22.3640
4	Marathon Oil	*******	14.8330	18.2930
8	McGraw Hill Inc.	34.2500	18.3330	21.7310
8	Mead Corporation	*******	14.9510	17.4270
5	Merck & Company	34.5630	27.0000	33.4350
2	Middle South Utilities Inc.	24.3330	22.6560	22.4640
8	Minnesota Mining & Manufacturing Co.	44.0160	31.6420	35.9030
8	Moore Corp.	25.6330	19.8300	19.8920
1	Motorola, Inc.	*******	21.2070	25.2800
6	National Biscuit Co. (NABISCO)	22.1790	20.3530	24.6770
1	National Cash Register Co. (NCR)	38.1680	21.1840	22.7540
6	National Dairy Prods. (Kraft Inc.)	19.6580	17.2480	17.1050
8	National Distillers & Chemical Corp.	13.0360	12.1250	13.2640
8	National Lead Co. (NL Industries)	22.9590	14.9180	16.0530
3	National Steel Corp.	*******	13.5850	15.5200
2	New York State Electric & Gas Co.	19.7670	18.2020	17.8120
2	Niagara Mohawk Power Corp.	19.5110	18.8270	19.6300
7	No. Amer. Aviation (Rockwell Intl.)	*******	17.5330	10.7870
7	North Amer. Car Corp. (Flying Tiger)	26.8000	17.3680	17.1550
2	Northern States Power Co.	22.0780	21.8460	21.2500
5	Norwich Phar. Co. (Morton-Norwich)	36.4620	24.3060	19.9310
2	Oklahoma Gas & Electric Co.	27.8660	26.0000	26.9740
7	Otis Elevator Co. (United Tech.)	26.7570	18.6970	15.3390
8	Owens-Corning Fiberglass Corp.	36.8480	23.0810	26.6320
2	Pacific Gas & Electric Co.	22.7500	20.2380	18.3820
6	Penney (J.C.) Co., Inc.	23.6470	18.7500	21.1240
5	Pfizer (Chas & Co.) Inc.	28.5000	24.5450	23.7350
3	Phelps Dodge Corp.	15.2500	13.7420	14.5270
8	Philip Morris Inc.	19.5580	12.4360	12.1110
4	Phillips Petroleum Co.	17.7650	14.6240	14.2700
1	Pitney-Bowes, Inc.	42.4140	24.6920	27.1010
8	Pittsburg Plate Glass (PPG Ind.)	16.6670	12.9860	13.6310
8	Polaroid Corp.	95.6520	51.2500	48.1520
8	Prentice Hall Inc.	47.0830	32.0930	27.9070
6	Procter & Gamble Co.	35.9800	25.0000	26.6250
2	Public Service of Colorado	25.7890	22.4000	22.6000
2	Public Service Electric & Gas Co.	18.8240	19.5740	19.0970
1	Radio Corp. of America (RCA Corp.)	*******	24.2110	31.6800
3	Republic Steel Corp.	*******	8.6563	11.3210
3	Reynolds Metals Co.	22.9850	14.6150	19.1040
8	Reynolds (R.J.) Tob. Co. (Rey. Ind.)	26.5830	13.1750	13.3070
5	Richardson-Merrell Inc.	31.1570	19.1740	14.6180
8	Rohm/Haas Co.	30.1640	24.8640	25.4590
4	Royal Dutch Petroleum Co.	*******	10.6100	11.2930
6	Safeway Stores, Inc.	20.4740	15.5930	17.5000
8	Scott Paper Co.	36.2770	25.5880	27.5930
6	Sears, Roebuck & Co.	32.2070	22.1580	27.1870

1964	1965	1966	1967	1968	1969
8.6441	10.4460	13.2000	10.8000	11.7000	8.5000
23.7070	20.7140	10.0000	14.2000	*******	*******
16.8420	13.2650	12.6000	14.4000	20.0000	10.9000
26.9640	33.8570	25.2000	31.3000	30.8000	23.2000
16.5000	14.5740	9.8000	10.5000	15.3000	11.4000
38.1730	39.1670	28.9000	30.0000	32.5000	34.8000
26.1330	23.7640	19.2000	18.6000	17.7000	14.2000
29.1450	30.9090	26.0000	31.7000	35.6000	29.7000
22.3740	25.2500	20.8000	35.5000	*******	*******
22.6040	35.7610	14.3000	26.0000	26.7000	22.9000
21.8690	18.5040	16.6000	13.0000	15.6000	15.1000
21.4130	21.3690	17.4000	31.7000	31.4000	33.2000
21.3580	17.3470	13.1000	13.3000	15.8000	13.0000
14.5210	15.0000	13.3000	10.8000	*******	*******
16.2360	14.5600	11.0000	14.0000	17.9000	*******
10.9070	15.8920	9.5000	9.2000	10.9000	9.6000
17.9210	18.5350	15.0000	12.8000	*******	*******
18.5960	19.0180	13.1000	11.8000	14.2000	9.1000
9.4956	9.9160	8.7000	*******	*******	*******
20.0000	18.4170	10.0000	10.9000	*******	*******
22.1230	17.9490	16.5000	13.2000	*******	*******
21.3290	22.3680	19.7000	27.1000	24.8000	20.6000
28.6360	23.5290	19.3000	19.3000	*******	*******
13.5550	15.9790	10.9000	14.3000	17.8000	14.9000
22.2110	22.5210	17.4000	23.0000	28.9000	*******
19.2960	18.4810	15.7000	14.4000	14.0000	11.2000
28.8170	22.3080	16.4000	19.4000	22.4000	18.8000
22.0000	27.2480	22.1000	22.7000	24.3000	26.4000
15.2990	12.8020	10.0000	9.0000	17.0000	9.1000
11.7670	12.9670	13.1000	*******	*******	*******
15.2860	14.4230	11.1000	14.8000	17.5000	12.6000
20.7330	22.1840	22.9000	28.4000	28.1000	25.0000
15.5370	15.0780	10.8000	13.0000	15.9000	*******
31.2070	93.3000	*******	55.8000	63.0000	50.0000
28.8460	31.1760	23.6000	26.9000	30.7000	27.0000
25.0770	20.7090	19.2000	20.9000	20.2000	22.0000
22.7780	19.5610	16.0000	13.1000	14.7000	10.6000
19.7530	17.8410	15.0000	12.7000	13.2000	9.6000
25.0930	32.0340	15.9000	21.2000	19.6000	13.9000
9.6591	11.0970	4.2000	*******	*******	*******
18.3550	20.7890	15.2000	15.2000	26.7000	12.0000
11.9620	13.0370	9.7000	*******	*******	*******
17.1480	21.5100	17.6000	19.3000	21.7000	22.9000
25.6220	22.4770	14.4000	*******	19.1000	*******
11.6350	10.7590	7.5000	10.2000	11.7000	8.9000
20.7640	14.7060	11.4000	12.6000	11.8000	*******
23.3620	23.9060	15.0000	16.9000	20.0000	19.4000
30.7740	26.9390	17.3000	23.8000	23.0000	21.9000

Table 1.A.1 (continued)

Industry Code		1961	1962	1963
4	Shell Oil Co.	15.7500	15.3500	18.0290
8	Singer Co.	*******	21.0830	25.7140
5	Smith Kline & French (Smithkline)	39.1890	30.7140	28.5000
4	Socony (Mobil Oil Corp.)	10.4850	12.5000	14.6210
2	Southern Co.	26.4460	23.4660	23.3510
2	Southwestern Public Service Co.	27.2000	26.9230	26.5790
1	Sperry Rand Corp.	*******	14.7300	25.0000
4	Standard Oil Co. of California	12.3030	14.3020	12.6600
4	Standard Oil Co. of Indiana	12.5710	10.9770	13.4470
4	Standard Oil of N.J. (Exxon)	13.9040	14.8750	17.7780
5	Sterling Drug Inc.	30.0000	23.9680	23.6960
7	Swift & Co. (Esmark)	12.6840	14.6850	15.4420
8	Talcott Nat. (Assoc. Fst. Cap. Corp.)	27.1710	19.6340	14.0130
2	Tampa Electric Co.	34.1180	29.3970	31.7190
4	Texaco Inc.	17.2560	16.6110	17.5000
8	Texas Gulf Sulphur Co. Inc.	16.6350	10.0880	18.2690
1	Texas Instruments, Inc.	37.5380	24.6600	28.5640
2	Texas Utilities Co.	30.9230	28.1510	28.7340
8	Union Carbide Corp.	23.4540	19.2140	22.2120
4	Union Oil Co. of California	14.8890	14.0280	16.0000
7	United Aircraft Corp. (United Tech.)	*******	13.9260	11.1760
7	U. S. Gypsum Co.	20.9500	15.3140	16.8840
8	U. S. Rubber (Uniroyal, Inc.)	13.0000	9.8182	10.6800
3	U. S. Steel Corp.	16.5260	9.9714	14.1670
5	Upjohn Inc.	33.2580	19.6270	29.0410
2	Virginia Electric & Power Co.	29.5240	26.4840	26.3430
1	Westinghouse Electric Corp.	17.6140	14.8840	15.7560
2	Wisconsin Electric Power Co.	*******	19.0830	17.9370
1	Xerox Corp.	*******	43.9930	77.2730
1	Zenith Radio Corp.	38.4210	26.3860	32.7420

Table 1.A.2   **Average Predicted Future Long-Term Growth Rate of Earnings Per Share $(\bar{g}_p)$ (percent)**

Industry Code		1961	1962	1963
7	A.C.F. Industries, Inc.	*******	5.6667	6.0000
1	Addressograph-Multigraph (AM Corp.)	10.0000	7.6000	7.8333
8	Air Reduction Co. (B.O.C. Fin. Corp.)	4.0000	4.6667	4.1667
2	Allegheny Power System Inc.	*******	4.3333	4.8750
8	Allied Chemical Corp.	3.0000	3.0000	4.0000
3	Alcan Aluminum Ltd.	10.0000	8.0000	7.7500
3	Aluminum Company of America	7.2500	8.2000	8.4000
4	Amerada Pet. (Amerada Hess)	4.5000	6.0000	5.0000
5	American Cyanamid Co.	4.0000	4.7500	4.0000
2	American Electric Power Co.	5.7500	6.0000	6.0000

1964	1965	1966	1967	1968	1969
19.5080	17.5170	13.0000	11.0000	14.5000	9.5000
19.2730	13.9230	9.8000	13.8000	17.4000	16.0000
28.5150	27.3250	17.6000	26.7000	17.9000	16.7000
16.3110	15.6050	11.8000	10.5000	14.1000	10.2000
26.2500	23.8390	13.2000	17.5000	16.3000	13.3000
27.1540	24.6970	18.9000	17.5000	16.7000	14.1000
13.5370	20.0000	18.8000	26.7000	21.4000	14.8000
15.6120	15.0000	10.7000	11.1000	11.9000	10.0000
16.3460	15.9240	12.3000	12.3000	13.4000	10.7000
19.0740	15.6830	11.3000	11.5000	13.2000	10.7000
23.7250	28.7720	22.8000	27.9000	27.2000	27.7000
19.2500	*******	*******	*******	*******	*******
11.6430	10.3620	8.8000	13.8000	*******	*******
32.3450	28.7990	24.2000	19.3000	24.1000	16.4000
19.8020	17.1010	13.1000	13.8000	13.2000	10.2000
18.5910	26.0360	10.6000	*******	*******	*******
29.1540	38.2320	28.6000	36.0000	40.8000	36.8000
28.0460	25.6770	21.9000	20.7000	20.0000	16.9000
21.5250	20.1470	13.1000	14.0000	17.0000	13.7000
17.8480	17.2880	11.3000	12.1000	12.8000	10.0000
11.9630	16.1030	18.8000	15.8000	12.7000	9.8000
15.6310	13.7820	14.7000	15.7000	14.3000	19.0000
13.1750	30.3680	13.0000	12.3000	21.1000	10.5000
10.2000	12.7440	10.0000	9.1000	12.9000	9.3000
25.6790	29.5100	23.4000	21.7000	24.3000	19.3000
27.3240	25.3850	22.9000	19.1000	17.6000	11.9000
20.2380	23.2710	13.4000	20.6000	19.4000	16.1000
17.7690	17.1230	13.8000	11.9000	*******	*******
51.2340	56.1110	33.0000	55.1000	49.5000	41.6000
21.7670	39.1130	14.5000	21.9000	20.8000	13.2000

1964	1965	1966	1967	1968	1969
5.6667	4.6667	7.0000	7.0000	7.1000	7.0000
7.4286	7.4286	8.3330	8.3330	10.1300	8.0000
2.2500	3.8000	4.0000	5.5000	8.6000	*******
4.4000	5.3000	5.0000	5.0000	5.0000	*******
4.4167	4.7143	4.0000	4.3330	4.8670	2.0000
4.8333	5.8333	4.3330	5.0000	8.9670	3.0000
6.0714	7.0000	4.3330	4.6670	8.2000	0.0000
7.6667	7.5000	5.5000	5.0000	9.6500	10.0000
5.5833	6.1667	6.3330	6.3330	5.7670	2.0000
6.5000	6.5625	7.1670	7.3330	7.3670	7.0000

Table 1.A.2 (continued)

Industry Code		1961	1962	1963
5	American Home Products Corp.	7.3333	6.2500	5.2000
8	Amer. Mach. & Foundry Co. (AMF Ind.)	9.5000	5.0000	4.2500
8	Amer. Nat. Gas Co. (Amer. Nat. Res.)	7.0000	6.0000	5.1250
3	Amer. Smelt. & Refin. (UV Ind.)	*******	3.3333	2.7500
8	American Telephone & Telegraph Co.	4.7500	4.9167	4.8333
8	American Tobacco (Amer. Brands, Inc.)	*******	4.0000	3.0000
3	Anaconda Co.	*******	1.6667	2.2500
3	Armco Steel Corp. (ARMCO Inc.)	2.5000	2.5000	3.6000
7	Armour & Co. (Esmark)	*******	4.0000	3.2500
4	Atlantic Richfield Co.	1.0000	2.0000	2.2500
8	Atlas Chem. Ind. Inc. (Imperial Ch.)	4.0000	4.6667	3.0000
2	Baltimore Gas & Electric Co.	*******	5.2500	4.9000
1	Beckman Instruments, Inc.	18.6670	14.1670	12.3330
8	Beneficial Finance Co.	5.5000	6.3333	6.0000
3	Bethlehem Steel Corp.	2.0000	3.0000	3.5000
7	Boeing Co.	*******	5.3333	5.0000
6	Borden Inc.	4.0000	4.6667	4.5000
2	Boston Edison Co.	3.0000	3.5000	4.6667
5	Bristol-Myers Co.	11.0000	10.6670	11.2860
1	Burroughs Corp.	*******	9.6667	4.6667
8	C.I.T. Financial Corp. (RCA Corp.)	4.0000	4.4000	3.8000
6	Campbell Soup Co.	7.6667	7.0000	6.5714
7	Caterpillar Tractor Co.	5.5000	7.0000	6.0000
2	Central & Southwest Corp.	6.5000	6.7000	6.6429
2	Cincinnati Gas & Electric Co.	5.0000	4.6667	5.0000
4	Cities Service Co.	3.0000	3.0000	3.0000
2	Cleveland Electric Illuminating Co.	4.6667	5.2500	3.7500
6	Colgate Palmolive Co.	7.0000	5.0000	6.0000
2	Consolidated Edison Co.	4.0000	4.1250	4.6000
2	Consumers Power Co.	4.5000	4.7500	5.1250
4	Continental Oil Co. (CONOCO)	4.6667	4.7500	4.6000
16	Corn Products Co. (CPC Intl. Inc.)	7.6667	7.6000	7.8000
8	Crown Zellerback	4.0000	3.3333	3.7500
1	Cutler-Hammer Inc. (Eaton Corp.)	7.0000	6.6667	4.6667
2	Dayton Power & Light Co.	*******	5.3333	5.5000
2	Detroit Edison Co.	7.0000	5.0000	4.3750
8	Dow Chemical	5.5000	5.3333	5.5000
2	Duquesne Light Co.	4.0000	3.6667	3.5000
8	Eastman Kodak Co.	7.2000	7.0000	6.8571
7	Ex-Cell-O Corp.	*******	5.0000	3.6667
6	Federated Dept Stores Inc.	6.0000	6.2000	5.6667
8	Firestone Tire & Rubber Co.	4.3333	3.7500	4.2000
2	Florida Power Corp.	8.2500	7.9000	7.6000
2	Florida Power & Light Co.	10.0000	8.9167	8.4286
6	Food Fair, Inc.	5.0000	3.0000	3.0000
7	Ford Motor Co.	5.0000	5.0000	4.2500
7	General Amer. Transp. Corp. (GATX)	5.5000	4.6667	4.5000
1	General Electric Co.	7.0000	8.0000	6.5000

1964	1965	1966	1967	1968	1969
6.0000	7.5000	7.0000	8.0000	9.5330	8.0000
3.4000	3.8000	3.5000	7.0000	9.0000	*******
5.2000	5.3333	6.5000	6.5000	6.7500	*******
2.4167	3.9167	4.3330	5.3330	13.3300	*******
4.9444	4.9375	5.0000	4.6670	5.3330	5.7500
2.5000	3.5000	4.0000	4.0000	4.0000	*******
1.2000	2.3333	4.5000	7.0000	14.4000	1.5000
2.5000	3.2857	4.5000	4.5000	7.4500	1.5000
3.2500	3.5000	5.0000	5.0000	5.0000	*******
4.5000	5.0714	5.6670	8.3330	11.1700	11.5000
3.3333	4.6667	7.0000	10.0000	10.0000	*******
4.8571	4.7143	4.8330	5.1670	5.8000	5.7500
11.0000	11.0000	11.0000	13.3300	12.2000	8.5000
6.5625	6.7500	6.0000	5.5000	6.8500	6.7500
1.8000	3.5833	4.5000	4.5000	7.5500	2.0000
4.2000	5.0000	11.3300	11.0000	13.5000	4.2500
5.1667	6.3750	6.3330	6.0000	6.4670	5.2500
5.1250	5.1000	5.5000	6.0000	6.0000	*******
11.7500	12.8750	14.0000	14.3300	15.0700	11.7500
3.6000	7.3333	7.7500	16.5000	24.7500	18.5000
2.8333	2.7857	2.5000	3.7500	3.9000	5.2500
6.3750	6.0000	6.5000	6.5000	5.3000	6.2500
7.2500	7.2500	9.0000	11.0000	12.0300	8.2500
6.7778	6.6667	7.0000	7.0000	6.9330	6.7500
5.1250	5.1000	5.5000	5.5000	7.2500	6.0000
3.7000	4.5833	4.1670	6.6670	7.9330	9.2500
4.4000	4.9167	5.6670	5.6670	7.0670	6.0000
4.9167	5.4167	5.8330	6.5000	8.6000	7.7500
5.2143	4.3571	4.6670	4.6670	4.4330	4.2500
5.5833	5.7500	6.0000	5.8330	7.2000	5.7500
6.5000	6.3125	5.0000	6.3330	7.0330	7.5000
7.2857	6.5000	6.3330	6.3330	5.2330	5.0000
4.4000	4.3333	5.3330	5.5000	5.5000	6.5000
6.4000	6.2500	6.0000	7.3330	6.9670	6.0000
5.1000	5.4167	5.2500	5.2500	7.3000	6.2500
4.8000	5.0000	5.3330	5.3330	6.1000	5.2500
6.1667	7.4286	6.3330	6.3330	9.7000	3.2500
3.8333	3.8750	4.5000	4.5000	4.0000	*******
7.1667	8.3333	9.3330	10.0000	14.6300	10.5000
3.6000	3.5000	5.0000	5.0000	8.0000	*******
6.8750	7.1111	7.6670	7.0000	9.3330	6.2500
4.5714	4.8571	5.0000	5.3330	7.6330	4.7500
8.2143	8.2143	8.5000	8.5000	8.0000	7.2500
7.6250	7.7500	8.5000	8.3330	8.1330	7.7500
2.7500	3.2000	3.5000	3.0000	4.0000	*******
4.6667	4.6000	3.5000	10.0000	5.5000	6.7500
5.2857	5.8333	6.0000	5.0000	*******	4.5000
5.5625	6.6875	6.5000	6.5000	6.6000	8.2500

Table 1.A.2 (continued)

Industry Code		1961	1962	1963
6	General Foods Corp.	8.2500	7.6667	7.5000
6	General Mills Inc.	2.0000	4.3333	4.2500
7	General Motors Corp.	3.0000	4.2000	3.8000
7	General Portland Cement Co.	4.0000	2.0000	2.8333
2	General Public Utilities Corp.	4.3333	4.5000	5.0000
8	General Telephone & Electronics	6.0000	6.3750	6.1000
8	Goodrich (B.F.) Co.	3.0000	2.6667	3.2500
8	Goodyear Tire & Rubber Co.	4.3333	4.0000	4.4000
6	Grand Union Co. (Cavenham Ltd.)	6.3333	3.1250	2.3333
6	Great Atlantic & Pacific Tea Co.	5.5000	4.3000	3.7500
4	Gulf Oil Corp.	3.6667	5.0000	4.4000
2	Gulf States Utilities Co.	6.6667	6.7500	6.6250
6	Heinz (H. J.) Co.	6.5000	6.3333	5.0000
8	Hercules Inc.	8.0000	7.5000	6.7500
1	Hewlett Packard Co.	17.5000	15.3330	14.5000
1	Honeywell Inc.	7.8000	6.3333	7.4286
8	Household Finance Corp.	5.0000	5.3333	4.7500
2	Houston Ltg. & Pow. Co. (Hous. Inds.)	7.2500	7.8000	8.4167
2	Idaho Power Co.	7.0000	6.0000	6.0000
7	Ideal Cement (Ideal Basic Ind. Inc.)	*******	4.6667	3.5000
2	Illinois Power Co.	6.0000	6.5000	6.2000
7	Ingersoll-Rand Co.	4.0000	3.3333	3.3333
3	Inland Steel Co.	2.3333	3.0000	2.8000
1	International Business Machines	17.0000	15.5000	15.0000
7	International Harvester Co.	*******	2.6667	2.8750
3	Intl. Nickel Co. Canada (INCO)	6.6667	7.2000	4.2000
8	International Paper Co.	2.5000	4.0000	4.2500
1	Intl. Telephone & Telegraph Corp.	10.0000	9.7500	8.8000
7	Johns-Manville Corp.	2.0000	2.7500	2.7500
3	Jones & Laug. Steel Corp. (LTV Corp.)	*******	4.0000	3.0000
3	Kaiser Aluminum & Chemical Corp.	*******	8.6667	9.0000
6	Kellogg Co.	8.0000	6.5000	7.2500
3	Kennecott Copper Corp.	2.0000	1.0000	1.2500
8	Kimberly-Clark Corp.	5.2500	4.3000	4.4000
6	Kroger Co.	3.5000	2.5000	3.6000
8	Liggett & Myers (Liggett Group)	5.0000	1.6667	0.7500
5	Lilly Eli Co.	8.0000	5.3333	6.6250
1	Litton Industries, Inc.	20.7500	17.8330	15.1430
7	Lockheed Aircraft Corp.	*******	7.0000	5.2500
2	Long Island Lighting Co.	7.0000	6.3333	6.8333
4	Marathon Oil	*******	4.6667	3.7500
8	McGraw Hill Inc.	8.5000	7.6667	7.7143
8	Mead Corporation	*******	3.6667	5.0000
5	Merck & Company	8.4000	7.0000	8.7143
2	Middle South Utilities Inc.	5.5000	5.3333	5.9000
8	Minnesota Mining & Manufacturing Co.	12.8000	11.0000	10.1430
8	Moore Corp.	8.0000	8.0000	7.7500
1	Motorola, Inc.	8.0000	7.5000	7.0000

1964	1965	1966	1967	1968	1969
7.3333	6.7778	6.6670	6.3330	6.2670	6.2500
4.8000	6.6667	9.0000	9.0000	11.6500	11.0000
4.4375	4.5000	3.1670	4.6670	4.7000	6.5000
3.5000	2.7500	5.0000	5.0000	16.0000	*******
5.1429	5.2857	4.7500	4.7500	4.8500	5.0000
6.9375	7.0000	8.6670	8.6670	10.7000	9.2500
3.6000	4.0000	4.5000	6.1670	5.1000	5.2500
4.8750	5.3750	5.1670	5.3330	7.2670	7.2500
2.6250	4.2000	5.5000	5.0000	11.0000	7.2500
3.0000	2.5714	2.0000	3.0000	1.1000	4.0000
6.0000	5.6875	5.7500	7.0000	7.0000	7.5000
6.7500	7.3571	7.5000	7.1670	8.1000	7.2500
4.2500	4.7500	5.8000	7.0000	10.6000	7.5000
7.1429	7.0000	6.3330	6.3330	8.0670	4.0000
12.0000	12.0000	13.5000	15.6700	18.9000	12.5000
6.7857	7.8750	7.6670	8.6670	9.7000	13.2500
5.5625	6.1111	5.0000	5.2500	11.1000	9.7500
8.5000	8.7500	8.5000	8.5000	8.8000	8.0000
6.5000	6.5833	6.5000	6.6670	8.0670	6.5000
3.8000	3.6000	*******	*******	9.0000	*******
5.6429	5.7857	6.1670	6.1670	6.8000	6.5000
3.2500	3.6000	4.5000	4.0000	8.0000	*******
2.5000	3.2857	4.0000	4.0000	2.2000	1.2500
15.1110	14.8890	15.0000	16.0000	15.3700	14.2500
3.1000	4.3333	5.3330	5.3330	8.6000	4.5000
5.3571	5.6429	7.3330	6.3330	5.9670	9.0000
4.1667	4.1667	4.3330	4.3330	5.6330	4.5000
9.0000	9.1429	11.0000	11.3300	11.7000	11.7500
3.2000	3.6667	4.0000	4.3330	8.3670	3.2500
1.5000	2.9167	2.6670	2.6670	5.2000	*******
4.1667	5.9167	5.5000	7.0000	12.5000	4.0000
8.3333	8.0000	7.0000	7.0000	8.9500	6.5000
2.5000	3.6667	3.6670	6.0000	7.6330	3.5000
4.4167	4.2857	4.5000	4.8330	4.8330	4.5000
3.4167	4.5714	4.0000	3.5000	4.8500	*******
1.0000	1.0000	3.0000	3.0000	4.0000	*******
6.7500	8.6429	9.7500	11.5000	15.0000	13.0000
13.1250	13.5000	17.0000	17.0000	14.9300	5.7500
3.2000	5.0000	9.0000	7.3330	7.1000	1.2500
6.8000	6.6000	6.5000	4.5000	6.5000	*******
5.5833	6.0833	5.1670	8.3330	9.5000	10.5000
8.0000	8.2500	8.6670	11.0000	12.0300	7.7500
3.8750	4.3000	5.2500	5.5000	6.3000	6.0000
9.0000	9.8889	10.3300	10.6700	14.7300	10.7500
6.5000	7.0714	7.8330	7.8330	8.0670	7.5000
9.1250	9.3750	10.2500	10.8300	10.5000	10.0000
7.4000	7.4000	8.0000	7.5000	7.0000	*******
7.7143	8.8750	10.6700	12.0000	14.7700	4.7500

Table 1.A.2 (continued)

Industry Code		1961	1962	1963
6	National Biscuit Co. (NABISCO)	4.0000	4.2500	5.4000
1	National Cash Register Co. (NCR)	9.0000	8.3333	7.0000
6	National Dairy Prods. (Kraft Inc.)	4.0000	3.8333	3.8750
8	National Distillers & Chemical Corp.	3.0000	3.3333	3.3333
8	National Lead Co. (NL Industries)	5.5000	4.2500	2.6250
3	National Steel Corp.	*******	3.6667	2.8750
2	New York State Electric & Gas Co.	6.0000	5.8333	5.3333
2	Niagara Mohawk Power Corp.	3.0000	4.0000	4.3750
7	No. Amer. Aviation (Rockwell Intl.)	*******	7.0000	5.0000
7	North Amer. Car Corp. (Flying Tiger)	9.0000	8.7500	5.2500
2	Northern States Power Co.	6.0000	5.0000	4.7500
5	Norwich Phar. Co. (Morton-Norwich)	10.7500	9.0000	8.0000
2	Oklahoma Gas & Electric Co.	6.0000	6.3333	6.5000
7	Otis Elevator Co. (United Tech.)	7.5000	6.7500	4.9000
8	Owens-Corning Fiberglass Corp.	9.0000	7.4000	6.8000
2	Pacific Gas & Electric Co.	5.6667	5.7500	5.4000
6	Penney (J.C.) Co., Inc.	3.5000	4.0000	3.7500
5	Pfizer (Chas & Co.) Inc.	8.6667	8.0000	8.2143
3	Phelps Dodge Corp.	2.0000	2.6667	2.2500
8	Philip Morris Inc.	5.0000	4.3333	4.0000
4	Phillips Petroleum Co.	4.0000	3.3333	3.2500
1	Pitney-Bowes, Inc.	9.0000	9.6000	9.4000
8	Pittsburg Plate Glass (PPG Ind.)	2.0000	2.6667	2.2500
8	Polaroid Corp.	17.2000	16.1670	17.3330
8	Prentice Hall Inc.	15.5000	13.6000	12.0000
6	Procter & Gamble Co.	9.0000	7.5000	6.2857
2	Public Service of Colorado	6.0000	7.4000	6.6000
2	Public Service Electric & Gas Co.	5.0000	5.6667	5.6667
1	Radio Corp. of America (RCA Corp.)	8.0000	8.2500	7.4000
3	Republic Steel Corp.	*******	3.0000	2.7500
3	Reynolds Metals Co.	7.5000	10.2500	9.5000
8	Reynolds (R.J.) Tob. Co. (Rey. Ind.)	12.0000	7.3333	4.7500
5	Richardson-Merrell Inc.	11.0000	8.0000	6.0000
8	Rohm/Haas Co.	7.7500	7.1667	7.2000
4	Royal Dutch Petroleum Co.	*******	4.7500	4.2500
6	Safeway Stores, Inc.	5.0000	2.8333	4.6000
8	Scott Paper Co.	6.7500	6.5000	6.3333
6	Sears, Roebuck & Co.	6.3333	6.5000	6.5000
4	Shell Oil Co.	3.3333	3.2500	3.2000
8	Singer Co.	*******	7.2500	6.3333
5	Smith Kline & French (Smithkline)	9.4000	9.3333	8.7143
4	Socony (Mobil Oil Corp.)	3.0000	4.3333	3.7500
2	Southern Co.	6.2500	6.5000	6.5000
2	Southwestern Public Service Co.	7.0000	6.6250	6.6250
1	Sperry Rand Corp.	*******	3.6667	4.2500
4	Standard Oil Co. of California	3.5000	4.5000	3.7500
4	Standard Oil Co. of Indiana	2.5000	1.6667	3.3333
4	Standard Oil of N.J. (Exxon)	4.3333	5.0000	4.8000

1964	1965	1966	1967	1968	1969
6.4286	6.4286	6.3330	6.0000	6.5670	6.5000
7.2222	7.1111	7.3330	8.0000	9.8670	10.0000
4.2857	4.7143	5.6670	5.6670	6.9670	8.0000
1.7500	2.2000	4.3330	5.3330	6.0000	*******
3.2857	3.5000	3.5000	5.0000	6.3000	*******
1.9000	3.2500	4.0000	4.6670	6.1670	1.2500
5.0000	5.0000	5.0000	5.0000	*******	*******
4.7500	4.6667	4.8330	4.8330	5.0330	4.2500
2.8000	1.9000	3.6670	4.0000	4.0000	*******
6.0000	7.0000	5.0000	5.0000	*******	*******
4.7000	4.7500	4.7500	4.7500	4.5000	*******
6.8000	7.8000	8.0000	8.5000	11.8500	6.0000
7.0000	7.3333	6.8330	6.8330	6.5000	*******
3.8000	4.6000	5.0000	5.0000	6.0000	6.0000
*******	6.5714	9.0000	7.5000	8.3500	*******
5.5000	5.4286	5.6670	5.6670	7.0000	5.5000
4.9286	6.0625	7.7500	8.0000	9.9330	8.7500
7.4444	7.8889	8.3330	9.0000	9.3330	9.0000
1.9167	2.5833	2.6670	4.6670	7.1000	6.5000
3.5000	4.3000	5.2500	7.0000	8.0000	*******
4.2143	5.2143	4.5000	7.3330	6.9670	8.2500
7.5833	7.5833	9.0000	8.6670	8.2000	10.0000
3.2000	4.0000	4.5000	4.5000	8.6500	*******
17.3330	18.5000	16.5000	19.3300	27.2300	16.7500
10.8000	10.4000	13.5000	15.0000	21.0500	12.0000
6.5000	6.3125	7.1670	7.5000	8.9500	7.0000
6.7857	6.5000	6.0000	6.0000	6.9000	5.7500
5.7500	5.7500	5.8330	5.8330	6.3330	6.0000
5.3333	6.8333	7.6670	8.0000	13.1000	7.5000
1.2000	2.6667	2.6670	3.0000	3.0000	*******
4.3000	5.7500	5.0000	5.6670	11.1000	3.7500
4.3333	4.1667	4.6670	4.5000	6.0000	*******
5.3333	6.1429	7.0000	7.5000	8.4000	9.2500
8.1429	8.5714	8.0000	11.0000	8.2500	*******
4.5000	4.6667	4.6670	6.3330	5.5330	6.5000
5.3333	5.0000	4.7500	4.5000	5.7000	*******
6.3333	6.3333	6.6670	5.8330	4.8000	4.5000
8.0000	8.5556	8.6670	7.0000	9.5330	8.0000
4.8125	5.5625	5.6670	7.6670	9.1330	6.0000
7.6000	6.4000	5.3330	8.0000	7.9000	8.7500
8.3333	8.6250	8.1670	7.1670	6.9670	4.0000
4.5000	5.2857	5.1670	6.5000	7.2670	6.2500
6.5000	6.8125	6.3330	6.8330	6.5670	6.5000
7.2000	7.4167	7.7500	7.7500	5.3500	7.0000
4.2000	4.5000	11.0000	11.0000	23.7000	8.0000
4.7143	5.3571	5.5000	5.1670	6.1330	7.2500
4.0714	4.3571	4.5000	7.0000	8.2330	4.5500
6.5625	5.9375	5.0000	5.1670	5.8670	5.0000

Table 1.A.2 (continued)

Industry Code		1961	1962	1963
5	Sterling Drug Inc.	7.0000	5.3333	6.6667
7	Swift & Co. (Esmark)	3.0000	2.5000	2.5000
8	Talcott Nat. (Assoc. Fst. Cap. Corp.)	10.5000	9.0000	6.8000
2	Tampa Electric Co.	9.5000	9.1250	8.8750
4	Texaco Inc.	5.6667	6.2000	5.4000
8	Texas Gulf Sulphur Co. Inc.	3.0000	2.0000	1.3333
1	Texas Instruments, Inc.	15.0000	9.0000	10.0000
2	Texas Utilities Co.	8.0000	7.9000	7.6000
8	Union Carbide Corp.	5.5000	4.8000	5.0000
4	Union Oil Co. of California	6.0000	3.3333	2.6667
7	United Aircraft Corp. (United Tech.)	*******	7.3333	5.0000
7	U. S. Gypsum Co.	5.0000	4.7500	4.3000
8	U. S. Rubber (Uniroyal, Inc.)	2.5000	2.5000	2.6667
3	U. S. Steel Corp.	1.6667	1.6667	3.0000
5	Upjohn Inc.	8.2000	6.1667	8.2857
2	Virginia Electric & Power Co.	7.5000	8.0000	7.5833
1	Westinghouse Electric Corp.	7.0000	6.2500	5.2000
2	Wisconsin Electric Power Co.	*******	4.0000	4.3333
1	Xerox Corp.	25.0000	22.6670	22.4290
1	Zenith Radio Corp.	12.0000	9.0000	9.2500

Table 1.A.3   **Average Predicted Earnings per Share for the Next Year Divided by Average Normalized Earnings for Current Year** $[(E_{t+1}/\overline{WE}) - 1]$

Industry Code		1961	1962	1963
7	A.C.F. Industries, Inc.	*******	0.1429	0.4506
1	Addressograph-Multigraph (AM Corp.)	0.0963	−0.0409	−0.0598
8	Air Reduction Co. (B.O.C. Fin. Corp.)	−0.0247	−0.0476	0.0069
2	Allegheny Power System Inc.	*******	*******	*******
8	Allied Chemical Corp.	0.1120	−0.0400	0.2178
3	Alcan Aluminum Ltd.	0.1083	−0.0969	0.1943
3	Aluminum Company of America	−0.0055	−0.0704	0.1218
4	Amerada Pet. (Amerada Hess)	−0.0895	−0.0027	0.1380
5	American Cyanamid Co.	0.0783	0.1129	0.1506
2	American Electric Power Co.	0.0577	0.0596	0.1374
5	American Home Products Corp.	0.0930	0.0565	0.0791
8	Amer. Mach. & Foundry Co. (AMF Ind.)	*******	*******	*******
8	Amer. Nat. Gas Co. (Amer. Nat. Res.)	−0.0296	0.0728	0.0581
3	Amer. Smelt. & Refin. (UV Ind.)	*******	−0.1111	−0.1445
8	American Telephone & Telegraph Co.	0.0365	0.0534	0.0408
8	American Tobacco (Amer. Brands, Inc.)	*******	−0.0291	−0.0118
3	Anaconda Co.	*******	−0.0110	−0.0556
3	Armco Steel Corp. (ARMCO Inc.)	−0.1219	−0.2570	0.0000
7	Armour & Co. (Esmark)	*******	*******	*******

1964	1965	1966	1967	1968	1969
7.1667	7.2500	7.1670	7.3330	9.3330	8.7500
2.2500	2.6667	5.0000	5.0000	5.0000	*******
4.6000	4.6667	5.0000	4.7500	5.0000	*******
9.2000	9.0833	9.5000	9.5000	11.1000	8.5000
7.0000	6.5625	7.1670	7.5000	8.3330	4.7500
18.7500	18.8000	11.5000	14.0000	8.0000	*******
8.8750	9.5000	12.0000	15.3300	18.1300	15.5000
7.9167	8.0833	8.1670	8.1670	7.8670	8.2500
5.5000	5.9444	5.5000	5.5000	5.2330	2.2500
5.6250	6.3333	5.6670	8.0000	12.3000	9.7500
4.2000	6.6000	12.0000	10.0000	12.1700	3.5000
3.6875	3.5714	3.6670	5.3330	11.6500	2.7500
3.8750	4.4000	5.7500	8.7500	4.9000	2.0000
1.8333	2.8333	2.3330	2.3330	3.5330	1.5000
7.6250	8.7143	8.3330	8.0000	7.8000	7.0000
7.3889	7.2222	7.3330	7.3330	7.4330	7.0000
4.6000	7.0000	6.6670	7.0000	11.5700	7.5000
4.6667	4.6250	4.0000	6.5000	*******	*******
23.8750	25.3330	22.6700	22.3300	27.7300	19.0000
8.1667	9.5000	10.6700	10.0000	12.8700	9.0000

1964	1965	1966	1967	1968
0.7073	0.4464	0.4290	0.0000	0.0960
− 0.0309	0.0896	0.0150	0.4000	0.0760
0.1187	0.2395	− 0.0100	0.0360	0.1350
*******	*******	− 0.0294	0.0000	*******
0.2292	0.1261	0.0000	0.0000	0.2360
0.3651	0.2623	0.2330	− 0.5800	0.0110
0.1221	0.3867	0.1430	0.9570	0.0000
0.2372	0.1130	− 0.0200	− 0.0200	0.0600
0.2396	0.1458	0.0000	0.1050	0.0390
0.0636	0.0463	0.0000	0.0000	0.0850
*******	0.1124	0.0000	0.0000	0.0930
*******	*******	0.0830	*******	*******
0.0612	0.0826	− 0.0161	0.0000	*******
0.1691	0.1458	0.2080	− 0.1791	0.0240
0.0660	0.0584	0.0430	0.0000	0.0810
0.0784	0.1186	− 0.0161	*******	*******
0.2917	0.5823	0.7140	0.0000	0.1630
− 0.0595	0.2228	0.0420	0.0000	− 0.1364
*******	*******	*******	*******	*******

Table 1.A.3 (continued)

Industry Code		1961	1962	1963
4	Atlantic Richfield Co.	0.0100	0.0211	−0.0412
8	Atlas Chem. Ind. Inc. (Imperial Ch.)	*******	*******	*******
2	Baltimore Gas & Electric Co.	*******	*******	*******
1	Beckman Instruments, Inc.	−0.0102	0.1010	−0.2098
8	Beneficial Finance Co.	0.0588	0.0704	0.0377
3	Bethlehem Steel Corp.	−0.0063	−0.3033	−0.2286
7	Boeing Co.	*******	−0.2121	−0.0679
6	Borden Inc.	0.0457	0.0043	0.0581
2	Boston Edison Co.	*******	*******	*******
5 .·	Bristol-Myers Co.	0.1020	0.1541	0.0812
1	Burroughs Corp.	*******	−0.0221	−0.2231
8	C.I.T. Financial Corp. (RCA Corp.)	0.0435	0.0332	0.0269
6	Campbell Soup Co.	0.0186	−0.0629	0.0089
7	Caterpillar Tractor Co.	0.0785	0.0471	0.2981
2	Central & Southwest Corp.	0.1035	0.0820	0.0939
2	Cincinnati Gas & Electric Co.	0.0780	0.0623	0.0145
4	Cities Service Co.	*******	*******	*******
2	Cleveland Electric Illuminating Co.	0.0942	0.0293	0.0610
6	Colgate Palmolive Co.	*******	*******	*******
2	Consolidated Edison Co.	*******	*******	*******
2	Consumers Power Co.	0.0331	0.0683	0.2126
4	Continental Oil Co. (CONOCO)	0.0935	0.0665	0.1930
6	Corn Products Co. (CPC Intl. Inc.)	0.0876	0.0795	0.1156
8	Crown Zellerback	−0.1349	0.0133	0.0494
1	Cutler-Hammer Inc. (Eaton Corp.)	−0.1125	−0.1043	−0.0260
2	Dayton Power & Light Co.	*******	*******	*******
2	Detroit Edison Co.	*******	*******	*******
8	Dow Chemical	0.0073	0.0756	0.1268
2	Duquesne Light Co.	*******	*******	*******
8	Eastman Kodak Co.	*******	*******	*******
7	Ex-Cell-O Corp.	*******	*******	*******
6	Federated Dept Stores Inc.	0.0227	−0.0087	0.1034
8	Firestone Tire & Rubber Co.	0.0180	−0.0496	0.0237
2	Florida Power Corp.	0.0357	0.0667	0.0666
2	Florida Power & Light Co.	0.0437	0.0400	0.0728
6	Food Fair, Inc.	*******	*******	*******
7	Ford Motor Co.	0.1371	−0.0447	0.0417
7	General Amer. Transp. Corp. (GATX)	0.0906	0.0190	0.0621
1	General Electric Co.	0.0149	−0.1356	−0.0370
6	General Foods Corp.	0.0852	0.0537	0.0315
6	General Mills Inc.	0.0227	0.0479	0.1282
7	General Motors Corp.	0.1789	0.1644	0.2235
7	General Portland Cement Co.	−0.0688	−0.1706	−0.0269
2	General Public Utilities Corp.	0.0938	0.1364	0.0686
8	General Telephone & Electronics	0.0927	0.0783	0.1725
8	Goodrich (B.F.) Co.	0.0895	−0.2025	−0.1447
8	Goodyear Tire & Rubber Co.	0.0426	−0.0691	0.0733
6	Grand Union Co. (Cavenham Ltd.)	*******	*******	*******

1964	1965	1966	1967	1968
− 0.0099	0.1061	0.0870	− 0.0206	0.3290
*******	*******	− 0.0333	*******	*******
*******	*******	− 0.0250	0.0000	0.0650
0.9811	− 0.0149	− 0.0278	0.1580	− 0.0447
0.1351	0.0901	− 0.0278	0.0000	0.0650
*******	0.0531	0.1070	− 0.1429	− 0.1429
0.0776	0.2476	0.0380	0.0000	− 0.1379
0.1087	0.0235	0.0000	0.0450	0.1710
*******	*******	0.0000	0.0360	*******
0.1037	0.0826	− 0.0294	0.0000	0.1030
− 0.0833	0.4933	0.1710	− 0.1923	0.2810
0.0285	0.0286	− 0.0185	− 0.1333	0.0660
0.0678	0.0303	− 0.0588	0.0000	− 0.0588
0.7259	0.3714	0.1820	0.0870	0.0850
0.0909	0.0482	− 0.0217	0.0000	0.0640
0.0760	0.1154	0.0000	0.0000	0.0750
*******	*******	0.0120	− 0.0217	0.1320
0.0965	0.1406	0.0000	0.0000	0.0730
*******	*******	− 0.0227	0.0000	0.0820
*******	*******	0.0000	0.0000	0.0480
0.1648	0.1038	− 0.0167	0.0000	0.1250
0.1294	*******	0.0180	0.0000	0.0580
− 0.0270	0.0471	− 0.0179	0.0770	0.1280
0.2324	0.1157	− 0.0405	0.0300	0.0280
0.1910	0.3217	0.0000	0.2310	0.2660
*******	*******	− 0.0263	0.0000	0.0430
*******	*******	− 0.0227	0.0000	0.0660
0.1952	0.1178	− 0.0132	0.0000	0.0940
*******	*******	0.0000	0.0000	*******
*******	*******	0.0000	0.0000	0.1280
*******	*******	*******	*******	*******
0.2435	0.1428	− 0.0278	0.0000	0.1250
0.1471	0.1725	0.2330	− 0.1429	0.0360
0.0953	0.0438	− 0.0227	0.0000	0.0360
0.0987	0.0390	0.0000	0.0000	0.0510
*******	*******	− 0.1471	0.0000	*******
0.1250	0.1589	− 0.1038	− 0.0909	− 0.0909
0.2395	0.2329	0.1880	0.0830	0.1360
0.0689	0.1718	− 0.1333	0.0000	0.1220
0.0137	0.0000	− 0.0366	0.0000	0.0420
0.2011	0.1393	− 0.0278	− 0.0476	0.2290
0.2584	0.1060	− 0.1912	− 0.0500	− 0.0948
− 0.1838	− 0.1161	− 0.2000	− 0.1000	*******
0.0411	0.0291	0.0000	0.0000	0.0470
0.2485	0.1349	0.0000	− 0.0417	0.1160
− 0.0996	0.0110	0.0780	0.0000	0.1110
0.1391	0.2073	0.1290	− 0.0789	0.0660
*******	*******	0.0000	0.0560	0.0750

Table 1.A.3 (continued)

Industry Code		1961	1962	1963
6	Great Atlantic & Pacific Tea Co.	*******	*******	*******
4	Gulf Oil Corp.	0.0417	−0.0112	0.1062
2	Gulf States Utilities Co.	*******	*******	*******
6	Heinz (H. J.) Co.	*******	*******	*******
8	Hercules Inc.	0.1675	0.0834	0.0784
1	Hewlett Packard Co.	0.0417	0.1181	0.0551
1	Honeywell Inc.	−0.0193	−0.1237	0.2218
8	Household Finance Corp.	0.2549	0.0856	0.0872
2	Houston Ltg. & Pow. Co. (Hous. Inds.)	0.0933	0.0769	0.1400
2	Idaho Power Co.	0.0230	0.0169	0.0917
7	Ideal Cement (Ideal Basic Ind. Inc.)	*******	0.0098	0.0133
2	Illinois Power Co.	0.0250	0.0588	0.0953
7	Ingersoll-Rand Co.	*******	*******	*******
3	Inland Steel Co.	0.1532	−0.0476	0.0677
1	International Business Machines	*******	*******	*******
7	International Harvester Co.	*******	−0.0484	0.1057
3	Intl. Nickel Co. Canada (INCO)	0.3941	0.0018	0.0765
8	International Paper Co.	0.0270	−0.1316	−0.0434
1	Intl. Telephone & Telegraph Corp.	0.1209	0.1652	0.1802
7	Johns-Manville Corp.	0.0640	−0.0389	0.1048
3	Jones & Laug. Steel Corp. (LTV Corp.)	*******	−0.2515	0.0746
3	Kaiser Aluminum & Chemical Corp.	*******	−0.0821	0.0045
6	Kellogg Co.	*******	0.1368	0.1356
3	Kennecott Copper Corp.	0.0000	−0.0557	−0.1346
8	Kimberly-Clark Corp.	−0.0348	−0.0365	0.0309
6	Kroger Co.	−0.0323	0.0430	0.0762
8	Liggett & Myers (Liggett Group)	*******	*******	*******
5	Lilly Eli Co.	−0.0040	0.0354	0.0758
1	Litton Industries, Inc.	0.0333	0.2169	0.1402
7	Lockheed Aircraft Corp.	*******	0.3078	0.2023
2	Long Island Lighting Co.	*******	*******	*******
4	Marathon Oil	*******	0.0417	0.2618
8	McGraw Hill Inc.	0.1750	0.0294	*******
8	Mead Corporation	*******	−0.0162	0.1003
5	Merck & Company	0.0706	0.0580	0.1507
2	Middle South Utilities Inc.	0.1000	0.0737	0.0570
8	Minnesota Mining & Manufacturing Co.	0.1093	0.0547	0.0710
8	Moore Corp.	*******	*******	*******
1	Motorola, Inc.	*******	0.1330	0.1383
6	National Biscuit Co. (NABISCO)	0.0256	0.0745	0.1255
1	National Cash Register Co. (NCR)	0.0576	−0.1408	−0.1435
6	National Dairy Prods. (Kraft Inc.)	0.0214	0.0168	−0.0105
8	National Distillers & Chemical Corp.	*******	*******	*******
8	National Lead Co. (NL Industries)	0.0982	−0.0601	0.0146
3	National Steel Corp.	*******	−0.0503	0.3440
2	New York State Electric & Gas Co.	*******	*******	*******
2	Niagara Mohawk Power Corp.	*******	*******	*******
7	No. Amer. Aviation (Rockwell Intl.)	*******	0.2171	0.1208

1964	1965	1966	1967	1968
*******	*******	− 0.0435	0.0000	0.0860
0.0992	0.0805	− 0.0093	0.0000	0.0830
*******	*******	− 0.0417	0.0000	0.1400
*******	*******	− 0.0143	− 0.0250	0.0750
0.1771	0.0246	− 0.3750	0.0000	0.0380
0.1146	0.2520	0.0000	0.1250	0.1590
− 0.4447	0.1959	− 0.2375	0.2900	0.1340
0.0870	0.1740	0.1520	− 0.1071	0.0880
0.1406	0.0568	− 0.0227	0.0000	0.0850
0.1429	0.0667	− 0.0227	0.0000	0.0700
− 0.0902	0.0000	*******	*******	*******
0.0684	0.0575	0.0000	0.0000	0.0710
*******	*******	*******	*******	*******
0.0051	0.0814	− 0.0156	− 0.0571	− 0.0976
*******	*******	− 0.1840	0.0140	0.1060
0.5914	0.2230	− 0.0135	0.0610	0.0320
0.1680	0.2197	− 0.0094	− 0.1667	0.0710
0.1166	0.0812	− 0.1200	0.0870	0.0480
0.1148	0.1041	0.0000	0.0000	0.1180
0.2341	0.0340	− 0.1333	0.0000	0.0880
0.0617	0.2115	0.1810	− 0.0769	0.0380
0.0725	0.3067	0.1330	− 0.1143	− 0.0036
0.1970	0.0385	0.0000	0.0000	0.0640
0.1246	0.4965	0.3700	− 0.1489	0.3710
0.0207	− 0.0163	− 0.1111	0.0000	0.1060
0.2400	0.0918	− 0.1600	0.0670	0.0570
*******	*******	0.0090	*******	*******
0.2101	0.2500	− 0.0152	0.0000	0.1160
0.0951	0.1912	− 0.0345	0.2070	0.4800
− 0.0079	− 0.0321	0.2000	0.1400	0.0710
*******	*******	− 0.4138	0.0000	*******
0.1947	0.0824	0.0400	0.0180	0.1270
0.2071	0.2343	0.0000	0.1330	0.0000
0.1818	0.1628	0.0000	0.0540	0.0470
0.2638	0.2187	− 0.0185	0.0000	0.0940
0.1493	0.0966	− 0.0385	0.0000	0.0770
0.1082	0.0783	*******	0.0000	0.1440
*******	*******	− 0.0641	0.0000	*******
0.2978	0.4692	− 0.0769	0.1110	0.1740
0.0841	0.0199	0.0000	0.0000	0.0420
− 0.0200	0.0069	− 0.0128	0.0240	0.2220
0.1531	0.0204	0.0000	0.0370	0.0850
*******	*******	0.0000	− 0.0278	*******
0.1348	0.0777	− 0.0500	0.0640	0.0920
0.0535	0.3358	0.0000	− 0.1400	− 0.0756
*******	*******	0.0000	0.0000	*******
*******	*******	0.0000	0.0000	0.1130
− 0.0205	− 0.0280	0.0910	*******	*******

Table 1.A.3 (continued)

Industry Code		1961	1962	1963
7	North Amer. Car Corp. (Flying Tiger)	0.1800	0.0351	0.1379
2	Northern States Power Co.	0.0552	0.0615	0.1324
5	Norwich Phar. Co. (Morton-Norwich)	0.1590	0.0159	0.0111
2	Oklahoma Gas & Electric Co.	0.1040	0.1047	0.2105
7	Otis Elevator Co. (United Tech.)	*******	*******	*******
8	Owens-Corning Fiberglass Corp.	0.0783	−0.0667	−0.0526
2	Pacific Gas & Electric Co.	0.0361	0.0746	0.0221
6	Penney (J.C.) Co., Inc.	0.0541	0.0087	0.0112
5	Pfizer (Chas & Co.) Inc.	0.0857	0.1039	0.0940
3	Phelps Dodge Corp.	0.0719	−0.0629	−0.0237
8	Philip Morris Inc.	0.0619	−0.0042	0.0464
4	Phillips Petroleum Co.	0.0555	−0.0175	−0.0268
1	Pitney-Bowes, Inc.	0.1609	0.0154	0.0628
8	Pittsburg Plate Glass (PPG Ind.)	0.1859	−0.0088	0.0000
8	Polaroid Corp.	0.4690	0.3826	0.2295
8	Prentice Hall Inc.	0.2592	0.1318	0.0853
6	Procter & Gamble Co.	0.1324	−0.0070	−0.0167
2	Public Service of Colorado	0.0329	0.0300	0.0900
2	Public Service Electric & Gas Co.	−0.0147	0.0567	0.1011
1	Radio Corp. of America (RCA Corp.)	*******	0.2337	0.3292
3	Republic Steel Corp.	*******	−0.3625	−0.0071
3	Reynolds Metals Co.	−0.1094	−0.2103	0.0064
8	Reynolds (R.J.) Tob. Co. (Rey. Ind.)	0.0875	0.0079	0.0425
5	Richardson-Merrell Inc.	0.0620	−0.0041	−0.0229
8	Rohm/Haas Co.	0.1068	0.1036	0.1878
4	Royal Dutch Petroleum Co.	*******	0.0455	0.0617
6	Safeway Stores, Inc.	0.0345	0.0339	0.0784
8	Scott Paper Co.	0.0529	0.0028	0.0926
6	Sears, Roebuck & Co.	0.1043	−0.0342	0.0938
4	Shell Oil Co.	0.0000	0.0514	0.1995
8	Singer Co.	*******	*******	*******
5	Smith Kline & French (Smithkline)	0.1027	0.0905	0.0933
4	Socony (Mobil Oil Corp.)	−0.0656	0.0745	0.1481
2	Southern Co.	0.0859	0.0735	0.0729
2	Southwestern Public Service Co.	*******	*******	*******
1	Sperry Rand Corp.	*******	−0.1892	0.0588
4	Standard Oil Co. of California	0.0202	0.0726	0.0036
4	Standard Oil Co. of Indiana	−0.0057	0.0378	0.0908
4	Standard Oil of N.J. (Exxon)	0.0152	0.0444	0.1848
5	Sterling Drug Inc.	−0.0195	0.0279	0.0261
7	Swift & Co. (Esmark)	*******	*******	*******
8	Talcott Nat. (Assoc. Fst. Cap. Corp.)	0.0789	0.0634	−0.1184
2	Tampa Electric Co.	*******	*******	*******
4	Texaco Inc.	0.0902	0.0772	0.1194
8	Texas Gulf Sulphur Co. Inc.	*******	*******	*******
1	Texas Instruments, Inc.	−0.1015	−0.0485	0.2163
2	Texas Utilities Co.	0.0795	0.0763	0.1329
8	Union Carbide Corp.	0.0604	−0.0014	0.0394
4	Union Oil Co. of California	0.0296	0.0383	0.1980

1964	1965	1966	1967	1968
0.3220	0.2696	0.0530	−0.0870	*******
0.0068	0.0086	−0.0238	0.0000	*******
0.1038	0.0611	0.0000	0.0000	0.1520
0.1364	0.0980	−0.0333	0.0000	*******
*******	*******	−0.0714	0.1000	0.0740
0.1032	0.0084	−0.0526	0.0000	0.0370
0.0634	0.0734	−0.0217	0.0000	0.0600
0.2258	0.1054	−0.0303	0.0290	0.0480
0.0889	0.1009	−0.0147	0.0000	0.0820
0.1739	0.2371	0.1490	−0.1250	0.3170
0.0281	0.0403	0.1150	*******	*******
0.0476	0.0678	0.0220	0.0000	0.2310
0.1111	0.0268	−0.2222	0.1200	0.1280
0.1186	0.1615	−0.0500	0.0000	0.0200
−0.0612	0.9666	*******	0.0440	0.1880
0.1538	0.2157	0.0000	0.0770	0.1920
0.0062	0.0060	−0.0132	0.0000	0.0350
0.0741	0.0526	0.0000	0.0000	0.0590
0.0732	0.0705	0.0000	0.0000	0.0380
0.1481	0.3898	−0.0185	0.0400	0.0850
−0.0757	0.1054	0.1330	*******	*******
0.1754	0.4281	0.1670	0.0610	0.4700
−0.0123	0.0370	−0.0286	*******	*******
0.0222	0.0604	0.0000	0.0000	0.0600
0.1470	0.0651	0.0000	*******	0.0680
0.0064	0.0253	−0.0114	0.0000	0.1190
0.1389	−0.0353	0.1430	0.1050	0.0450
0.0991	0.1111	0.0000	0.0630	0.0670
0.1005	0.0041	−0.0385	0.1250	0.1110
0.1557	0.1262	0.0000	0.0000	0.0580
*******	*******	−0.0638	0.0400	0.1430
0.1287	0.0994	0.0000	−0.3548	0.0690
0.0900	0.0952	0.0000	0.0000	0.0980
0.1200	0.0714	−0.3182	0.0000	0.0630
*******	*******	−0.0556	0.0000	0.0260
0.1463	0.1136	0.0940	1.3750	0.1360
0.0390	0.0610	0.0000	0.0000	0.0840
0.1418	0.1354	0.0130	0.0230	0.0630
0.1376	0.0226	−0.0179	−0.0339	0.0640
0.0667	0.0877	−0.0278	0.0000	0.3800
*******	*******	*******	*******	*******
−0.0714	−0.0580	0.0000	*******	*******
*******	*******	0.0000	0.0000	0.1640
0.0634	0.0819	0.0090	0.0000	0.0670
*******	*******	−0.3250	*******	*******
0.2692	0.3481	0.0000	0.3330	0.1880
0.0966	0.0495	0.0000	0.0000	0.0930
0.1450	0.1809	0.000	0.0000	0.1320
0.2969	0.2915	−0.0111	0.0000	0.0980

Table 1.A.3 (continued)

Industry Code		1961	1962	1963
7	United Aircraft Corp. (United Tech.)	******	−0.1611	−0.0902
7	U. S. Gypsum Co.	−0.0513	−0.0497	0.0229
8	U. S. Rubber (Uniroyal, Inc.)	0.1765	−0.1313	−0.0947
3	U. S. Steel Corp.	0.1053	−0.3780	−0.0584
5	Upjohn Inc.	0.0606	0.0235	0.1037
2	Virginia Electric & Power Co.	0.0286	0.1077	0.0697
1	Westinghouse Electric Corp.	−0.2216	−0.2064	−0.2525
2	Wisconsin Electric Power Co.	******	0.0493	0.0667
1	Xerox Corp.	0.8600	0.5312	0.6000
1	Zenith Radio Corp.	0.1009	0.0883	0.2258

Table 1.A.4   **Dividend-Payout Ratio Based on Normalized Earnings** $(D/\overline{NE})$

Industry Code		1961	1962	1963
7	A.C.F. Industries, Inc.	******	0.5291	0.5556
1	Addressograph-Multigraph (AM Corp.)	0.4444	0.4091	0.4348
8	Air Reduction Co. (B.O.C. Fin. Corp.)	0.6849	0.6803	0.6897
2	Allegheny Power System Inc.	******	0.7176	0.7148
8	Allied Chemical Corp.	0.7200	0.7200	0.7129
3	Alcan Aluminum Ltd.	0.5000	0.4364	0.4800
3	Aluminum Company of America	0.5275	0.4660	0.4615
4	Amerada Pet. (Amerada Hess)	0.5347	0.5333	0.5781
5	American Cyanamid Co.	0.6956	0.6667	0.6429
2	American Electric Power Co.	0.7308	0.7088	0.7230
5	American Home Products Corp.	0.6698	0.6696	0.6598
8	Amer. Mach. & Foundry Co. (AMF Ind.)	0.5500	0.6000	0.6429
8	Amer. Nat. Gas Co. (Amer. Nat. Res.)	0.5333	0.5517	0.6237
3	Amer. Smelt. & Refin. (UV Ind.)	******	0.5111	0.4107
8	American Telephone & Telegraph Co.	0.6188	0.6261	0.6025
8	American Tobacco (Amer. Brands, Inc.)	******	0.5825	0.5882
3	Anaconda Co.	******	0.5494	0.5208
3	Armco Steel Corp. (ARMCO Inc.)	0.5505	0.6742	0.6667
7	Armour & Co. (Esmark)	******	0.4870	0.4828
4	Atlantic Richfield Co.	0.4400	0.5053	0.4948
8	Atlas Chem. Ind. Inc. (Imperial Ch.)	0.4615	0.5106	0.6154
2	Baltimore Gas & Electric Co.	******	0.7000	0.7077
1	Beckman Instruments, Inc.	******	******	******
8	Beneficial Finance Co.	0.3647	0.4112	0.4174
3	Bethlehem Steel Corp.	0.8276	0.7267	0.5454
7	Boeing Co.	******	0.4848	0.5714
6	Borden Inc.	0.5272	0.5484	0.5519
2	Boston Edison Co.	0.6897	0.7167	0.6769
5	Bristol-Myers Co.	0.4898	0.4918	0.4615
1	Burroughs Corp.	******	0.5882	0.6154
8	C.I.T. Financial Corp. (RCA Corp.)	0.5833	0.6061	0.6337

1964	1965	1966	1967	1968
− 0.1111	0.0784	0.2790	0.0000	− 0.0625
− 0.0119	− 0.1337	− 0.1447	0.0000	0.0950
0.0317	1.3857	0.2500	− 0.1500	0.1580
− 0.2025	0.0305	0.0140	− 0.1556	− 0.0809
0.0864	0.0980	− 0.0172	0.0000	0.0740
0.0348	0.0403	0.0000	0.0000	0.0910
0.1508	0.3040	− 0.1429	0.0590	0.0810
0.0262	0.1507	0.0000	0.0000	*******
0.4494	0.1042	− 0.1667	0.1090	0.1900
0.0489	0.4328	− 0.1212	0.0380	0.1080

1964	1965	1966	1967	1968	1969
0.6537	0.5643	0.6000	0.6000	0.6600	0.6000
0.4536	0.4906	0.4500	0.4000	0.5200	0.4200
0.7194	0.5988	0.6000	0.6000	0.8100	*******
0.7286	0.6968	0.7000	0.7000	*******	*******
0.6429	0.6387	0.6500	0.6000	0.6700	0.5400
0.4815	0.4955	0.5000	0.5000	0.2300	0.5600
0.4248	0.4667	0.4500	0.4000	0.9000	0.3500
0.5385	0.5556	0.5500	0.6000	0.6000	0.1200
0.6250	0.5375	0.6500	0.6000	0.6600	0.6200
0.7151	0.7000	0.7000	0.8000	0.7700	0.7400
0.6539	0.6230	0.6500	0.6000	0.6000	0.5900
0.6923	0.7200	0.5000	*******	*******	*******
0.6531	0.6238	0.6500	0.6000	*******	*******
0.6176	0.5833	0.5000	0.5000	0.8900	*******
0.6240	0.5926	0.6500	0.6000	0.6500	0.6500
0.6274	0.5593	0.5500	*******	*******	*******
0.5208	0.6329	0.5000	0.5000	0.5800	0.4400
0.5556	0.6218	0.6000	0.6000	0.5500	0.5300
0.3500	*******	*******	*******	*******	*******
0.4753	0.4484	0.4000	0.3000	0.4900	0.4700
0.6000	0.4516	0.5000	*******	*******	*******
0.7200	0.7013	0.7000	0.7000	0.7000	0.6400
*******	*******	0.1500	0.1000	0.4100	0.4000
0.4216	0.4427	0.5000	0.5000	0.4200	0.3800
0.4412	0.5310	0.5500	0.5000	0.5100	0.5600
0.3448	0.2857	0.5000	0.3000	0.2800	0.2400
0.5480	0.5177	0.5500	0.5000	0.6900	0.6600
0.6884	0.6809	0.7500	0.8000	*******	*******
0.4667	0.4602	0.5000	0.5000	0.6200	0.5300
0.6250	0.5333	0.4000	0.4000	0.2300	0.1800
0.6154	0.6095	0.6000	0.6000	0.5900	0.5700

Table 1.A.4 (continued)

Industry Code		1961	1962	1963
6	Campbell Soup Co.	0.4969	0.4914	0.5238
7	Caterpillar Tractor Co.	0.4651	0.4546	0.5000
2	Central & Southwest Corp.	0.6963	0.6646	0.6743
2	Cincinnati Gas & Electric Co.	0.6383	0.5849	0.6473
4	Cities Service Co.	0.5714	0.5217	0.5138
2	Cleveland Electric Illuminating Co.	0.6281	0.5926	0.6197
6	Colgate Palmolive Co.	0.5283	0.4667	0.4884
2	Consolidated Edison Co.	0.7317	0.7186	0.7218
2	Consumers Power Co.	0.6887	0.6747	0.6805
4	Continental Oil Co. (CONOCO)	0.6182	0.5343	0.5588
6	Corn Products Co. (CPC Intl. Inc.)	0.6486	0.6265	0.6222
8	Crown Zellerback	0.5714	0.7200	0.6729
1	Cutler-Hammer Inc. (Eaton Corp.)	0.5000	0.4908	0.5195
2	Dayton Power & Light Co.	*******	0.7094	0.7051
2	Detroit Edison Co.	*******	0.7586	0.7742
8	Dow Chemical	0.6078	0.6274	0.5907
2	Duquesne Light Co.	0.7375	0.7515	0.7420
8	Eastman Kodak Co.	0.6977	0.5509	0.6219
7	Ex-Cell-O Corp.	*******	0.4921	0.5039
6	Federated Dept Stores Inc.	0.5000	0.5130	0.5447
8	Firestone Tire & Rubber Co.	0.3806	0.4126	0.4126
2	Florida Power Corp.	0.6429	0.6533	0.6523
2	Florida Power & Light Co.	0.4874	0.4968	0.4941
6	Food Fair, Inc.	0.5029	0.5373	0.5538
7	Ford Motor Co.	0.3871	0.4417	0.4286
7	General Amer. Transp. Corp. (GATX)	0.7031	0.6686	0.6703
1	General Electric Co.	0.6838	0.5634	0.5797
6	General Foods Corp.	0.5614	0.5760	0.5926
6	General Mills Inc.	0.7273	0.6575	0.6154
7	General Motors Corp.	0.8130	0.8054	0.9412
7	General Portland Cement Co.	0.6750	0.7059	0.7164
2	General Public Utilities Corp.	0.7312	0.7210	0.7176
8	General Telephone & Electronics	0.7415	0.6696	0.6588
8	Goodrich (B.F.) Co.	0.5789	0.5570	0.5789
8	Goodyear Tire & Rubber Co.	0.3745	0.4043	0.4255
6	Grand Union Co. (Cavenham Ltd.)	0.3636	0.4286	0.4528
6	Great Atlantic & Pacific Tea Co.	0.4748	0.6362	0.5676
4	Gulf Oil Corp.	0.3273	0.4328	0.4671
2	Gulf States Utilities Co.	0.7143	0.6540	0.6892
6	Heinz (H. J.) Co.	0.3738	0.3571	0.3884
8	Hercules Inc.	0.4370	0.4412	0.4412
1	Hewlett Packard Co.	*******	*******	*******
1	Honeywell Inc.	0.5161	0.4624	0.4762
8	Household Finance Corp.	0.4706	0.4531	0.4480
2	Houston Ltg. & Pow. Co. (Hous. Inds.)	0.4741	0.4359	0.4600
2	Idaho Power Co.	0.6552	0.6780	0.7000
7	Ideal Cement (Ideal Basic Ind. Inc.)	*******	0.5246	0.6667
2	Illinois Power Co.	0.6875	0.6941	0.6857

1964	1965	1966	1967	1968	1969
0.5288	0.5333	0.5500	0.5000	0.6500	0.7100
0.5000	0.4396	0.5000	0.5000	0.5900	0.4500
0.6649	0.6494	0.6500	0.6000	0.7200	0.6700
0.6456	0.6349	0.7500	0.8000	0.7000	0.6700
0.4818	0.4206	0.4500	0.4000	0.5300	0.5100
0.6316	0.6361	0.7000	0.7000	0.7400	0.7400
0.4706	0.4722	0.5000	0.5000	0.4900	0.4900
0.6911	0.7200	0.9500	0.9000	0.6900	0.7000
0.7033	0.6717	0.7000	0.7000	0.7300	0.7100
0.4941	0.5000	0.5000	0.5000	0.5300	0.5200
0.6061	0.5882	0.6500	0.6000	0.7200	0.6900
0.6789	0.6612	0.6000	0.6000	0.6200	0.6500
0.4494	0.3826	0.5500	0.5000	0.7500	0.6000
0.7226	0.6956	0.7000	0.7000	0.6600	0.7200
0.7273	0.6842	0.7500	0.8000	0.7400	0.7100
0.5833	0.5197	0.5500	0.5000	0.5300	0.5500
0.7549	0.7273	0.8500	0.8000	*******	*******
0.5340	0.5169	0.6500	0.6000	0.4900	0.5000
0.5000	0.4533	*******	*******	*******	*******
0.5524	0.4960	0.5500	0.4000	0.5300	0.5000
0.4314	0.4404	0.4000	0.4000	0.3700	0.3900
0.6514	0.6421	0.6500	0.6000	0.6100	0.5500
0.4982	0.4767	0.5500	0.5000	0.4400	0.5300
0.6000	0.5454	0.6000	0.6000	*******	*******
0.4444	0.4286	0.4500	0.4000	0.4400	0.4800
0.6711	0.6494	0.6500	0.6000	0.7300	0.6600
0.6423	0.5897	0.7000	0.7000	0.7000	0.8600
0.5480	0.5385	0.5500	0.5000	0.5700	0.5900
0.5977	0.5000	0.5500	0.5000	0.4600	0.4700
0.8517	0.8400	0.7500	0.8000	0.7400	0.7400
0.7059	0.7143	0.6000	0.8000	*******	*******
0.7123	0.6937	0.8500	0.8000	0.7400	0.8000
0.6836	0.5889	0.7000	0.7000	0.6900	0.6700
0.5058	0.4835	0.5000	0.5000	0.5500	0.5600
0.4311	0.4404	0.4500	0.4000	0.3900	0.3800
0.4000	0.3105	0.5000	0.5000	0.3000	0.3700
0.5901	0.6409	0.6500	0.6000	0.7400	0.6300
0.4564	0.4512	0.4500	0.5000	0.5000	0.4800
0.7086	0.6927	0.7000	0.7000	0.7000	0.6800
0.3670	0.3871	0.4000	0.4000	0.3600	0.4000
0.5333	0.4598	0.5000	0.5000	0.4500	0.5200
*******	0.1990	0.1000	0.1000	0.1200	0.1900
0.1934	0.3964	0.4000	0.4000	0.3300	0.2800
0.4672	0.4331	0.5000	0.4000	0.3900	0.3500
0.4727	0.4543	0.5000	0.5000	0.5500	0.5000
0.7302	0.6667	0.6500	0.6000	0.7400	0.7400
0.6557	0.6667	*******	*******	*******	*******
0.7179	0.6667	0.7000	0.7000	0.7300	0.7400

Table 1.A.4 (continued)

Industry Code		1961	1962	1963
7	Ingersoll-Rand Co.	0.9195	0.9302	0.9143
3	Inland Steel Co.	0.5161	0.5079	0.5156
1	International Business Machines	0.2556	0.2791	0.3366
7	International Harvester Co.	*******	0.6194	0.5854
3	Intl. Nickel Co. Canada (INCO)	0.5424	0.5588	0.6667
8	International Paper Co.	0.5568	0.5407	0.5493
1	Intl. Telephone & Telegraph Corp.	0.4651	0.4348	0.3960
7	Johns-Manville Corp.	0.6400	0.6667	0.6667
3	Jones & Laug. Steel Corp. (LTV Corp.)	*******	0.5988	0.4975
3	Kaiser Aluminum & Chemical Corp.	*******	0.5217	0.4931
6	Kellogg Co.	*******	0.5660	0.5763
3	Kennecott Copper Corp.	0.7692	0.8333	0.6154
8	Kimberly-Clark Corp.	0.5101	0.5401	0.5714
6	Kroger Co.	0.7097	0.7097	0.6286
8	Liggett & Myers (Liggett Group)	0.7692	0.7042	0.7813
5	Lilly Eli Co.	0.8065	0.7874	0.7289
1	Litton Industries, Inc.	*******	*******	*******
7	Lockheed Aircraft Corp.	*******	0.2981	0.3586
2	Long Island Lighting Co.	0.6578	0.6653	0.6182
4	Marathon Oil	*******	0.5267	0.5463
8	McGraw Hill Inc.	0.6300	0.5098	0.5385
8	Mead Corporation	*******	0.6602	0.6602
5	Merck & Company	0.6214	0.6261	0.6107
2	Middle South Utilities Inc.	0.7000	0.6687	0.6493
8	Minnesota Mining & Manufacturing Co.	0.4262	0.4776	0.5000
8	Moore Corp.	0.4304	0.4546	0.4430
1	Motorola, Inc.	*******	0.3448	0.3200
6	National Biscuit Co. (NABISCO)	0.7179	0.6965	0.6796
1	National Cash Register Co. (NCR)	0.3478	0.3158	0.3478
6	National Dairy Prods. (Kraft Inc.)	0.5480	0.5503	0.5789
8	National Distillers & Chemical Corp.	0.5714	0.6000	0.6667
8	National Lead Co. (NL Industries)	0.7692	0.7104	0.7602
3	National Steel Corp.	*******	0.6038	0.5280
2	New York State Electric & Gas Co.	0.5954	0.6202	0.5958
2	Niagara Mohawk Power Corp.	0.7826	0.7551	0.7407
7	No. Amer. Aviation (Rockwell Intl.)	*******	0.5263	0.4494
7	North Amer. Car Corp. (Flying Tiger)	0.5600	0.5474	0.5517
2	Northern States Power Co.	0.7662	0.7569	0.7765
5	Norwich Phar. Co. (Morton-Norwich)	0.6461	0.5833	0.5833
2	Oklahoma Gas & Electric Co.	0.7643	0.7314	0.7368
7	Otis Elevator Co. (United Tech.)	0.5405	0.5378	0.6102
8	Owens-Corning Fiberglass Corp.	0.4348	0.4040	0.4211
2	Pacific Gas & Electric Co.	0.6133	0.6222	0.5882
6	Penney (J.C.) Co., Inc.	0.7059	0.6522	0.6742
5	Pfizer (Chas & Co.) Inc.	0.4857	0.4935	0.5060
3	Phelps Dodge Corp.	0.7500	0.7547	0.7101
8	Philip Morris Inc.	0.6372	0.6102	0.5902
4	Phillips Petroleum Co.	0.5152	0.5564	0.5781

1964	1965	1966	1967	1968	1969
0.8421	0.6780	*******	*******	*******	*******
0.5000	0.5634	0.5500	0.5000	0.4900	0.5700
0.3878	0.4040	0.4000	0.4000	0.3400	0.4800
0.5806	0.4852	0.6000	0.6000	0.6700	0.7800
0.6875	0.6932	0.6000	0.6000	0.6000	0.8800
0.6187	0.6250	0.6000	0.6000	0.7100	0.6000
0.3443	0.3288	0.4000	0.4000	0.3700	0.3600
0.6107	0.5223	0.6500	0.6000	0.6000	0.4800
0.4115	0.4493	0.6500	0.6000	0.6800	*******
0.5217	0.4800	0.5000	0.5000	0.3600	0.3500
0.6061	0.5641	0.5500	0.5000	0.6400	0.6400
0.6154	0.6291	0.6000	0.6000	0.6100	0.4800
0.5517	0.5229	0.6000	0.6000	0.5500	0.4700
0.6027	0.5020	0.6000	0.6000	0.4900	*******
0.7752	0.7905	0.7500	*******	*******	*******
0.7652	0.5957	0.6500	0.6000	0.4700	0.4800
*******	*******	0.0000	0.0000	0.0000	0.0000
0.3616	0.3571	0.4300	0.4000	0.5200	0.4800
0.6276	0.6222	0.7500	0.8000	*******	*******
0.5263	0.5059	0.5000	0.4000	0.5100	0.5300
0.5714	0.5714	0.5500	0.5000	0.5800	0.6000
0.6182	0.5271	0.6000	0.6000	0.5300	0.5500
0.7231	0.6667	0.6000	0.6000	0.7500	0.7800
0.6187	0.5573	0.7000	0.7000	0.6800	0.6600
0.5263	0.5000	0.5000	0.5000	0.4900	0.5000
0.4566	0.4267	0.4000	0.4000	*******	*******
0.2367	0.2174	0.3000	0.2000	0.2200	0.1800
0.6280	0.6086	0.6500	0.6000	0.6800	0.8100
0.3478	0.3153	0.4000	0.4000	0.3300	0.2800
0.5926	0.5306	0.5500	0.5000	0.6000	0.6100
0.6575	0.6087	0.6000	0.6000	*******	*******
0.7303	0.6736	0.7500	0.8000	0.8600	*******
0.4042	0.5427	0.5000	0.5000	0.5800	0.5600
0.6059	0.6586	0.7500	0.8000	*******	*******
0.7017	0.7714	0.9500	0.9000	0.7100	0.7300
0.4035	0.4538	0.5000	*******	*******	*******
0.5627	0.5643	0.5000	0.5000	*******	*******
0.7562	0.7385	0.7000	0.7000	*******	*******
0.5468	0.4968	0.6000	0.6000	0.4800	0.4900
0.7091	0.6431	0.7000	0.7000	*******	*******
0.5719	0.5399	0.6000	0.6000	0.7400	0.6800
0.4211	0.4370	0.4500	0.4000	0.5200	*******
0.6084	0.5975	0.7000	0.7000	0.6000	0.5500
0.6452	0.5914	0.5500	0.5000	0.4800	0.4500
0.5111	0.4771	0.5000	0.5000	0.5400	0.5300
0.6739	0.6897	0.6500	0.6000	0.6300	0.4600
0.5783	0.5275	0.5500	*******	*******	*******
0.5714	0.5256	0.5500	0.5000	0.6500	0.7600

Table 1.A.4 (continued)

Industry Code		1961	1962	1963
1	Pitney-Bowes, Inc.	0.4966	0.4923	0.4638
8	Pittsburg Plate Glass (PPG Ind.)	0.5641	0.5521	0.5357
8	Polaroid Corp.	0.0870	0.0714	0.0580
8	Prentice Hall Inc.	0.4444	0.3721	0.3721
6	Procter & Gamble Co.	0.5216	0.5088	0.5167
2	Public Service of Colorado	0.5474	0.6000	0.6400
2	Public Service Electric & Gas Co.	0.6029	0.6383	0.6323
1	Radio Corp. of America (RCA Corp.)	*******	0.4126	0.4262
3	Republic Steel Corp.	*******	0.6250	0.5714
3	Reynolds Metals Co.	0.2985	0.3077	0.2985
8	Reynolds (R.J.) Tob. Co. (Rey. Ind.)	0.4667	0.5079	0.5197
5	Richardson-Merrell Inc.	0.3107	0.3306	0.3053
8	Rohm/Haas Co.	0.1611	0.1963	0.2469
4	Royal Dutch Petroleum Co.	*******	0.3781	0.4000
6	Safeway Stores, Inc.	0.5276	0.5424	0.4925
8	Scott Paper Co.	0.6383	0.6274	0.6148
6	Sears, Roebuck & Co.	0.5405	0.4748	0.4861
4	Shell Oil Co.	0.4400	0.4400	0.5000
8	Singer Co.	*******	0.5167	0.5113
5	Smith Kline & French (Smithkline)	0.6757	0.6429	0.6667
4	Socony (Mobil Oil Corp.)	0.4592	0.5000	0.5253
2	Southern Co.	0.7229	0.6955	0.6936
2	Southwestern Public Service Co.	0.6960	0.7462	0.7368
1	Sperry Rand Corp.	*******	0.0000	0.0000
4	Standard Oil Co. of California	0.4270	0.4313	0.4255
4	Standard Oil Co. of Indiana	0.3200	0.4138	0.4000
4	Standard Oil of N.J. (Exxon)	0.6301	0.6250	0.6433
5	Sterling Drug Inc.	0.6154	0.5714	0.5565
7	Swift & Co. (Esmark)	0.5441	0.5766	0.5664
8	Talcott Nat. (Assoc. Fst. Cap. Corp.)	0.4895	0.4878	0.5263
2	Tampa Electric Co.	0.5961	0.5655	0.5875
4	Texaco Inc.	0.4662	0.4966	0.5250
8	Texas Gulf Sulphur Co. Inc.	0.7692	0.3860	0.3077
1	Texas Instruments, Inc.	*******	0.2330	0.2723
2	Texas Utilities Co.	0.6277	0.6027	0.5975
8	Union Carbide Corp.	0.6956	0.6857	0.6636
4	Union Oil Co. of California	0.4422	0.4422	0.4371
7	United Aircraft Corp. (United Tech.)	*******	0.5369	0.5229
7	U. S. Gypsum Co.	0.6000	0.6283	0.6231
8	U. S. Rubber (Uniroyal, Inc.)	0.5177	0.5333	0.5207
3	U. S. Steel Corp.	0.6316	0.6286	0.5333
5	Upjohn Inc.	0.4485	0.4776	0.4822
2	Virginia Electric & Power Co.	0.6191	0.6154	0.6030
1	Westinghouse Electric Corp.	0.5454	0.5581	0.5581
2	Wisconsin Electric Power Co.	*******	0.6433	0.6349
1	Xerox Corp.	0.2000	0.1528	0.1818
1	Zenith Radio Corp.	0.6158	0.5783	0.5806

1964	1965	1966	1967	1968	1969
0.4800	0.4506	0.5000	0.5000	0.0000	0.5200
0.5424	0.5208	0.5500	0.5000	0.5700	*******
0.0408	0.1040	*******	0.1000	0.1600	0.1600
0.4135	0.4392	0.4000	0.4000	0.5200	0.4300
0.5169	0.5373	0.5500	0.5000	0.6000	0.5700
0.5704	0.6035	0.7500	0.8000	0.6200	0.6400
0.6518	0.6318	0.8000	0.8000	0.6200	0.5800
0.4074	0.4610	0.4500	0.3000	0.4300	0.4200
0.4546	0.5161	0.6000	*******	*******	*******
0.2632	0.3116	0.3000	0.3000	0.5500	0.4000
0.5538	0.5482	0.5500	*******	*******	*******
0.2963	0.2685	0.3000	0.3000	0.3700	0.3600
0.2345	0.2219	0.2000	*******	0.2700	*******
0.4436	0.4658	0.4500	0.4000	0.4500	0.4600
0.5167	0.4706	0.5000	0.5000	0.5000	*******
0.6207	0.5813	0.6000	0.6000	0.6700	0.6000
0.4762	0.4612	0.5500	0.5000	0.5000	0.4700
0.4918	0.4626	0.4500	0.4000	0.4800	0.5300
0.4848	0.4862	0.6000	0.6000	0.5300	0.5000
0.6139	0.6491	0.6000	0.0000	0.6900	0.7100
0.4978	0.4919	0.5000	0.5000	0.5400	0.5000
0.6920	0.6536	0.7000	0.7000	0.7100	0.7000
0.7139	0.7212	0.7500	0.8000	0.8200	0.8500
0.0000	0.0000	0.0000	0.0000	0.1800	0.2100
0.4255	0.4282	0.4500	0.4000	0.4500	0.4900
0.5115	0.5210	0.5000	0.4000	0.5200	0.6400
0.6349	0.6146	0.6000	0.6000	0.6400	0.6400
0.5412	0.5333	0.6000	0.6000	0.5600	0.5300
0.5833	*******	*******	*******	*******	*******
0.5714	0.5797	0.5000	0.6000	*******	*******
0.5650	0.5098	0.6000	0.6000	0.6200	0.5600
0.4949	0.5213	0.5000	0.5000	0.4800	0.5300
0.1454	0.1143	0.4000	*******	*******	*******
0.2462	0.2210	0.2500	0.1000	0.3300	0.2700
0.5793	0.5583	0.6000	0.6000	0.5900	0.5600
0.6102	0.5882	0.7000	0.7000	0.7500	0.6800
0.4229	0.3559	0.3500	0.3000	0.3000	0.4700
0.3653	0.2745	0.3200	0.4000	0.3500	0.4500
0.6214	0.6632	0.6500	0.8000	0.3300	0.9800
0.4656	0.8748	0.4500	0.4000	0.8400	0.3600
0.4000	0.4878	0.6500	0.6000	0.7100	0.6000
0.4938	0.4706	0.5000	0.5000	0.6800	0.6200
0.6197	0.6051	0.7000	0.7000	0.6500	0.6400
0.5714	0.4673	0.6500	0.6000	0.5300	0.4800
0.6523	0.6137	0.7000	0.7000	*******	*******
0.2234	0.1667	0.2500	0.3000	0.3000	0.2900
0.5345	0.6452	0.5500	0.5000	0.5500	0.6500

Table 1.A.5   **Variance of the Long-Term Growth Forecasts (σ_p^2)**

Industry Code		1961	1962	1963
7	A.C.F. Industries, Inc.	*******	2.5166	2.0000
1	Addressograph-Multigraph (AM Corp.)	2.3094	1.6733	1.4720
8	Air Reduction Co. (B.O.C. Fin. Corp.)	1.4142	1.5275	1.6073
2	Allegheny Power System Inc.	*******	0.5774	0.8539
8	Allied Chemical Corp.	1.4142	1.0000	2.1602
3	Alcan Aluminum Ltd.	*******	7.2111	7.6322
3	Aluminum Company of America	2.7538	5.6745	6.3087
4	Amerada Pet. (Amerada Hess)	2.1213	1.7321	1.4142
5	American Cyanamid Co.	2.0000	1.5000	0.8165
2	American Electric Power Co.	0.5000	0.7071	0.6325
5	American Home Products Corp.	1.1547	1.5000	1.0954
8	Amer. Mach. & Foundry Co. (AMF Ind.)	2.1213	1.0000	1.8930
8	Amer. Nat. Gas Co. (Amer. Nat. Res.)	*******	1.0000	1.0308
3	Amer. Smelt. & Refin. (UV Ind.)	*******	4.9329	2.8723
8	American Telephone & Telegraph Co.	0.5000	0.6646	0.7528
8	American Tobacco (Amer. Brands, Inc.)	*******	0.0000	0.0000
3	Anaconda Co.	*******	2.8868	3.3040
3	Armco Steel Corp. (ARMCO Inc.)	2.1213	2.3805	3.7815
7	Armour & Co. (Esmark)	*******	1.4142	0.9574
4	Atlantic Richfield Co.	*******	1.0000	0.5000
8	Atlas Chem. Ind. Inc. (Imperial Ch.)	*******	2.0817	2.0000
2	Baltimore Gas & Electric Co.	*******	0.5000	0.7416
1	Beckman Instruments, Inc.	2.3094	1.4720	2.5820
8	Beneficial Finance Co.	0.7071	1.5275	0.8165
3	Bethlehem Steel Corp.	*******	4.3589	5.0662
7	Boeing Co.	*******	2.3094	3.3665
6	Borden Inc.	0.0000	0.5774	0.5774
2	Boston Edison Co.	*******	0.5774	0.5774
5	Bristol-Myers Co.	1.7321	1.2111	1.3801
1	Burroughs Corp.	*******	5.5076	1.5275
8	C.I.T. Financial Corp. (RCA Corp.)	1.7321	1.3416	1.6432
6	Campbell Soup Co.	0.5774	0.6325	0.7868
7	Caterpillar Tractor Co.	0.7071	1.8708	1.5811
2	Central & Southwest Corp.	0.5774	0.4472	0.4756
2	Cincinnati Gas & Electric Co.	*******	0.5774	0.0000
4	Cities Service Co.	*******	2.0000	0.0000
2	Cleveland Electric Illuminating Co.	1.1547	0.9574	0.5000
6	Colgate Palmolive Co.	*******	1.0000	1.8257
2	Consolidated Edison Co.	*******	0.2500	0.5477
2	Consumers Power Co.	0.7071	0.9574	0.6291
4	Continental Oil Co. (CONOCO)	2.0817	1.5000	1.3416
6	Corn Products Co. (CPC Intl. Inc.)	1.1547	0.8944	0.8367
8	Crown Zellerback	*******	2.0817	2.0616
1	Cutler-Hammer Inc. (Eaton Corp.)	*******	3.5119	1.5275
2	Dayton Power & Light Co.	*******	0.5774	0.5774
2	Detroit Edison Co.	*******	0.7071	0.4787
8	Dow Chemical	2.3805	1.5275	1.4142
2	Duquesne Light Co.	*******	0.5774	0.5000

1964	1965	1966	1967	1968
1.1547	2.5166	*******	*******	*******
1.2724	1.3973	4.3330	5.3330	6.2530
1.7078	0.8367	0.0000	4.5000	5.1200
0.8944	0.9747	0.0000	0.0000	0.0000
1.3571	1.4960	1.0000	2.3330	1.0530
1.5055	3.3116	4.3330	4.0000	62.1000
1.7895	2.8284	4.3330	2.3330	43.3200
3.9328	2.0736	0.5000	0.0000	14.0500
1.5626	1.3292	0.3333	0.3333	1.1630
0.5976	0.6232	0.0833	0.0833	0.1033
1.2247	1.4142	0.0000	1.0000	8.0530
1.1402	0.8367	0.5000	*******	*******
1.0368	0.9832	0.2500	0.2500	0.1250
1.7440	1.2813	0.3333	5.3330	*******
0.6346	0.4173	0.0000	0.3333	0.3333
1.0488	1.0488	0.0000	0.0000	*******
1.7889	1.3663	4.5000	2.0000	81.9200
1.3784	1.7995	0.5000	0.5000	12.0100
2.2174	2.3805	*******	*******	*******
3.2787	2.5565	1.3330	12.3300	29.0800
2.0817	5.0332	18.0000	*******	*******
0.6268	0.6986	0.0833	0.5833	3.3700
3.4641	2.8284	13.0000	33.3300	25.7200
1.2374	1.0351	0.0000	0.5000	1.4450
1.3038	1.7440	0.5000	0.5000	41.4100
2.9496	1.2247	57.3300	21.0000	*******
0.9832	1.5059	0.3333	1.0000	0.2533
0.2500	0.7416	0.2500	0.0000	0.0000
1.6690	1.7269	1.0000	1.3330	12.8100
2.5100	4.3205	78.1300	4.5000	91.1300
0.4082	0.5670	0.5000	0.1250	0.0200
0.7440	1.0690	0.5000	0.5000	5.7800
1.2817	1.2817	7.0000	21.000	19.2000
0.6667	0.5000	0.0000	0.0000	0.0133
0.2500	0.2236	0.0000	0.0000	6.1250
0.6708	1.0206	0.0833	1.3330	6.4130
0.6519	0.8010	0.0833	0.0833	5.2630
1.3571	1.2007	3.0830	5.2500	0.7200
0.9940	1.1073	0.3333	0.3333	0.9633
0.6646	0.6124	0.2500	0.0833	4.3200
2.7124	2.0863	0.0000	1.3330	4.2030
0.4880	0.7559	0.3333	0.3333	5.0630
2.3022	1.6330	2.3330	1.7500	1.7500
2.5100	2.8723	4.0000	9.3330	6.8030
0.2236	0.4916	0.1250	0.1250	6.4800
0.5701	0.9487	0.0833	0.0833	2.2300
1.4720	1.5119	2.3330	2.3330	9.6700
0.2887	0.2500	0.5000	0.5000	*******

Table 1.A.5 (continued)

Industry Code		1961	1962	1963
8	Eastman Kodak Co.	0.8367	0.8944	1.0690
7	Ex-Cell-O Corp.	*******	2.6458	2.0817
6	Federated Dept Stores Inc.	1.4142	0.8367	1.0328
8	Firestone Tire & Rubber Co.	0.5774	0.5000	1.0954
2	Florida Power Corp.	0.9574	0.7416	0.5477
2	Florida Power & Light Co.	1.2247	1.1143	0.5345
6	Food Fair, Inc.	*******	1.0000	1.0000
7	Ford Motor Co.	*******	1.4142	1.2583
7	General Amer. Transp. Corp. (GATX)	0.7071	0.5774	0.5774
1	General Electric Co.	0.8165	1.5811	1.0488
6	General Foods Corp.	1.7078	1.0328	0.8367
6	General Mills Inc.	*******	3.2146	2.0616
7	General Motors Corp.	0.0000	2.1679	1.3038
7	General Portland Cement Co.	*******	1.7321	1.2583
2	General Public Utilities Corp.	1.1547	1.0000	0.0000
8	General Telephone & Electronics	0.8165	1.3769	1.5969
8	Goodrich (B.F.) Co.	0.0000	0.5774	1.8930
8	Goodyear Tire & Rubber Co.	0.5774	1.4142	2.0736
6	Grand Union Co. (Cavenham Ltd.)	1.1547	1.3150	1.1547
6	Great Atlantic & Pacific Tea Co.	0.8660	1.4832	1.7819
4	Gulf Oil Corp.	0.5774	1.0000	1.1402
2	Gulf States Utilities Co.	1.5275	0.5000	0.4787
6	Heinz (H. J.) Co.	0.7071	0.5774	0.0000
8	Hercules Inc.	3.3665	1.9748	1.6047
1	Hewlett Packard Co.	4.9497	2.4221	2.5884
1	Honeywell Inc.	1.7889	1.2111	1.7182
8	Household Finance Corp.	*******	1.5275	1.2583
2	Houston Ltg. & Pow. Co. (Hous. Inds.)	0.5000	0.8367	0.6646
2	Idaho Power Co.	*******	1.0000	1.0000
7	Ideal Cement (Ideal Basic Ind. Inc.)	*******	2.0817	1.7321
2	Illinois Power Co.	1.0000	0.5774	0.4472
7	Ingersoll-Rand Co.	1.4142	0.5774	0.5774
3	Inland Steel Co.	1.5275	2.0000	2.1679
1	International Business Machines	0.7071	1.8708	1.6330
7	International Harvester Co.	*******	1.1547	0.8539
3	Intl. Nickel Co. Canada (INCO)	2.5166	3.9623	0.4472
8	International Paper Co.	2.1213	2.0000	2.0616
1	Intl. Telephone & Telegraph Corp.	2.8284	4.3493	1.9235
7	Johns-Manville Corp.	1.4142	1.2583	1.2583
3	Jones & Laug. Steel Corp. (LTV Corp.)	*******	5.1962	4.0000
3	Kaiser Aluminum & Chemical Corp.	*******	7.3711	7.1181
6	Kellogg Co.	*******	1.2910	0.9574
3	Kennecott Copper Corp.	*******	1.0000	1.8930
8	Kimberly-Clark Corp.	0.3536	0.9747	0.5477
6	Kroger Co.	0.7071	0.5000	1.8166
8	Liggett & Myers (Liggett Group)	*******	1.5275	0.9574
5	Lilly Eli Co.	2.8284	1.5275	2.4958
1	Litton Industries, Inc.	2.9861	2.7869	1.9518

1964	1965	1966	1967	1968
0.6124	1.8708	1.3330	4.0000	68.4000
1.1402	1.2910	*******	*******	*******
0.8345	0.7817	0.3333	1.0000	6.3330
0.8381	0.9449	7.0000	8.3330	29.8000
0.8092	0.8092	2.0000	2.0000	0.0000
0.7440	0.4629	0.5000	0.3333	0.6533
0.9574	0.8367	0.5000	2.0000	*******
0.7528	1.3874	9.7500	*******	0.5000
1.1127	1.3292	*******	*******	*******
1.1160	1.4865	1.7500	1.7500	2.2800
0.7071	1.2019	0.3333	0.3333	0.4133
1.9235	1.3663	2.0000	2.0000	14.0500
0.9039	1.0000	7.5830	20.3300	4.1700
1.0000	2.0616	*******	12.5000	*******
0.3780	0.4880	0.1250	0.1250	0.0450
1.0836	1.1547	1.3330	1.3330	9.6700
1.3416	1.2649	6.2500	13.5800	7.6300
1.6421	1.5980	8.0830	8.3330	24.4100
1.4930	1.3038	0.5000	0.0000	72.0000
1.2649	0.9759	2.0000	0.0000	7.2200
1.2247	1.0329	0.1250	3.0000	52.6800
0.7583	0.8522	0.7500	0.5833	1.3300
1.7078	1.2583	1.2800	2.0000	*******
0.8522	0.8165	2.3330	2.3330	3.2130
3.1091	3.1091	4.5000	4.3330	29.2300
3.2642	1.1260	1.3330	8.3330	14.1700
1.2374	1.1667	0.0000	0.1250	74.4200
0.6455	0.6124	0.7500	0.7500	0.5700
1.0000	0.6646	0.7500	0.5833	5.7630
0.8367	0.8944	*******	*******	*******
0.7480	0.9063	0.5833	0.5833	1.4700
0.5000	0.8944	4.5000	*******	*******
1.7559	1.7762	0.0000	0.0000	1.2800
1.2693	1.2693	0.0000	3.0000	2.2030
0.7416	1.6330	4.3330	4.3330	25.4800
1.1073	1.2488	6.3330	1.3330	0.9033
1.3292	1.3292	2.3330	2.3330	9.0030
1.6330	1.4639	1.0000	1.3330	2.4700
1.4832	1.0328	1.0000	0.3333	20.3000
0.5000	1.6253	5.3330	5.3330	20.4800
3.0605	3.1689	4.5000	18.0000	60.5000
0.8165	0.6325	0.0000	0.0000	7.6050
1.6583	1.8619	4.3330	16.0000	24.0000
1.0206	0.9940	2.2500	2.5830	2.5830
1.0206	0.7868	0.0000	0.5000	1.4450
1.2247	1.2247	*******	*******	*******
1.6047	2.6882	3.1250	0.5000	18.0000
1.8077	1.8516	13.0000	13.0000	2.8130

Table 1.A.5 (continued)

Industry Code		1961	1962	1963
7	Lockheed Aircraft Corp.	*******	2.6458	1.5000
2	Long Island Lighting Co.	*******	0.5774	0.2887
4	Marathon Oil	*******	3.7859	2.2174
8	McGraw Hill Inc.	1.2910	1.3663	1.4960
8	Mead Corporation	*******	2.5166	3.1623
5	Merck & Company	1.1402	1.7889	1.4960
2	Middle South Utilities Inc.	0.7071	0.5774	0.2236
8	Minnesota Mining & Manufacturing Co.	1.9235	2.0976	2.4103
8	Moore Corp.	0.0000	1.0000	1.5000
1	Motorola, Inc.	*******	2.0817	1.6330
6	National Biscuit Co. (NABISCO)	1.4142	0.9574	1.8166
1	National Cash Register Co. (NCR)	2.1213	2.3381	1.9149
6	National Dairy Prods. (Kraft Inc.)	0.0000	0.2887	0.2500
8	National Distillers & Chemical Corp.	*******	1.5275	2.5166
8	National Lead Co. (NL Industries)	1.9149	1.7078	1.7970
3	National Steel Corp.	*******	4.7258	3.4248
2	New York State Electric & Gas Co.	*******	1.2583	1.154?
2	Niagara Mohawk Power Corp.	*******	0.8165	0.4787
7	No. Amer. Aviation (Rockwell Intl.)	*******	2.1602	1.8257
7	North Amer. Car Corp. (Flying Tiger)	4.2426	4.8563	1.5000
2	Northern States Power Co.	*******	0.0000	0.5000
5	Norwich Phar. Co. (Morton-Norwich)	0.9574	1.2247	1.8257
2	Oklahoma Gas & Electric Co.	*******	1.5275	0.5000
7	Otis Elevator Co. (United Tech.)	0.7071	0.5000	1.4318
8	Owens-Corning Fiberglass Corp.	2.1602	1.5166	1.3038
2	Pacific Gas & Electric Co.	0.5774	0.5000	0.8944
6	Penney (J.C.) Co., Inc.	0.7071	1.0000	0.9574
5	Pfizer (Chas & Co.) Inc.	1.1547	1.4142	0.6986
3	Phelps Dodge Corp.	*******	3.0551	2.6300
8	Philip Morris Inc.	*******	0.5774	0.0000
4	Phillips Petroleum Co.	0.0000	0.5774	0.5000
1	Pitney-Bowes, Inc.	0.0000	1.5166	1.6733
8	Pittsburg Plate Glass (PPG Ind.)	1.0000	1.5275	2.5000
8	Polaroid Corp.	5.1186	6.4936	6.8605
8	Prentice Hall Inc.	3.5355	1.3416	1.8974
6	Procter & Gamble Co.	1.5811	1.2247	1.1127
2	Public Service of Colorado	0.0000	1.6733	1.5166
2	Public Service Electric & Gas Co.	0.0000	1.1547	0.5774
1	Radio Corp. of America (RCA Corp.)	*******	4.5735	1.8166
3	Republic Steel Corp.	*******	3.6056	4.8563
3	Reynolds Metals Co.	3.5355	7.5443	6.8557
8	Reynolds (R.J.) Tob. Co. (Rey. Ind.)	*******	1.5275	1.2583
5	Richardson-Merrell Inc.	1.8257	1.8257	1.2247
8	Rohm/Haas Co.	3.4034	2.4014	2.5884
4	Royal Dutch Petroleum Co.	*******	1.5000	0.5000
6	Safeway Stores, Inc.	1.4142	1.0408	0.8944
8	Scott Paper Co.	0.9574	1.0488	1.2111
6	Sears, Roebuck & Co.	2.3094	1.0488	1.0408

1964	1965	1966	1967	1968
1.9235	3.6056	28.0000	6.3330	4.0300
0.4472	0.5477	0.2500	15.2500	0.5000
3.5835	3.1689	0.5833	4.3330	14.2500
0.9258	1.1650	9.3330	21.0000	36.6000
2.0966	1.9235	1.1250	0.5000	3.3800
1.5119	1.6159	1.3330	2.3330	68.2100
0.6455	0.6075	0.0833	0.0833	1.2130
1.5526	0.9161	3.1250	2.5830	4.5000
0.5477	0.5477	1.0000	0.5000	*******
1.3801	2.7484	9.3330	28.0000	17.7600
1.1339	1.1339	2.3330	1.0000	0.2633
2.1667	1.6915	4.3330	9.0000	12.6500
0.7559	0.7569	0.3333	0.3333	2.8030
1.5000	1.6432	2.3330	1.3330	*******
1.3801	0.7638	0.5000	8.0000	27.3800
1.2450	1.8371	2.0000	2.3330	15.0800
1.0000	1.0000	*******	*******	*******
0.7583	0.5164	0.0833	0.0833	0.0033
1.6432	1.7464	1.3330	*******	*******
2.7080	2.4495	*******	*******	*******
0.4472	0.4183	0.1250	0.1250	*******
0.8367	0.4472	0.0000	0.5000	6.8850
1.0954	1.0328	0.0833	0.0833	0.5000
1.3038	1.8166	*******	*******	*******
*******	1.2724	2.0000	0.5000	26.6500
0.5000	0.5345	0.3333	0.3333	3.0000
1.6938	1.1476	0.1250	0.0000	6.8130
0.5271	0.7817	0.3333	3.0000	1.3330
1.2813	0.6646	0.3333	14.3300	22.2300
0.5774	1.3038	3.1250	*******	*******
1.0746	1.1495	0.2500	6.3330	3.8030
0.9174	0.9174	9.0000	9.3330	10.9200
2.1679	1.7889	4.5000	4.5000	80.6500
6.0553	7.0071	84.5000	16.3300	*******
1.7889	1.6733	4.5000	0.0000	73.2000
1.0351	0.9613	1.0830	0.2500	1.8050
0.4880	0.5000	0.0000	0.0000	1.6200
0.6124	0.6124	0.5833	0.5833	0.0833
3.1411	1.7224	4.3330	4.0000	82.0300
0.8367	1.5055	2.3330	*******	*******
3.2326	2.5642	9.0000	9.3330	75.7300
0.8165	0.9832	0.3333	0.5000	*******
0.5164	1.2150	2.0000	0.5000	0.3200
1.5736	1.8127	8.0000	*******	15.1300
0.5477	0.8165	1.3330	2.3330	7.4530
1.3663	0.5774	0.1250	0.5000	0.9800
1.2247	1.0000	1.3330	0.0833	1.7200
1.0000	1.1304	0.3333	3.0000	4.8530

Table 1.A.5 (continued)

Industry Code		1961	1962	1963
4	Shell Oil Co.	0.5774	0.5000	0.4472
8	Singer Co.	*******	2.0616	0.5774
5	Smith Kline & French (Smithkline)	1.6733	1.0328	1.6036
4	Socony (Mobil Oil Corp.)	*******	2.3094	0.9574
2	Southern Co.	0.9574	0.5477	0.5477
2	Southwestern Public Service Co.	*******	0.4787	0.4787
1	Sperry Rand Corp.	*******	3.2146	3.3040
4	Standard Oil Co. of California	0.7071	1.7321	0.5000
4	Standard Oil Co. of Indiana	0.7071	0.5774	2.3094
4	Standard Oil of N.J. (Exxon)	2.5166	1.5811	1.3038
5	Sterling Drug Inc.	0.0000	0.5774	2.0817
7	Swift & Co. (Esmark)	*******	0.7071	0.5774
8	Talcott Nat. (Assoc. Fst. Cap. Corp.)	1.9149	1.2649	0.8367
2	Tampa Electric Co.	0.7071	0.6291	0.2500
4	Texaco Inc.	1.1547	0.8367	1.1402
8	Texas Gulf Sulphur Co. Inc.	*******	1.7321	1.5275
1	Texas Instruments, Inc.	3.5590	3.3466	3.2660
2	Texas Utilities Co.	1.0000	0.7416	0.6519
8	Union Carbide Corp.	1.9149	1.3038	0.8944
4	Union Oil Co. of California	*******	2.5166	0.5774
7	United Aircraft Corp. (United Tech.)	*******	7.5719	4.0825
7	U. S. Gypsum Co.	0.0000	1.7078	1.7176
8	U. S. Rubber (Uniroyal, Inc.)	0.7071	0.7071	0.5774
3	U. S. Steel Corp.	1.5275	1.5275	3.4641
5	Upjohn Inc.	1.3038	2.4833	2.4976
2	Virginia Electric & Power Co.	0.5774	0.7071	0.4916
1	Westinghouse Electric Corp.	0.0000	4.9244	1.9235
2	Wisconsin Electric Power Co.	*******	0.0000	0.5774
1	Xerox Corp.	0.0000	6.4083	3.9940
1	Zenith Radio Corp.	*******	1.4142	2.2174

1964	1965	1966	1967	1968
1.6890	1.3999	1.3330	0.3333	8.2530
1.5166	0.5477	1.3330	8.0000	2.4200
1.2247	1.3025	0.0833	3.5830	1.0030
1.0488	1.4100	0.5833	2.2500	4.0130
0.7559	0.3720	1.3330	0.0833	0.2633
0.7583	0.6646	1.1250	1.1250	19.8500
0.8367	1.3229	2.0000	2.0000	*******
1.6036	1.2488	0.2500	1.0830	4.0530
1.3048	0.9449	0.2500	4.0000	11.2600
1.5222	1.2660	0.0000	1.0830	4.0530
1.6021	1.1726	4.0830	4.3330	6.3330
2.0616	2.5166	*******	*******	*******
2.7928	1.1547	2.0000	0.1250	*******
0.4472	0.4916	0.5000	0.5000	2.4200
1.4142	0.9797	1.0830	0.2500	1.3330
22.5000	23.9730	84.5000	*******	*******
2.0310	2.1381	12.0000	6.3330	38.4500
0.8010	0.6646	0.0833	0.0833	0.5033
1.3844	1.2360	0.2500	0.2500	1.1630
3.0923	3.2146	0.3333	4.0000	*******
3.0332	0.8944	52.0000	21.0000	96.5800
0.7039	0.7868	1.3330	6.3330	0.2450
1.7500	1.8166	3.1250	10.1300	*******
1.3292	1.6021	1.3330	1.3330	8.0530
1.6850	1.7043	6.3330	0.0000	0.1200
0.4859	0.4410	0.3333	0.3333	0.2633
1.5166	2.3664	5.3330	7.0000	66.5600
0.5774	0.4787	*******	12.5000	*******
3.3991	4.7170	6.3330	6.3330	*******
1.4720	3.2094	4.3330	4.0000	28.6500

2   Consensus, Accuracy, and Completeness of the Earnings Growth Forecasts

We study in this chapter the nature of the forecasts made by security analysts that were described in chapter 1. To do so we look at three questions: (*a*) To what extent are the forecasts of different analysts similar to each other and to forecasts that might be produced by some explicit, "objective" methods? (*b*) How accurate are the forecasted growth rates when compared with the quantities that were later realized? (*c*) Are the forecasts complete in the sense that they use all information which should have been readily available to the forecasters when they formulated their predictions? This last question is related to whether we can reasonably consider the forecasts to represent "rational" expectations. Relative to many investigations of expectations in other fields,[1] this study is characterized by having comparatively few predictors and by covering predictions made over a period of slightly less than a decade. This is balanced, however, by the study's access to a large number of forecasts from each predictor.

2.1 Importance of a Study of Growth Forecast Accuracy

Financial theorists have emphasized for years the importance of expectational variables in the valuation of common stocks. Accordingly the price of a share should be determined primarily by investors' current expectations about the firm's future performance and profitability, particularly the anticipated growth rate of earnings and dividends per share. Modern financial literature emphasizes the link between anticipated risk

---

1. A number of studies of anticipations data have been collected by Zarnowitz (1967). Some more recent work on the assessment of expectations or forecasts has been done by Mincer (1969), Pesando (1975), Pearce (1978), and Friedman (1980).

and return; and the capital-asset pricing model, developed by Sharpe (1964), Lintner (1965), and Mossin (1966), has become a widely used approach to security valuation. Central to this approach is expected return, even though its nature has not been stressed. Empirical studies of price-earnings ratios of common stocks (including those described in chapter 4) find that the most important explanatory variables are expectational ones, especially those measuring the anticipated future growth rate of the corporation.[2] Other empirical investigators who have studied the determination of stock-price changes have similarly put heavy emphasis on the importance of variables measuring the growth of the firm. For example, Nerlove (1968) found that two of the most important variables explaining differences in the actual price performance of individual common stocks over both short and long periods were the growth of sales and earnings and the retention of earnings, which is related to future growth. Nerlove's results suggest that growth forecasts are needed in order to predict differential returns from individual common stocks.

This analytical emphasis is matched by efforts in the financial community of security analysts to forecast the future earnings and dividends and to judge the risk levels of the companies they study. Thus financial theorists, practitioners, and empirical researchers all agree on the importance of these expectational inputs in determining the prices of common stocks. A study of growth forecasts would seem to be of critical importance in understanding how capital markets value different securities.

2.2 Agreement among Predictors

The extent to which the different growth-rate projections are in agreement is described and summarized in this section. As chapter 1 explained, the growth forecasts estimated by security analysts are of two types: (a) long-run forecasts representing the anticipated average annual rate of growth expected to occur over the next five years, and (b) forecasts of earnings per share for the following year. We converted the latter into one-year percentage rates of growth by using the average "normalized" earnings estimates of the analysts as a common base.

Forecasts of long-term growth made by nine predictors were available during the 1961–65 period while eleven forecasters provided short-term growth estimates. However, data were not available from each forecaster in each of the five years, and ten of the eleven forecasters of short-term

2. The classic statement of the anticipations view of the determination of share valuation may be found in Williams (1938). This position is also adopted in the standard textbook in the field, Graham et al. (1962). The emphasis on the importance of earnings growth may also be found in Gordon (1962), Holt (1962), and Malkiel (1963).

growth were different from the forecasters of long-term growth. More limited numbers of forecasts were available for the period 1966–69.

The question of the extent of agreement among predictors is important in the development of the capital-asset pricing model. It has been usual in that literature to assume that all market participants have identical expectations concerning all security returns. Similarly, most economic theories that embody expectations, including most of the "rational expectations" literature, implicitly assume that all participants hold the same expectations. Our data make possible for the first time an examination of this assumption with respect to predictions formed for judging the values of common stocks.

2.2.1 Comparisons of Different Predictions

We start by considering the extent of agreement between each pair of predictors with respect to the relative growth prospects of companies by calculating correlation and rank correlation coefficients. These measures ignore any disagreements concerning the expected overall average rates of growth or concerning dispersion of growth rates among companies.

Table 2.1 gives the correlations among the long-term growth predictions. Below the main diagonals of the table we report the product-moment correlations; we present the Spearman rank correlations above the diagonals. Each correlation is based on all the observations (companies) available for each pair of forecasters. Correlations are calculated in the usual way. The correlation matrix with elements consisting of these separate correlations need not be positive definite. Only results for the

Table 2.1   **Agreement among Long-Term Growth Predictors**

			1961		
Predictor	1	2	3	6	8
1	***	.78	.87	.83	.81
2	.82	***	.67	.58	.74
3	.95	.79	***	.93	.76
6	.90	.77	.97	***	.71
8	.85	.73	.74	.76	***

			1962			
Predictor	1	2	4	5	6	7
1	***	.78	.75	.39	.73	.70
2	.85	***	.74	.61	.82	.80
4	.89	.82	***	.69	.82	.61
5	.57	.63	.85	***	.72	.44
6	.83	.86	.86	.77	***	.67
7	.84	.86	.83	.67	.82	***

Table 2.1 (continued)

					1963			
Predictor	1	2	3	4	5	6	7	
1	***	.81	.70	.72	.38	.69	.80	
2	.84	***	.81	.76	.54	.75	.82	
3	.83	.83	***	.75	.45	.86	.70	
4	.85	.76	.89	***	.75	.81	.74	
5	.55	.57	.71	.90	***	.76	.57	
6	.79	.77	.89	.88	.88	***	.72	
7	.88	.85	.83	.83	.66	.76	***	

					1964				
Predictor	1	2	3	4	5	6	7	8	9
1	***	.79	.73	.71	.76	.77	.63	.77	.66
2	.83	***	.76	.86	.77	.83	.66	.79	.78
3	.90	.91	***	.77	.79	.77	.67	.69	.83
4	.83	.87	.95	***	.62	.77	.49	.69	.61
5	.86	.86	.81	.84	***	.71	.72	.79	.66
6	.76	.79	.77	.85	.86	***	.70	.73	.58
7	.48	.52	.82	.64	.81	.73	***	.62	.66
8	.91	.90	.92	.89	.85	.79	.82	***	.67
9	.81	.89	.93	.81	.83	.63	.76	.88	***

					1965				
Predictor	1	2	3	4	5	6	7	8	9
1	***	.72	.63	.64	.74	.75	.52	.78	.53
2	.80	***	.79	.80	.78	.80	.64	.73	.68
3	.84	.89	***	.79	.79	.81	.67	.73	.73
4	.82	.87	.94	***	.72	.79	.82	.67	.71
5	.84	.85	.80	.86	***	.77	.66	.66	.49
6	.78	.77	.79	.87	.83	***	.66	.69	.66
7	.47	.46	.79	.84	.50	.71	***	.49	.62
8	.90	.88	.91	.90	.82	.76	.81	***	.54
9	.90	.88	.97	.95	.90	.88	.92	.91	***

NOTE. Simple correlations in lower left, Spearman rank correlations in upper right.

years 1961 through 1965 are shown because of the limited numbers of forecasters available in later periods. Table 2.2 presents the corresponding figures for the short-term predictors. In the tables the long-term predictors are numbered 1 through 9 while the short-term predictors are designated A through K. This serves to emphasize that the short- and long-term predictors are not the same.

Tables 2.1 and 2.2 do suggest considerable consensus. The correlations are generally significantly different from zero well beyond conventionally used significance levels. However, the lack of agreement they reveal is substantial and possibly more striking. Agreement tended to be greatest among the long-term predictors, but the average correlation coefficient was only about three-fourths. This suggests that only half the variance in one individual's predictions can typically be "explained" by agreement with those of another. Agreement was substantially less among the short-term predictors. Even ignoring predictor E, which made comparatively few forecasts and showed a tendency toward lower agreement, the average pairwise correlation coefficient was not much above one-half.

No great differences are evident when rank correlations are used rather than product-moment ones. The rank correlations may be aggregated

Table 2.2   **Agreement among Predictors of Short-Term Growth Rates**

1961

Pred.	A	B	C	D	E	G	H	I	K
A	***	.51	.71	.80	.48	.72	.67	.66	.68
B	.67	***	.54	.67	.54	.53	.85	.62	.59
C	.71	.69	***	.61	.41	.52	.49	.55	.52
D	.74	.83	.76	***	.65	.53	.80	.81	.73
E	.48	.45	.39	.83	***	.37	.71	.48	.74
G	.61	.78	.57	.82	.65	***	.35	.62	.54
H	.54	.92	.50	.77	.71	.39	***	.55	.61
I	.71	.79	.70	.81	.48	.78	.63	***	.70
K	.69	.80	.78	.86	.80	.71	.62	.77	***

1962

Pred.	A	B	C	D	E	G	H	I	K
A	***	.68	.57	.56	.15	.33	.81	.69	.51
B	.91	***	.36	.49	.03	.44	.54	.52	.63
C	.43	.71	***	.57	.07	.44	.64	.61	.61
D	.49	.72	.70	***	.26	.34	.44	.62	.54
E	.03	− .04	.15	.12	***	.33	.47	.27	.47
G	.54	.80	.73	.54	.67	***	.56	.55	.35
H	.82	.63	.69	.39	.13	.61	***	.59	.49
I	.75	.76	.77	.49	.13	.74	.74	***	.49
K	.79	.95	.86	.73	.75	.68	.55	.78	***

1963

Pred.	A	B	C	D	E	F	G	H	I	K
A	***	.69	.53	.56	.27	.62	.62	.81	.67	.70
B	.85	***	.45	.34	.17	.69	.58	.65	.66	.76
C	.55	.57	***	.28	.36	.44	.66	.58	.48	.66
D	.58	.17	.44	***	.26	.67	.48	.65	.55	.55
E	.49	− .03	.25	.53	***	− .25	.53	.33	.49	.41
F	.57	.83	.64	.72	− .29	***	.59	.82	.67	.74
G	.71	.85	.79	.50	.70	.71	***	.70	.64	.75
H	.91	.62	.68	.69	.43	.85	.81	***	.77	.76
I	.74	.88	.61	.64	.68	.80	.73	.88	***	.70
K	.60	.79	.70	.51	.63	.74	.84	.73	.80	***

Table 2.2 (continued)

Pred.	A	B	C	D	E	F	G	H	I	K
					1964					
A	***	.82	.60	.82	.19	.82	.51	.78	.48	.76
B	.89	***	.47	.64	.55	.79	.53	.78	.57	.80
C	.48	.75	***	.49	.81	.50	.45	.55	.43	.78
D	.75	.79	.61	***	.09	.73	.68	.72	.58	.77
E	.25	.31	.25	.17	***	.28	.36	.13	.29	.55
F	.48	.89	.67	.81	.24	***	.49	.71	.55	.68
G	.42	.75	.73	.74	.34	.70	***	.60	.63	.53
H	.91	.81	.72	.82	−.11	.77	.80	***	.70	.62
I	.50	.80	.88	.78	.46	.72	.78	.86	***	.65
K	.54	.88	.89	.85	.52	.80	.62	.75	.85	***

Pred.	A	B	C	D	E	F	G	H	I	J	K
						1965					
A	***	.84	.69	.51	.53	.71	.65	.82	.65	.72	.71
B	.93	***	.67	.57	.46	.77	.78	.69	.84	.79	.82
C	.47	.80	***	.61	.86	.67	.71	.83	.63	.75	.82
D	−.06	.61	.48	***	.41	.54	.71	.80	.70	.62	.71
E	.53	.76	.85	.54	***	.54	.48	.52	.66	.01	.74
F	.64	.84	.71	.39	.69	***	.64	.80	.78	.92	.88
G	.31	.80	.47	.69	.47	.58	***	.89	.81	.81	.86
H	.86	.86	.89	.85	.50	.82	.83	***	.86	.72	.90
I	.28	.90	.66	.65	.62	.58	.83	.80	***	.60	.86
J	.94	.92	.74	.86	−.01	.97	.87	.84	.85	***	.87
K	.44	.89	.87	.64	.56	.91	.88	.93	.88	.91	***

NOTE. Simple correlation coefficients in lower left, Spearman rank correlations in upper right.

using Kendall's coefficient of concordance (W).[3] Values for this statistic are reported in table 2.3 for selected groups of long- and short-term predictors where substantial overlap occurred in the companies covered. This table reveals on a simultaneous, nonparametric basis much the same results as those shown by the correlations. Agreement certainly is present, but it is far from being complete. Possibly surprisingly, the short-term concordances are typically not much smaller than the long-term ones.

A rather different way of looking at the agreement among predictors is to see how much of the variation in one forecaster's predictions can be associated with those of the other predictors as a group. Doing so sensibly requires use only of the companies for which all the predictors being

3. Kendall's W is a statistic measuring the amount of association among several rankings. It varies between zero (no association) and unity (perfect agreement). It can be expressed as a linear function of all pairwise Spearman rank correlation coefficients. For further discussion, see, e.g., Siegel (1956, pp. 229–38).

Table 2.3   **Kendall's Coefficient of Concordance for Ranks
of Companies by Different Predictors**

A. Long-Term Growth

	Predictors				
Year	(1,2,4)	(1,2,5)	(1,2,4,5)	(1,2,4,5,6)	(1,2,4,5,6,7)
1962	.826	.792	.784	.817	.775
1963	.833	.832	.815	.778	.788
1964	.850	.838	.803	.796	.736
1965	.806	.813	.792	.792	.757

B. Short-Term Growth

	Predictors		
Year	(A,B,C)	(A,B,D)	(A,B,C,D)
1961	.734	.798	.762
1962	.787	.776	.736
1963	.641	.736	.629
1964	.781	.886	.776
1965	.797	.790	.738

compared provided forecasts.[4] Only a limited number of the predictors could be included, and even so the number of companies is severely restricted. The statistic we use is the multiple correlation coefficient R for each predictor with the set of other predictors being compared. The results are presented in table 2.4, which also indicates the predictors that were included in the comparisons and the number of observations that were available.

The values of the multiple correlation coefficients are, of course, higher than those of the simple correlations. Even so, among the long-term predictors they also reveal that each predictor still has a considerable amount of variation that is not associated with the predictions of the others. The most noticeable aspect of the short-term predictions is that now the multiple correlation coefficients are more nearly of the same size as those for the long-term predictions. Correspondingly, the increase in the correlation coefficients obtained by proceeding from the simple to the multiple correlations is comparatively greater for the short-term than for the long-term predictions. This finding is not an artifact of the different observations used. When the simple correlations are calculated using only those companies from which the multiple correlations are calculated, the simple correlation coefficients have much the same values as

4. The fact that the correlation matrices in tables 2.1 and 2.2 need not be (and are not always) positive definite means that we cannot sensibly calculate multiple correlations on the basis of the simple correlations calculated for different companies.

Table 2.4   Multiple Correlations of Predictors with Several Others

A. Long-Term Growth

Pred.	1961	1962	1963	1964	1965
1	.88	.92	.93	.94	.89
2	.84	.89	.88	.94	.93
4	***	.96	.95	.91	.94
5	***	.95	.93	.94	.92
6	.85	.87	.95	.92	.91
7	***	.92	.92	.85	.86
8	.83	***	***	***	***
No. observations	22	27	24	77	101

B. Short-Term Growth

Pred.	1961	1962	1963	1964	1965
A	.76	.93	.77	.95	.92
C	.92	.95	.83	.92	.93
D	.98	.89	.82	.93	.96
G	.92	.89	.93	.95	.95
I	.91	.93	.96	.96	.93
K	.90	.92	.94	.96	.96
No. observations	24	29	28	25	26

NOTE. Table entries are multiple correlations of each predictor with the others listed. ***
entries not included in the calculations.

those shown in tables 2.1 and 2.2 and the short-term predictors still tend to be less than the long-term predictors.

The reasons for these findings are not entirely clear. The results suggest that roughly as much common information is used in forming the short-term as the long-term forecasts, but that there appear to be greater differences in how various types of information are combined in the short-term than in the long-term forecasts. We shall investigate in section 2.2.4 below the extent to which these associations may represent some common underlying factors.

Correlation coefficients measure only one aspect of agreement. They ignore any differences in the average levels of forecasts. The average forecasts of the different predictors appeared to be of roughly the same magnitude. However, they did tend to differ significantly from each other, even though the averages of different pairs of predictors were calculated from the companies for which both made forecasts. Significant differences also tended to be found when central tendency was measured by the medians of the observations. These differences are in addition to the lack of agreement indicated by the correlation coefficients and concordances, and strongly support the finding of considerable heterogeneity of expectations.

While we have treated long-term and short-term forecasts as being basically different, one might nevertheless suspect that little difference

Table 2.5		Correlations of Long- and Short-Term Growth Predictions (1965)							
Pred.	1	2	3	4	5	6	7	8	9
A	.17	.09	.51	.18	.26	.30	.38	.60	.35
B	.60	.64	.73	.74	.65	.71	.62	.63	.71
C	.21	.37	.42	.50	.30	.46	.57	.07	.48
D	.29	.37	.54	.52	.27	.28	.38	.27	.60
E	.38	.42	.66	.85	.53	.61	.64	.45	.09
F	.45	.53	.74	.64	.53	.50	.62	.62	.74
G	.43	.35	.61	.51	.57	.55	.57	.58	.69
H	.30	.34	.34	.44	.13	.32	.58	.42	.57
I	.43	.32	.61	.56	.56	.49	.55	.65	.73
J	.65	.72	.77	.77	.70	.71	.76	.60	.71
K	.57	.52	.53	.64	.65	.65	.78	.50	.52

may be evident in practice. This suspicion is strengthened by noting that only one predictor was able to supply both types of forecast in the same year; other predictors formed either short- or long-term forecasts but not both. Correlating the long- with the short-term predictions bears out this supposition only partially, however. The values for 1965 shown in table 2.5 provide a typical example. The correlation coefficients vary considerably among the pairs of predictors; but on average the values are lower than those found among the short-term predictions, and so a fortiori they are lower than those of the long-term predictors. Thus there is little systematic tendency for the long- and short-term predictions to show close associations.

2.2.2 Changes in Predictions

Our data set allows us to observe changes in predictions over time. This permits us to investigate the extent to which each predictor is influenced by the previous forecasts it made. The correlations are shown in table 2.6.

Table 2.6		Correlations of Predictions over Time							
			A. Long-Term Growth Rates						
Year	1	2	3	4	5	6	7	8	9
1961/62	.97	.86	***	***	***	.92	***	***	***
1962/63	.95	.96	***	.96	.82	.91	.97	***	***
1963/64	.97	.87	.94	.89	.73	.97	.71	***	***
1964/65	.96	.89	.99	.93	.95	.95	.90	.98	.88

			B. Short-Term Growth Rates						
Year	A	B	C	D	E	F	G	H	I	K
1961/62	.28	.45	.40	.12	.45	***	.29	.02	.32	.46
1962/63	.27	.69	.04	.23	.59	***	.37	.13	.28	.61
1963/64	.65	.49	.37	.33	.62	.44	.39	.26	.37	.45
1964/65	.44	.52	.65	.47	.67	.40	.42	.61	.56	.35

For the long-term growth predictions these correlations were quite high, being generally in excess of 0.9. These values tended to be considerably higher than the correlations with the forecasts made by other predictors at the same time; that is, a forecaster of long-term growth tended to be more in agreement with his own prior views than with those of other predictors.

The correlations over time of the short-term predictions also shown in table 2.6 were typically a great deal smaller than those for the long-term predictions, averaging 0.4. Though there were exceptions, particularly in the case of predictor *E*, the pattern found for the long-term predictors that these correlations over time were generally higher than the contemporaneous correlations with other predictors was far less evident.

These findings raise the question of the extent to which forecasters were in agreement with each other about the *changes* in their forecasts. The correlations for the differences of 1965 predictions from the 1964 ones are shown in table 2.7. They reveal a pattern also present in the other years. In these comparisons the correlations were low for the long-term predictions, suggesting that alterations in the expectations were not all based on information common to all or interpreted similarly. Correlations were much higher among the short-term predictions (re-

Table 2.7   **Correlations of Changes of Predictions (1964–65)**

A. Long-Term Growth Rates

Pred.	1	2	3	4	5	6	7	8	9
1	1.00								
2	.22	1.00							
3	.06	.02	1.00						
4	−.09	.25	.02	1.00					
5	.25	.18	.07	.05	1.00				
6	.05	.21	.09	−.01	.27	1.00			
7	.10	−.02	.10	−.12	−.01	.21	1.00		
8	−.10	.18	.03	−.03	−.12	.06	.07	1.00	
9	−.15	−.05	−.26	.19	.04	−.34	.27	.21	1.00

B. Short-Term Growth Rates

Pred.	A	B	C	D	E	F	G	H	I	K
A	1.00									
B	.81	1.00								
C	.46	.70	1.00							
D	.17	.38	.39	1.00						
E	.52	.77	.47	.22	1.00					
F	.77	.78	.53	.46	.44	1.00				
G	.37	.53	.19	.48	.33	.25	1.00			
H	.67	.40	.50	.33	.25	.53	.53	1.00		
I	.17	.77	.54	.42	.34	.42	.67	.70	1.00	
K	.78	.87	.88	.39	.59	.83	.51	.71	.87	1.00

versing the pattern found for the predictions themselves) and were comparable in magnitude to the correlations of the forecasts themselves shown in table 2.2.

2.2.3 Industrial Classification and the Predictions

One might suspect that the correlations among the predictors reflect little more than consensus concerning the industries that are expected to grow relatively quickly rather than agreement about the relative rates of growth of firms within industries. This possibility was investigated by decomposing the correlation coefficient into two parts, one due to correlation within industries (r_w) after removing correlation of industry averages, and the other due to correlation among the industry means (r_a). That is,

(2.2-1) $$r = r_w + r_a,$$

where

(2.2-2) $$r_w = \frac{\sum\limits_{j=1}^{J} \sum\limits_{i=1}^{N_j} (X_{ij} - \bar{X}_j)(Y_{ij} - \bar{Y}_j)}{\left[\sum\limits_{j=1}^{J} \sum\limits_{i=1}^{N_j} (X_{ij} - \bar{X})^2 \sum\limits_{j=1}^{J} \sum\limits_{i=1}^{N_j} (Y_{ij} - \bar{Y})^2 \right]^{1/2}}$$

and

(2.2-3) $$r_a = \frac{\sum\limits_{j=1}^{J} N_j (\bar{X}_j - \bar{X})(\bar{Y}_j - \bar{Y})}{\left[\sum\limits_{j=1}^{J} \sum\limits_{i=1}^{N_j} (X_{ij} - \bar{X})^2 \sum\limits_{j=1}^{J} \sum\limits_{i=1}^{N_j} (Y_{ij} - \bar{Y})^2 \right]^{1/2}},$$

with

X_{ij}, Y_{ij} the ith observations in the jth class (industry),
N_j the number of observations in the jth class,
J the number of classes,
$\bar{X}_j, \bar{Y}_j$ the averages within the classes, and
$\bar{X}, \bar{Y}$ the overall averages.

This decomposition indicated that agreement concerning industry growth rates is not the major factor accounting for the correlations among the forecasts. The values for 1965 are shown in table 2.8. Entries above the diagonal in that table show the values of r_a using the industrial classification obtained from the participating firms. As a comparison with tables 2.1 and 2.2 shows, only a small part of the correlations among the predictions is due to correlations among the industry means, a pattern not specific just to the year for which results are shown.

The decomposition we have just been considering does not yield the partial correlation coefficient holding industrial classification constant

Table 2.8   Industrial Classification and Forecast Agreement (1965)

A. Long-Term Forecasts

Pred.	1	2	3	4	5	6	7	8	9
1	***	.27	.20	.26	.29	.27	.10	.26	.34
2	.77	***	.30	.30	.36	.34	.14	.29	.36
3	.82	.82	***	.41	.31	.32	.25	.31	.51
4	.83	.83	.91	***	.37	.39	.27	.31	.43
5	.81	.78	.69	.79	***	.33	.16	.20	.34
6	.74	.68	.68	.81	.76	***	.16	.28	.39
7	.47	.40	.73	.79	.44	.71	***	.18	.34
8	.87	.84	.88	.88	.78	.69	.77	***	.29
9	.81	.79	.92	.86	.83	.81	.82	.88	***

B. Short-Term Forecasts

Pred.	A	B	C	D	E	F	G	H	I	J	K
A	***	.30	.14	.16	.19	.64	.17	.18	.08	.47	.17
B	.86	***	.61	.51	.56	.52	.49	.56	.40	.66	.44
C	.45	.57	***	.34	.42	.33	.25	.33	.15	.38	.33
D	−.19	.27	.33	***	.24	.33	.37	.38	.22	.64	.42
E	.48	.59	.73	.39	***	.29	.37	.01	.21	.02	.11
F	.65	.71	.55	.22	.71	***	.22	.26	.28	.59	.43
G	.22	.57	.36	.51	.26	.50	***	.35	.29	.46	.32
H	.84	.64	.87	.80	.55	.77	.68	***	.15	.64	.41
I	.23	.83	.63	.55	.52	.44	.69	.77	***	.46	.26
J	.90	.57	.54	.82	.04	.73	.87	.58	.69	***	.50
K	.37	.85	.74	.37	.61	.77	.67	.81	.80	.69	***

NOTE. Values of r_a are above diagonal created by asterisks; values of partial correlations holding industry classification constant are below diagonal.

although the numerator of r_w in equation (2.2-2) is the numerator of that partial correlation coefficient. These partial correlations are shown below the main diagonal in table 2.8. Roughly speaking, they are of the same magnitude as the simple correlations of tables 2.1 and 2.2. Especially in the case of the short-term predictions, they vary extensively across the predictors. This finding again suggests that the forecasters are not all following uniform procedures in arriving at their predictions. Although, in principle, part of this variation might arise from the need to use different sets of companies when comparing different pairs of predictors, equally wide variations appeared when only a common set of companies was used for the comparison.

These findings should not be taken to indicate that there is not a large association between the predictions and the industry classification. The values of R^2 obtained by regressing the predictions on industry dummy variables are shown in table 2.9. They indicate that there are very strong and significant associations. This is a particularly striking feature of the long-term predictions where values above 0.9 occur quite often and all

Table 2.9 **Industrial Classification and Forecast Variation: Values of R^2 for Regressing Growth Rates on Industry Dummies**

A. Long-Term Growth

	Predictor								
Year	1	2	3	4	5	6	7	8	9
1961	.42	.88	.89	***	***	.89	***	.85	***
1962	.77	.87	***	.89	.80	.91	.91	***	***
1963	.78	.85	.82	.89	.83	.90	.92	***	***
1964	.80	.85	.91	.83	.85	.86	.66	.91	.90
1965	.82	.88	.90	.87	.86	.87	.64	.92	.83

B. Short-Term Growth

	Predictor										
Year	A	B	C	D	E	F	G	H	I	J	K
1961	.36	.68	.67	***	.56	***	.39	.74	.46	***	.62
1962	.27	.35	.32	.24	.60	***	.34	.22	.18	***	.41
1963	.34	.45	.49	.45	.74	.41	.37	.43	.39	***	.55
1964	.48	.63	.32	.40	.62	.64	.34	.66	.30	***	.49
1965	.24	.79	.48	.68	.57	.58	.62	.68	.48	.74	.66

the values for some predictors are above 0.8. Although industry associations are usually less pronounced for the short-term predictions, they are a highly important feature of these forecasts as well.

We conclude that while there exists a high association of forecasts with industry classification, it is not the primary factor accounting for the correlations between predictors. Thus the overall pattern is not one in which forecasters tend to agree on industry effects but not on other across-company variations; instead, they are in at least as much disagreement about industry effects as about other ones.

One may wonder whether correlations among individual forecasters varied over different industry groups. Such variation might indicate that certain industry groups are more difficult to forecast in some *ex ante* sense. The correlations among forecasters tended to be lowest in the "cyclical" industry group and highest for the electric utility companies. These differences were significant for all pairs of predictions considered. Ranking the correlations over industries and then comparing these ranks among predictors showed substantial concordance over the ordering of the correlations.[5]

5. The test for individual pairs of predictions was the likelihood-ratio test. Note that the ranking comparison is not based on independent observations, so a statistical test of the concordance is not appropriate. The hypothesis that the correlations are all zero within industries could, however, be rejected well beyond conventional significance levels.

2.2.4 Factor-analytic Investigation of Agreement

The analysis of the growth-rate expectations by industry classification was partly suggested by the notion that the predictions in part depend on simpler, more basic, and less diverse information than that specific to each firm. Thus it might be supposed that if one knew the fortunes of an industry group, one would know a good deal about the fortunes of each firm in it. One might want to carry this idea further and suppose that the predictions can be regarded as having a strong underlying core of information from which each predictor made its own further adjustments independent of the others. To investigate this hypothesis, we employ the standard factor-analysis model.

a) A Factor Model for Predictions

The basic idea is that each predictor forms its forecasts for the companies surveyed on the basis of the values of a few factors that affect all the companies. Let ϕ_{jk} be the value of the kth factor (out of K) for the jth company. These ϕ_{jk} are assumed to be random variables. The model then supposes that each forecast made by predictor i for company j, g_{ji}, can be expressed as

$$(2.2\text{-}4) \qquad g_{ji} = \sum_{k=1}^{K} \phi_{jk} a_{ki} + e_{ji}.$$

Here the a_{ki} are coefficients which have different values for different predictors but which assume the same values for every company in the forecasts of the ith predictor. The e_{ji} are random variables for which it is assumed that

$$(2.2\text{-}5) \qquad E(e_{ji}) = 0$$

and

$$(2.2\text{-}6) \qquad E(e_{ji} e_{mk}) = \sigma_i^2 \quad i = k,\ j = m$$
$$= 0 \qquad \text{otherwise.}$$

The important part of assumption (2.2-6) is that the e_{ji} for different predictors, i and k, are uncorrelated. The assumptions of homoscedasticity and lack of correlation across companies are used to determine the sizes of tests, but they are not a critical requirement for data to exhibit the type of variance-covariance matrix that is characteristic of the common-factor model.

The quantity ϕ_{jk} is interpreted most easily when there is only one of them for each company, that is, when $K = 1$. Then we might think of ϕ_{jk} as representing the (best) forecast that would be made for the company on the basis of commonly available information. The e_{ji} might then be taken to be specific or idiosyncratic information (or for that matter pure guesswork) used by the predictor i. The model assumes that this component of the predictor's forecasts is uncorrelated with the corresponding components of the forecasts of each of the other predictors. The a_{ki} contain the weightings of the two types of information. They could have the same values for each predictor.

When there is more than one factor, we might interpret the model as also reflecting the dependence of earnings on various aspects of the state of the economy, as, for example, real growth, inflation, etc. Different predictors might be in agreement over the extent to which each firm is sensitive to variations in these general conditions, but each might be using different predictions of what economic conditions will obtain. For example, the forecasters may agree that U.S. Steel's earnings growth would be positively influenced by the growth in GNP. Nevertheless, they may differ in their forecasts for U.S. Steel's earnings growth because they do not agree on the growth of GNP. Similarly, all forecasters may agree that an increase in the rate of inflation may depress the earnings for Consolidated Edison but may differ in their inflation forecasts. The a_{ki} now represent the different predictions of generally important economic variables made by the individual forecasters, and the ϕ_{jk} may be interpreted as the extent to which earnings growth depends on the various economic variables.

b) Relation to a Factor Model for Earnings

This interpretation of the model for earnings-growth forecasts complements nicely a related model for earnings growth or, more generally, for returns to securities that is sometimes used in valuation models. We shall see in chapter 3 that a common-factor model has important implications for the structure of security prices. Let x_{jt} be the value of the variable of interest for company j at time t and f_{kt} be the value of the kth factor at time t. (In the security-valuation model x_{jt} initially is the return to security j, but it might instead be earnings growth.) The model for x_{jt} is

$$(2.2\text{-}7) \qquad x_{jt} = \mu_j + \sum_{k=1}^{K} \gamma_{jk} f_{kt} + \epsilon_{jt},$$

where the f_{kt} might represent national income, inflation, or other generally relevant aspects of the economic environment. The μ_j and γ_{jk} are parameters specific to the firms while now ϵ_{jt} is a random disturbance. A forecast of x_{jt} could sensibly be made by forecasting f_{kt} and then using equation (2.2-7), with ϵ_{jt} taken to be zero. We might therefore consider the parameters μ_j and γ_{jk} to be the factors ϕ_{jk} of the prediction model (2.2-4), while the a_{ki} represent different forecasters' predictions of f_{kt} at a particular time as well as the weighting given to the typical common value of the firm-specific expectation μ_j.

From our previous discussion it may seem unreasonable to assume that the predictors should all know the values of ϕ_{jk} if they cannot even agree on the predicted values of major economic variables. However, the model could be extended to be

(2.2-8) $$g_{ji} = \sum_{k=1}^{K} (\phi_{jk} + \eta_{jki})a_{ki} + e_{jk},$$

where the η_{jki} are independent random variables uncorrelated across predictors. Now the ϕ_{jk} can be regarded as an average value held by predictors rather than ones on which all predictors agree implicitly. Since we can write equation (2.2-8) as

(2.2-9) $$g_{ji} = \sum_{k=1}^{K} \phi_{jk}a_{ki} + \left(\sum_{k=1}^{K} \eta_{jki}a_{ki} + e_{ji} \right)$$
$$= \sum_{k=1}^{K} \phi_{jk}a_{ki} + e_{ji}',$$

the model (2.2-4) remains formally appropriate provided that (2.2-6) holds for the augmented disturbance e_{ji}'. The theoretical implications for security valuation of diversity of expectations of the form (2.2-8) in the model (2.2-7) will be investigated in chapter 3.

c) Empirical Findings

Only a small number of factors can be identified from data for the limited number of predictors available, especially when the assumption of different variances for different predictors is made in (2.2-6).[6] However, for most years two factors are identifiable since the hypothesis that $K \leq 2$ imposes testable restrictions on the variance-covariance matrices of the predictors.

The major question is whether a common-factor model fits the data at all. Because of the small number of predictors, this amounts to asking whether only two factors can account for the observed correlations between predictors. Rejecting this hypothesis would not necessarily indicate that the model is inappropriate, but could arise from there being a (small) number of additional factors. As the discussion of the interpretation of the ϕ_{jk} indicated, particular interest focuses on the hypothesis that there is only one factor.

---

6. Identifiability and estimation of the factor-analysis model are discussed by Anderson and Rubin (1956).

Missing observations cause a major problem for the analysis. It is not at all clear that the fact of omission of a company from the list of those for whom a forecaster supplied predictions is a random event unconnected with the values predicted by others. Instead, it may be related to the values of the predictions—or to the extent to which some underlying factor about which there is uncertainty affects the company. As with the calculation of multiple correlation coefficients for table 2.4, it is necessary to base calculations on companies for which each of the included predictors made forecasts. The predictors that could be included and the number of observations are indicated in table 2.10. They are the same as those used in table 2.4.

It is of course quite possible for the model to describe some predictors and not others. No systematic search was made to try to find those predictors (if any) which it might fit; instead, the selection of the predictors included in the analysis was based on there being an overlap in the companies for which predictions were made.

Table 2.10   **Summary of Common-Factor Model**

A. Long-Term Predictions

	1961[†]	1962	1963	1964	1965
	Contributions of Two Factors to Predictors' Variances				
Pred.					
1	.84	.86	.86	.90	.81
2	.74	.86	.67	.90	.89
4	***	.94	.91	.87	.90
5	***	.97	.91	.89	.86
6	.74	.76	.90	.87	.85
7	***	.89	.97	.98	.98
8	.69	***	***	***	***
No. observations	22	27	24	77	101
	Significance Levels beyond Which Hypothesis Cannot Be Rejected				
No. Factors					
$K \leq 2$	***	.45	.01	.16	.09
$K = 1$	.12	.01	.00	.00	.00

B. Short-Term Predictions

	Contributions of Two Factors to Predictors' Variances				
Pred.	1961	1962	1963	1964	1965
A	.58	.90	.97	.90	.97
C	.84	.93	.55	.82	.87
D	.99	.80	.47	.86	.95
G	.98	.97	.85	.97	.89
I	.82	.86	.99	.94	.85
K	.78	.89	.83	.97	.92
No. observations	24	29	28	25	26

[†]Only one factor identifiable.

The findings of the (asymptotic) test[7] of the hypotheses are summarized in table 2.10 in terms of the smallest significance levels at which the hypotheses could be rejected.[8] The hypothesis of two factors could not be tested for the 1961 long-term predictions because only four predictors could be analyzed together. In most other cases, particularly among the short-term predictions, the hypothesis could only be rejected at high levels. This includes the long-term predictions in 1964 and 1965 where a

7. The tests are likelihood-ratio ones, in which one assumes that all random quantities have the normal distribution.

8. These quantities are sometimes referred to as "prob-vals." See Wonnacott and Wonnacott (1979).

fairly large number of observations are available. The predictions for 1963, however, provided a strong exception. Expressing these results differently, we find that usually it would be reasonable to ascribe the correlations among predictors to a pair of underlying factors.

The finding of two common factors does not necessarily indicate that there are only two factors present in the behavioral models underlying (2.2-4) and (2.2-7). If the values of a_{ki} for two or more factors (k) were the same for all predictors (i) (e.g., because they do all use the same forecasts of the important economic variables), then the test would aggregate these different factors into a single composite factor. The results just obtained may partly arise because such aggregation provides a sufficiently good approximation that more factors cannot be detected with the modest numbers of observations used.

The hypothesis of only one common factor receives little support from the data. It is rejected strongly except in a couple of instances, one of which is the long-term predictions of 1961, where only four predictors could be included and only one factor can be identified. The finding that one factor is not usually sufficient suggests that the correlations among predictors do not arise from just a single source, and indicates that the model (2.2-7) may be a fruitful way of considering how the forecasting process should be regarded.

d) Importance of the Common Factors

These findings suggest that the agreement among the forecasts of different predictors arises from their dependence on a set of common factors. The extent of this dependence may be summarized by considering the proportion of the variance of the forecasts of each predictor that can be attributed to two factors. Let $\bar{\phi}_k$ and $\bar{g}_i$ be the means of the kth factor and of the ith predictor's forecasts. The factor analysis then provides an estimate of

$$\sum_{j=1}^{J} \left(\sum_{k=1}^{K} (\phi_{jk} - \bar{\phi}_k) a_{ki} \right)^2,$$

which we can divide by $\sum_{j=1}^{J} (g_{ji} - \bar{g})^2$ to provide a quantity analogous to R^2. The values of these ratios are shown in table 2.10.

A large part of the variance of the predictors can be ascribed to dependence on the common factors. As table 2.10 reveals, there is a considerable amount of variation in the magnitude of these quantities among predictors and across years. Nevertheless, quite high values do prevail: most entries are above 0.8, values of 0.9 are common, and even values above 0.95 are found. This still leaves considerable diversity of expectations, but does indicate a very solid core of common information. It is worth noting that many of the largest values occur for the short-term predictions.

e) Extension of the Model

These findings spur a number of further investigations. One of the quantities which the factors represent does not seem to be the industry averages. When we analyzed the residuals using different industry means, levels of significance very similar to those of table 2.10 were obtained and models with only one factor still tended to be rejected strongly.

Taking the difference of one year's forecast from the forecast of the preceding year, where the forecasts are expressed by equation (2.2-4), we obtain

$$(2.2\text{-}10) \qquad g_{jit} - g_{jit-1} = \sum_{k=1}^{K} (\phi_{jkt} - \phi_{jkt-1})a_{kit} + \sum_{k=1}^{K} \phi_{jkt-1}$$

$$\times (a_{kit} - a_{kit-1}) + e_{jit} - e_{jit-1}.$$

The common-factor model would therefore continue to be appropriate for these differences if only the ϕ_{jk} or the a_{ki} changed. If both changed, the number of common factors would increase beyond the number that could be identified in our data. The three years in which changes in the long-term predictions could be analyzed produced even larger significance levels beyond which the two-factor model could not be rejected than those of table 2.10 for the predictions themselves. It is noteworthy that this was particularly true for the 1962–63 changes and the 1963–64 ones, since the model did not fit the predictions well in 1963. By contrast, the model was usually rejected beyond the 0.10 level with the changes in short-term predictions.

f) Summary of Factor-analytic Investigation

In sum, we find that the factor model (2.2-4) appears to describe well some of the predictions, but not all. Furthermore, some predictors may use the same values of the factors each year, though changing the predicted value of the underlying common variables. When five years of data are available for a predictor, two factors are still identifiable, but only one can be identified when not more than four years are available. Analyzing the long-term growth forecasts of predictors 1, 2, and 6 in this way led in each case to not rejecting at the 0.05 level the hypothesis of two factors. For these predictors and for the others for which only four years were available, the hypothesis of just one factor could be rejected easily. The results for the short-term predictors were similar: the only one for which the two-factor hypothesis could be rejected was C. Conditioning on the industry would lead to not rejecting the hypothesis in this case as well as in the others. No support was found for the model with only one factor.

Thus it appears reasonable to conclude that a factor model is consistent with the process by which our predictors have formed their expectations.

The forecasters may first have made predictions of important economic factors such as GNP growth, inflation, etc., and then attempted to estimate how each of these factors would affect each specific company. Disagreements among the forecasters could result either from different predicted values for the factors or from different views concerning how the factors affect specific company results.

2.2.5 Predictions and Past Growth Rates

Comparing the predictions with previous growth rates provides added perspective on the agreement among forecasters. However, past growth rates are not so well defined that their measurement is unambiguous. Instead, a number of different calculations may be made to estimate past growth. Of at least as much relevance as such objective calculations are the perceptions of past growth actually held by forecasters. We were fortunate in having had some of these perceptions supplied to us.

Correlations of eight historical growth rates of earnings per share with each other and with the predictions are shown in table 2.11 for 1963. Four of these past growth rates were supplied by participating firms, though not in all years. They represent the firm's perception of the growth of earnings per share that had occurred in various preceding periods. The other growth rates were calculated as coefficients in the regressions of the logarithms of earnings per share on time over the previous four, six, eight, and ten years. We also investigated with very similar results other measures based on the first differences of the logarithms of earnings per share and on linear trends.

The specific definitions of the eight historical growth rates were:

g_{p1} = four- to five-year historical growth rate supplied by predictor 1,

g_{p2} = eight- to ten-year historical growth rate supplied by predictor 1,

g_{p3} = one-year historical growth rate supplied by predictor 4,

g_{p4} = six-year historical growth rate supplied by predictor 4,

g_{c1} = log-regression trend fitted to last four years,

g_{c2} = log-regression trend fitted to last six years,

g_{c3} = log-regression trend fitted to last eight years,

g_{c4} = log-regression trend fitted to last ten years.

Values for g_{p3} were available only for 1962 and 1963.

The correlations in the first part of table 2.11 are indicative of the problems of assessing growth rates unambiguously. The different percep-

Table 2.11   **Correlations of Past Perceived, Past Calculated, and Predicted Growth Rates (1963)**

	g_{p1}	g_{p2}	g_{p3}	g_{p4}	g_{c1}	g_{c2}	g_{c3}	g_{c4}
				Past Growth				
g_{p1}	1.00							
g_{p2}	.66	1.00						
g_{p3}	.36	.43	1.00					
g_{p4}	.78	.82	.56	1.00				
g_{c1}	.54	.31	.10	.43	1.00			
g_{c2}	.79	.55	.03	.56	.68	1.00		
g_{c3}	.89	.74	.07	.76	.43	.77	1.00	
g_{c4}	.78	.88	.15	.96	.40	.67	.92	1.00
			Predicted Long-Term Growth					
1	.79	.85	.33	.78	.59	.62	.76	.82
2	.69	.73	.41	.75	.53	.52	.65	.68
3	.78	.68	.57	.77	.63	.57	.57	.58
4	.79	.82	.71	.79	.65	.70	.76	.79
5	.59	.56	.75	.75	.37	.25	.17	.26
6	.78	.90	.80	.90	.55	.65	.78	.85
7	.84	.82	.42	.80	.64	.70	.78	.81
			Predicted Short-Term Growth					
A	.15	.36	.62	.51	− .17	− .06	− .02	− .02
B	.43	.50	.65	.46	.44	.37	.37	.46
C	.10	.02	.51	.17	.10	− .13	− .21	− .19
D	.36	.22	.48	.43	− .13	− .01	.08	.06
E	.48	.60	.69	.34	− .15	− .09	.29	.48
F	.64	.50	.62	.64	.15	.46	.33	.29
G	.45	.45	.56	.33	.03	.10	.20	.20
H	− .16	− .07	.55	.32	− .10	− .15	− .35	− .28
I	.41	.45	.54	.45	− .04	.07	.12	.16
K	.36	.39	.62	.51	.06	.07	.32	.36

tions are not more highly correlated with each other than were different predictions, with the correlation being weakest between the one-year perceptions and the longer-term ones. The correlations among the calculated growth rates are of a similar order of magnitude as those among the perceived growth rates, and the same is true of the correlations of the calculated growth rates with the longer-term predictions. Their associations with the one-year perceived growth rates tend to be particularly weak.

The correlations of long-term growth predictions with historical growth rates are generally high. Indeed, they are not much different from those found in comparing the predictions with each other. Among the perceived past growth rates, the correlations are apt to be lowest with g_{p3}, the growth rates perceived to have occurred over the most recent year. For the calculated growth rates, the correlations tended to increase with the length of time over which the growth rates were calculated.[9]

The correlations relating the short-term predictions with the calculated growth rates tend to be considerably smaller and are negative in many cases. Correlations of short-term predictions with the past perceived growth rates tend to be stronger and are particularly so with the one-year past perceived growth. The values, however, are still not very large. Security analysts do not appear to rely simply on historical growth rates in forecasting for the year ahead. It seems more likely that they are also emphasizing a number of important economic factors and their own study of industry and company relationships to these factors.

The comparisons of past with predicted long-term growth rates might suggest that the apparent agreement among the predictors reflects little more than at least some use by all of them of the historic figures. In investigating this possibility, we calculated the partial correlations among the predictions, holding past calculated growth rates, past perceived growth rates, and both sets of growth rates constant. The first two sets of partial correlations were not much smaller than the simple correlations. Holding both sets constant produced partial correlations that were considerably smaller than the simple correlations, though almost all were still significant beyond the 0.05 level. Thus, while a substantial part of the agreement among predictors appears to result from their use of historic growth figures, there is also evidence of similarity in the adjustments that different security analysts tend to make to past growth rates.

We may well ask what is the relationship of the past growth figures to the common-factor model for which we found some support among the predictions. In particular, can we regard these past growth rates as representing one of the factors? The hypothesis that the same factor model applies to the past growth rates and to the predictions could be decisively rejected, partly because the factor hypothesis can be rejected among the past growth rates themselves, both perceived and calculated.

More mixed results were obtained when only one perceived and one calculated growth rate were used with the predictions. When these were used together with the short-term forecasts, significant rejection of the hypothesis of at most three factors occurred in all years except 1965. With the long-term forecasters of table 2.10, the hypothesis would be rejected very strongly in 1963 and 1964 but would be accepted in other years. Again, correlation between the two measures of past growth may be part of the problem. However, using only one past rate, perceived or calcu-

9. This effect was also found when the calculated growth rates were based on either (1) the regression of earnings per share on time or (2) the appropriate root of the ratio of earnings per share at the end of the period to earnings at the beginning.

lated, with but two factors produced again the same sort of ambiguous results.

2.2.6 Predictions and Price-Earnings Ratios

We complete our examination of agreement among various predictions by comparing the forecasts with the price-earnings ratios of the corresponding securities observed at about the times the predictions were being made. By utilizing a normative valuation model (for example, one of those cited in footnote 2), it is possible to calculate an implicit growth rate from the market-determined price-earnings multiple of a security. Thus comparisons of the predictions with the price-earnings ratios may be interpreted as examining the relationship between the forecasts and the growth rates expected by the market.

Correlations with two versions of the price-earnings ratio are shown in table 2.12 for 1965. The prices (P) used were the closing prices for the last day of the year. The earnings were either the actual earnings (E) or the average of the "normalized" or trend-earnings figures $(\overline{NE})$ supplied by the predictors. The correlation coefficients in the table are about the same as those obtained when the forecasts were compared with each

Table 2.12   Correlations of Price-Earnings Multiples and Predictions (1965)

Pred.	P/E	$P/\overline{NE}$
Long-Term		
1	.81	.72
2	.80	.81
3	.81	.60
4	.88	.85
5	.84	.85
6	.91	.83
7	.71	.54
8	.83	.66
9	.87	.78
Short-Term		
A	.31	.31
B	.74	.65
C	.46	.53
D	.31	.17
E	.44	.72
F	.61	.60
G	.47	.46
H	.33	.40
I	.50	.51
J	.58	.65
K	.61	.66

other. The correlations tend to be much higher for the long-term forecasts than for the short-term ones. Since price-earnings multiples should
be affected by several variables other than expected growth rates (and so
are not simply predictions), this exercise underscores the extent of disagreement among the forecasters.

2.3 The Accuracy of the Predictions

Three approaches are taken to evaluate the accuracy of the predictions. The first involves correlation of predictions and realizations and
investigates the extent to which the relative predicted rates of company
growth are associated with the relative rates of growth that occurred. This
association can be high even if there are major differences between the
predicted and realized rates of growth. The second approach to evaluation involves the appraisal of the accuracy of the various forecasts in more
absolute terms. The third type of appraisal is a comparison of the forecasts with extrapolation of various previously experienced growth rates.

All comparisons concerned rates of growth rather than the levels of
earnings per share in order to avoid misleading scale effects. In particular, all per-share realizations were converted into annual percentage rates
of change from the average values of the estimated normalized earnings
per share as of the dates the predictions were made. No conversion of the
long-term predictions was necessary since all the five-year forecasts were
originally recorded as percentage rates of growth, but the short-term
forecasts did require conversion, as was described in chapter 1. Although
every effort was made to ensure that the predicted and realized values
used the same concepts and conventions, small differences may remain.

2.3.1 Correlations of Predictions with Realizations

Correlation coefficients summarizing the forecasting ability of the
short-term predictors from 1961 through 1968 are presented in table 2.13.
Corresponding figures for the long-term predictors are shown in table
2.14. The goodness of the forecasts was assessed by calculating and
presenting Spearman rank correlation coefficients as well as product-
moment correlations. We also indicate the number of companies for
which forecasts and realizations could be compared.

By and large, the correlations of predicted and realized growth rates
are fairly low. Nevertheless, with few, minor exceptions, the correlations
are positive and most of them are significantly different from zero. The
values tend to be smaller than correlations found with the other predictors, a feature especially of the long-term predictions. On average, the
correlations for the long-term predictors are higher than for the short-
term ones, although the differences are slight in 1963 and 1964. Except
for the 1961 long-term predictions, the averages are below 0.5. They are

Table 2.13   Correlations of Earnings Growth Forecasts of Security Analysts with Realized One-Year Earnings Growth for the Year Following the Forecast

Pred. Short-Term (one-year) Forecasts	1961 Predictions			1962 Predictions			1963 Predictions			1964 Predictions			1965 Predictions		
	r	ρ	No.	r	ρ	No.	r	ρ	No.	r	ρ	No.	r	ρ	No.
A	.47	.22	109	.18	.21	112	.21	.21	112	.34	.36	111	.33	.42	112
B	.40	.20	63	.41	.25	64	.52	.27	64	.51	.37	62	.58	.39	66
C	.20	.15	106	.03	.11	126	.45	.47	126	.52	.34	128	.43	.40	129
D	.29	.21	186	.03	.06	192	.04	.02	184	.59	.33	115	.15	.24	117
E	.87	.68	30	.63	.39	32	.44	.57	31	.40	.49	35	.55	.57	36
F	***	***	***	***	***	***	.42	.27	74	.44	.28	74	.57	.47	76
G	.49	.24	143	.01	.09	146	.31	.13	166	.33	.14	161	.15	.16	163
H	.25	.30	42	.44	.38	48	.19	.28	55	.63	.35	54	.39	.45	56
I	.56	.20	176	.34	.16	187	.20	.18	191	.34	.24	191	.27	.35	194
J	***	***	***	***	***	***	***	***	***	***	***	***	.44	.28	52
K	.36	.36	87	.29	.25	88	.34	.15	88	.35	.36	87	.54	.43	88
Correlation with no. predictions	−.21	−.60	***	−.73	−.78	***	−.59	−.62	***	−.41	−.76	***	−.55	−.56	***

Pred.	1966 Predictions			1967 Predictions			1968 Predictions		
	r	ρ	No.	r	ρ	No.	r	ρ	No.
L	***	***	***	***	***	***	.10	−.09	108
M	.14	−.15	165	.10	.05	155	.04	−.08	142
N	.23	.18	154	.28	.21	151	.30	.23	150

NOTE. *r* = correlation coefficient. ρ = Spearman's rho. No. = number of observations.

Table 2.14   Comparison of Five-Year Earnings Growth Forecasts of Security Analysts with Realizations

Pred.	1961 Predictions vs. 1961–66 Growth			1962 Predictions vs. 1962–67 Growth			1963 Predictions vs. 1963–68 Growth			1964 Predictions vs. 1964–69 Growth			1965 Predictions vs. 1965–70 Growth		
	r	ρ	No.	r	ρ	No.	r	ρ	No.	r	ρ	No.	r	ρ	No.
1	.50	.09	119	.24	.03	175	.21	−.02	173	.27	.18	173	.40	.33	168
2	.33	.16	116	.32	.16	173	.25	.11	171	.35	.33	167	.34	.29	165
3	.80	.41	42	***	***	***	.48	.31	122	.53	.46	67	.33	.15	72
4	***	***	***	.75	.39	57	.75	.46	59	.50	.49	123	.40	.35	121
5	***	***	***	.49	.34	172	.42	.29	172	.68	.28	103	.37	.32	145
6	.55	.21	37	.62	.49	62	.69	.40	37	.43	.30	163	.31	.33	158
7	***	***	***	.57	.37	61	.51	.32	60	.38	.27	173	.42	.36	163
8	.36	.21	60	***	***	***	***	***	***	.66	.57	54	.64	.59	55
9	***	***	***	***	***	***	***	***	***	.40	.22	39	.53	.40	45
Correlation with no. predictions	−.73	−.56	***	−.86	−.78	***	−.87	−.79	***	−.59	−.42	***	−.66	−.31	***

Pred.	1966 Predictions vs. 1966–71 Growth			1967 Predictions vs. 1967–72 Growth			1968 Predictions vs. 1968–73 Growth			1969 Predictions vs. 1969–74 Growth		
	r	ρ	No.	r	ρ	No.	r	ρ	No.	r	ρ	No.
2	.38	.40	112	.10	.23	108	.11	.16	107	.05	.09	118
3	.09	.29	160	.09	.23	148	.14	.14	137	.18	−.12	129
6	.15	.16	162	.36	.33	153	.21	.32	156	***	***	***

NOTE. r = correlation coefficient. ρ = Spearman's rho. No. = Number of Observations considerably lower for some of the short-term predictions. The rank correlations furthermore tend to be lower than the product-moment ones.

One pronounced feature of the correlations is an inverse relationship between correlations of predictions with realizations and the number of companies for which predictions are made. As tables 2.13 and 2.14 reveal, the coefficients calculated between the number of companies and the correlations of predictions with realized growth rates are all negative and are generally quite substantial.

These results do not necessarily indicate that those who chose to forecast fewer companies were thereby able to make superior forecasts. Instead, it partly arises from a serious anomaly of our data. The simple correlation coefficients of tables 2.13 and 2.14 probably give a more favorable impression of predictive ability than is justified. Two or three companies in our study turned out to be rapid growers and also reasonably easy to predict. Were these companies omitted, the correlations (especially the product-moment ones) would decline substantially. For example, the correlation coefficients decline quite sharply if IBM, Polaroid, and Xerox are dropped from the sample. The importance of a few outliers in boosting the reported correlation coefficients thus weakens the evidence in favor of superior forecasting ability, since most forecasters did include these more spectacular performers.

2.3.2 Accuracy of the Predictions

Our second approach to the evaluation of the accuracy of the forecasts is based on an inequality coefficient similar to that developed by Theil (1966). This coefficient is given by

$$(2.3\text{-}1) \qquad T = \sum_{i=1}^{N} (P_i - R_i)^2 \Big/ \sum_{i=1}^{N} R_i^2,$$

Where P_i is the predicted and R_i the realized growth rate for the ith company. This coefficient gives a comparison between perfect prediction ($T = 0$) and a naive prediction of zero growth for all corporations ($T = 1$). Thus the higher the inequality coefficient, the worse the predictions. It is even possible, of course, for the inequality coefficient to be greater than unity. In such a case, the predictor would have done better simply to predict no growth for all companies.

Values of this statistic are shown in table 2.15. They are based on comparisons of the long-term forecasts with the subsequent realized growth rates over five years and the short-term forecasts with the subsequent one-year changes (all adjusted to the same base). Table 2.15 thus employs the same sets of data as do tables 2.13 and 2.14.

Values of the inequality coefficient for the long-term predictions show some tendency to drift upward over the period 1961–66. The nature of the

Table 2.15   Inequality Coefficients for Assessing Accuracy of Predictions

A. Long-Term Forecasts vs.
Five-Year Realizations

Pred.	1961–66	1962–67	1963–68	1964–69	1965–70
1	.38	.53	.56	.74	.85
2	.39	.49	.53	.70	.92
3	.28	***	.43	.33	.62
4	***	.22	.21	.53	.94
5	***	.35	.39	.29	.88
6	.32	.39	.43	.67	1.01
7	***	.34	.33	.69	1.04
8	.39	***	***	.40	.81
9	***	***	***	.37	.83
Correlation with no. of predictions	.73	.71	.66	.89	.66

Pred.	1966–71	1967–72	1968–73	1969–74
2	1.17	.90	.64	.63
3	1.36	.96	1.29	.85
6	1.40	.88	.69	***

B. Short-Term Forecasts vs.
One-Year Realizations

Pred.	1961–62	1962–63	1963–64	1964–65	1965–66
A	1.11	1.01	.73	.59	1.03
B	.80	.80	.46	.44	.49
C	1.10	1.00	.51	.55	1.26
D	1.41	1.07	.82	.49	.77
E	.16	.36	.37	.47	.52
F	***	***	.60	.49	.49
G	.70	1.24	.66	.75	.88
H	1.61	.79	.72	.36	.66
I	.63	.84	.74	.75	1.17
J	***	***	***	***	.77
K	.81	.73	.56	.57	.50
Correlation with no of predictions	0.49	0.70	0.68	0.90	0.74

Pred.	1966–67	1967–68	1968–69
L	***	***	.97
M	1.09	.97	.95
N	1.37	.91	1.21

statistic is such that given absolute differences between predicted and realized growth are treated more favorably when realized growth is high so that the figures might not be considered fully comparable from one year to the next. However, the change is impressive. In 1966 each of the three predictors which furnished data would have done better (on this criterion) simply to have predicted no growth at all. Subsequently, some improvement did occur. Though much less pronounced than differences between years, considerable variations also exist among predictors. As we already found with the correlations, the inequality coefficients are strongly correlated with the number of companies for which the predictor made forecasts. These correlations are all positive, again indicating that average forecast success tended to weaken as the number of forecasts made increased.

The inequality coefficients for one-year forecasts tended to be weaker than for the long-term ones. Quite commonly, values greater than unity occurred. There was again considerable variation from year to year, but no patterns are evident. Pronounced differences occur between forecasters, but these again are strongly related to the number of forecasts made.

The performance of predictor E, especially in the early years, appears to be particularly strong. However, this superiority is largely illusory. Predictor E tended to concentrate on large, relatively stable companies, and, we suspect, predictions were made only when there was a priori reason to believe that the forecasts would be reliable. The validity of this conjecture is suggested by observing that all the other forecasters did better for the set of companies for which predictor E made forecasts than for the larger set. At the same time, as noted earlier, it was the case that predictor E's forecasts tended to be less correlated with others. This tendency continued when the other correlations were also based on the same limited set of companies.

We may put the general findings into perspective by noting that a naive forecast based on predicting that, for each company, earnings growth would equal the past growth rate of GNP would have given lower inequality coefficients than the short-term forecasts. Such a naive forecast, of course, would not identify any relative differences among companies. On this criterion, the long-term forecasts are slightly stronger than the naive forecast. A naive prediction of average long-term GNP growth tended to produce slightly higher inequality coefficients than our predictors. As we shall see in section 2.4, there was a tendency in the early years for the forecasters to underestimate the realized growth. In later years, however, we did not find any systematic evidence of underestimation of change.

2.3.3 Analysis of the Forecasts by Industrial Category

We can extend the inequality-coefficient analysis to investigate the extent to which errors in prediction were related to (1) errors in predicting the average growth of the sample firms, (2) errors in predicting the average growth rate of particular industries, and (3) errors in predicting the growth rates of firms within industries. To accomplish this, we decompose the numerator of (2.3-1) into three parts. The first comes from the average prediction for all companies not being equal to the average realization. The second part reflects differences among the average industry predictions not being equal to the corresponding differences among average industry realizations. The third arises from the differences in predictions for the corporations within an industry not being the same as the differences in realizations.

Let P_{kj} and R_{kj} be the predicted and realized growth rates for the kth company ($k = 1, \ldots, N_j$) in the jth industry ($j = 1, \ldots, J$). We can write the numerator of (2.3-1) as

$$(2.3\text{-}2) \qquad \sum_{j=1}^{J} \sum_{k=1}^{N_j} (P_{kj} - R_{kj})^2 = \left[\sum_{j=1}^{J} N_j (\bar{P} - \bar{R})^2 \right]$$

$$+ \left[\sum_{j=1}^{J} N_j [(\bar{P}_j - \bar{P}) - (\bar{R}_j - \bar{R})]^2 \right]$$

$$+ \left[\sum_{j=1}^{J} \sum_{i=1}^{N_j} [(P_{kj} - \bar{P}_j) - (R_{kj} - \bar{R}_j)]^2 \right].$$

Here, $\bar{P}_j$ and $\bar{R}_j$ are the averages for the jth industry and $\bar{P}$ and $\bar{R}$ are the overall means. The three terms in square brackets represent the decomposition referred to above. The proportions of T arising from these three sources will be called T^M, T^{BI}, and T^{WI}, respectively, for mean errors, between-industry errors, and within-industry errors.

Failure to forecast industry means (T^{BI}) accounted for only a very small proportion of the inequality coefficient. The main sources of inequality were the within-industry errors. Table 2.16 shows the results for 1963 for the long-term predictors. Similar findings were made for other years and for the short-term predictors.

The correlations of predictions with future growth rates within industries permit us to assess which industries were most difficult to forecast in an *ex post* sense. This difficulty is indicated in table 2.17. To calculate this table, we first ranked each predictor's correlation coefficients between its forecasts and the realizations over the eight industry groups. The industry for which the predictor had the worst correlation (that is, the most difficulty) was given a rank of unity. Table 2.17 presents the sums of the ranks for each industry based on the predictors which furnished enough forecasts to calculate correlation coefficients in each of the industries.[10] If the difficulty rankings for all predictors were identical, the rank totals

---

10. Only three long-term predictors could be included in 1962, four in 1963, and six in 1964 and 1965. Three short-term predictors were included in 1961 and 1962, and four were included in 1963, 1964, and 1965.

Table 2.16   Analysis of Forecasts by Industrial Category:
                    1963 Predictions vs. 1963–68 Actual Earnings

Pred.	Correlation	T	T^M	T^{BI}	T^{WI}	No. of Observations
1	.21	.75	.32	.23	.63	173
2	.25	.73	.31	.20	.62	171
3	.48	.66	.31	.18	.55	122
4	.75	.46	.05	.21	.41	59
5	.42	.62	.12	.17	.58	172
6	.69	.45	.07	.11	.43	37
7	.51	.58	.16	.22	.51	60
g_{p1}	.42	.65	.07	.26	.59	153
g_{p2}	.39	.71	.09	.32	.63	131
g_{p3}	.47	.66	.04	.19	.63	121
g_{p4}	.45	.77	.04	.17	.75	156

would be 4 for the most difficult industry (in years when there were four predictors compared), 8 for the next most difficult, and so on. In this case, the coefficient of concordance (Kendall's W) would be unity. The values of Kendall's W were significantly different from zero beyond the 0.05 level for most of the years as were differences between industries for the correlation coefficients for most of the predictors.[11] These findings indicate that there were industry differences. For the long-term predictions, correlation coefficients between forecasts and realizations tended to be highest in the oil, food and stores, and "cyclical" industries. For the short-term predictions, there was really no industry that was particularly easy to predict compared with the others; that is, prediction performances were uniformly mediocre across industries.

The electric utility industry turned out to be one of the more difficult industries for which to make long-term forecasts. This would come as a distinct surprise to the participating security analysts who claimed at the outset that they had some reservations about their abilities to predict earnings for the metals and other "cyclical" companies, but had confidence that they could make accurate predictions for the utilities.[12] It turned out that the long-term predictions for the utility industry were considerably worse than for the metals and "cyclicals."

In general, we had little success in associating forecasting performance with industry or company characteristics. Forecasting differences between industries were only moderately related to the average realized

11. The latter was tested on the basis of the asymptotic distribution of the correlation coefficient and the assumption that the data were distributed normally.

12. This confidence was also reflected in the fact that for the electric utility industry there was high agreement among the forecasters, whereas agreement was relatively low for the cyclical group.

Table 2.17   Rank Totals of Correlations of Predictors and Realizations Summed over Predictors

A. Long-Term Forecasts

Industry	1962 Forecast vs. 1962–67 Earnings Growth	1963 Forecast vs. 1963–68 Earnings Growth	1964 Forecast vs. 1964–69 Earnings Growth	1965 Forecast vs. 1965–70 Earnings Growth	1966 Forecast vs. 1966–71 Earnings Growth	Total
Electrical & electronics	23.0	26.0	29.0	33.0	16.0	127.0
Electric utilities	14.0	19.0	36.0	34.0	21.0	124.0
Metals	14.0	17.0	28.0	28.0	9.0	96.0
Oils	3.0	5.0	8.0	9.0	11.0	36.0
Drugs & specialty chems.	17.0	26.0	34.0	42.0	17.0	136.0
Food & stores	8.0	10.0	16.0	26.0	21.0	81.0
Cyclical	10.0	16.0	22.0	16.0	4.0	68.0
Miscellaneous	19.0	25.0	43.0	28.0	9.0	124.0
Kendall's W	.76†	.62†	.59†	.50†	.71†	.46†

B. Short-Term Forecasts vs. One-Year Earnings Growth

Industry	1961	1962	1963	1964	1965	Total
Electrical & electronics	9.0	17.0	24.0	24.0	16.0	90.0
Electric utilities	11.0	20.0	20.0	11.0	12.0	74.0
Metals	5.0	13.0	14.0	27.0	27.0	86.0
Oils	10.0	14.0	16.0	16.0	9.0	65.0
Drugs & specialty chems.	21.0	14.0	26.0	17.0	27.0	105.0
Food & stores	21.0	9.0	4.0	11.0	24.0	69.0
Cyclical	16.0	13.0	17.0	18.0	12.0	76.0
Miscellaneous	15.0	8.0	23.0	20.0	17.0	83.0
Kendall's W	.61†	.28	.51†	.33	.53†	.85§

†Significant at .05 level.

industry growth rates over the forecast period or to the variances of earnings about the realized growth rates.[13]

2.3.4 Comparison with Extrapolation of Past Growth

The picture that emerges thus far is one of rather mediocre performance by our sample of forecasters. Short-term forecasting performance may fairly be described as poor; long-term forecasting success was only slightly better. A variety of supplementary tests will help us to buttress these conclusions and to appraise more fully security analysts' ability to forecast.

The record of the forecasters raises the question whether any naive forecasting device based on historical data yields as good forecasts as the painstaking efforts of the security analysts. Several alternative historical growth rates were compared with the predictors' forecasts in order to assess their forecasting abilities better. To do so, we used historical log-linear growth rates for pretax cash earnings per share, the g_c variables already used in section 2.2.5. We also tried various averages of first ratios of cash earnings. In all, almost a dozen different mechanical methods for calculating past earnings growth were used, but none of them was satisfactory. We also examined four past-growth perceptions supplied to us by some of the predictors.

Analyses comparable to those shown in tables 2.13, 2.14, and 2.15 were performed using these past growth rates as predictors. The calculated growth rates were virtually uncorrelated with the one-year realizations, uniformly giving correlation results comparable to the weakest of the short-term forecasts. The only virtue of these predictions was that they gave inequality coefficients that were less than unity. The longer-term past perceived rates gave similar findings. However, the one-year past perceptions were somewhat stronger predictors in the two years in which they were available. Even so, their highest correlation with the realizations was only 0.44.

The past growth rates, calculated or perceived, gave somewhat stronger results when used to predict growth rates over five years. In some instances, they were stronger than some explicit forecasts. This was not, however, generally the case, and on balance the security analysts tended to produce stronger predictions. Again, past perceived growth

---

13. One might at least expect forecasting difficulty to be related to company risk. To investigate this possibility, the corporations were classified according to the quality ratings supplied by two of the predicting firms. There was a tendency for the correlations to be lowest (and negative) in the poorest-quality grouping, but they did not get systematically higher with quality; the highest correlations tended to occur in the middle groupings. When the corporations were classified by a high, medium, or low price-earnings multiple; or past growth rates of earnings; or future growth rates of earnings, sales, or assets, no pronounced or significant patterns emerged.

rates were stronger predictors than calculated ones. Overall we can conclude that mechanically calculated growth rates are not very effective predictors, tending to be inferior to the predictions of the analyst. This finding is similar to that of Little (1962) for British corporations and of Lintner and Glauber (1972) for U.S. ones that growth does not tend to persist. By contrast, analysts' perceived past growth rates were somewhat effective as predictors for the periods of our study, especially those representing earnings growth over a reasonably long period of time. Indeed, the best of the past perceptions of growth were about as reliable predictors as were the individual analyst's explicit predictions.

We noted earlier that price-earnings ratios may be considered to contain implicit forecasts of earnings growth. When we compared the price-earnings multiple and the multiple calculated on the basis of average estimates of "normalized" earnings per share with realized earnings growth, it was evident that the ratios are generally as good predictors as either forecasts based on historical data or those made by many analysts. To put the point in a different way, there did not seem to be any more information in the predictions themselves than was already impounded in market prices.

2.4 Are the Expectations "Rational"?

A major question to ask of any expectations data is whether they are "rational." Unfortunately, our data are not really suitable for investigating this subject properly. In consequence, the tests that we do conduct are at best only slightly indicative of whether the rational-expectations hypothesis is appropriate. Fortunately, the analyses may be of interest in any case to indicate further features of our data and of the quantities being predicted.

The difficulty with our data for the rational-expectations hypothesis is that they are primarily cross-sectional. Nine years of annual data would be of rather limited use for time-series analysis even if we had data for all our forecasters in all years. However, some predictors were in the sample for only two or three years. Even when a predictor's forecasts were available throughout all the period or most of it, the firm did not cover each of the companies in our sample in all years. In consequence, our data were not suitable for many obvious tests of forecast rationality.

To accomplish any investigation, we shall have to treat the forecasts made for different companies as providing a random sample of forecasts. Such an assumption would also have been implicit in the comparisons made in section 2.3 had formal inferences been drawn from them, but it does not seem to be entirely suitable for our data.

We found earlier in analyzing the forecasts that a model in which earnings varied with a few important quantities, such as perhaps the overall growth of the economy, may provide a useful way of looking at the formation of predictions. Later we shall suggest that a similar model is useful for realizations. All the realizations over a particular period are presumably based on the same values of these key variables. If their realized values differ from the predicted ones, these few failures in predicting the common factors will show up as common elements of the differences of the predictions from the realizations. In particular, each realization may differ in a systematic way from its expected value depending on all information available at the time the forecasts were made. However, a factor analysis involving the realizations and predictions is not sensible since it presumes that the predictors have no ability to forecast the firm-specific variations. That is, forecasters may well have predictive ability beyond their assessment of the common variables.

The second problem is that differences between realizations and forecasts may be correlated across firms, affecting the significance levels and powers of tests. This would also arise from the first problem. There is no obvious a priori structure to impose on such correlations, and we lack observations sufficient to estimate them. Hence we shall have to make the standard cross-sectional assumption of independent residuals.

We can also expect heteroscedasticity to be a problem with cross-section data of the sort we have been using. In other words, we can expect some companies to be harder to predict than others so that residual variances should vary among companies. We have no basis, however, for specifying the form of the heteroscedasticity for Aitken estimation.[14] As a result, we used the ordinary least-squares estimates. To prevent the misleading inferences that may result fron heteroscedasticity, however, we use the variance-covariance matrix suggested by White (1980) in performing our tests. This allows specifically for the effects of heteroscedasticity without requiring us to specify its form.

A critical requirement for considering a forecast to be "rational" in the sense used by Muth (1961) is that the mathematical expectation of the realization conditional on the forecast should be the forecast;[15] i.e., we can express the realized growth over period t $(g_{r,t})$ as

---

14. Routine use of a quadratic function of the independent variables as an "explanation" of the heteroscedasticity could (and did) produce some negative estimates or tiny positive ones that, if used, would have dominated the Aitken estimates.

15. The criterion is not as simple or straightforward as it often appears. There is a problem with what is being forecast—that is, about the quantity for which an expectation is formed—and this affects the criterion. Explicitly, if the expectations refer to a nonlinear function of the quantity it is assumed is being predicted, then the expected value of the transformed quantity is not usually the transformation of the expected quantity. In our case this is particularly relevant because the five-year growth could be expressed in terms other than the annual rates of growth we use. If the rational-expectations hypothesis holds for the annual rates of growth, it will not hold for the total proportionate increase over five years.

$$(2.4\text{-}1) \qquad g_{r,t} = {}_t g_{p,t-1} + u_t,$$

where ${}_t g_{p,t-1}$ is the predicted growth rate for period t, made in period $t-1$, and u_t is a random variable with mean zero uncorrelated with ${}_t g_{p,t-1}$. Following Theil (1966) and Friedman (1980), who tested the "rationality" of interest-rate forecasts, we regress the realizations $(g_{r,t})$ on the forecasters' predictions $({}_t g_{p,t-1})$ according to

$$(2.4\text{-}2) \qquad g_{r,t} = a + b_t g_{p,t-1} + u_t$$

and investigate the null hypothesis of unbiasedness defined by

$$(2.4\text{-}3) \qquad H_0 : (a,b) = (0,1).$$

The results of testing H_0 for the long-term predictors are summarized in table 2.18 in terms of the significance levels beyond which H_0 cannot be rejected. We can reject a finding of unbiasedness in the majority of cases. This is not a uniform pattern, however. Few rejections occurred for the 1964–69 predictions. By contrast, the hypothesis is rejected for all predictors in the 1965–70 comparisons.

The estimates of equation (2.4-2) corresponding to these results are shown in table 2.19. While one cannot ascribe the rejection of hypothesis (2.4-3) simply to one coefficient or the other, the problem seems to involve both coefficients. Rather surprisingly, there is no clear-cut pattern to the rejection. It is not, for instance, the case that the a coefficients tend always to be positive or the b coefficients to be less than unity. Unfortunately, it is not appropriate to aggregate these results over time. The five-year nature of the forecasts and of the realizations means that successive values of u_t may very well be correlated. For this reason also,

Table 2.18   **Significance Levels beyond Which Hypothesis (2.4-3) Cannot Be Rejected**

Pred.	1961	1962	1963	1964	1965
1	.000	.000	.000	.511	.000
2	.000	.000	.000	.059	.000
3	.087	***	.000	.375	.008
4	***	.009	.071	.036	.000
5	***	.001	.024	.419	.000
6	.191	.135	.433	.225	.000
7	***	.064	.098	.311	.000
8	.000	***	***	.021	.000
9	***	***	***	.298	.000

Pred.	1966	1967	1968	1969
2	.000	.000	.034	.015
3	.000	.000	.000	.000
6	.000	.000	.000	***

NOTE. Significance levels are results of asymptotic χ^2 tests allowing for heteroscedasticity.

Table 2.19   **Long-Term Predictors' Estimates of Equation (2.4-2) (standard errors adjusted for heteroscedasticity in parentheses)**

	Predictor					
	2		3		6	
Year	a	$b-1$	a	$b-1$	a	$b-1$
1961/66	.06[†]	−.20	−.03	.48	−.03	.48
	(.02)	(.34)	(.07)	(.66)	(.07)	(.61)
1962/67	.04[†]	−.08	****	****	−.05	.79[†]
	(.01)	(.28)	****	****	(.03)	(.39)
1963/68	.05[†]	−.32	.03[†]	.11	−.04	.43
	(.01)	(.27)	(.01)	(.18)	(.03)	(.35)
1964/69	−.01	.34	−.02	.30	−.04	.52
	(.02)	(.25)	(.01)	(.21)	(.02)	(.31)
1965/70	−.04[†]	.16	−.00	−.26	−.03[†]	−.19
	(.01)	(.20)	(.01)	(.16)	(.01)	(.17)
1966/71	−.10[†]	.55	−.03	−.67	−.04	−.49
	(.03)	(.42)	(.03)	(.44)	(.02)	(.25)
1967/72	.03	−.74[†]	.02	−.73[†]	−.03	−.18
	(.03)	(.37)	(.02)	(.27)	(.03)	(.39)
1968/73	.05[†]	−.74[†]	.05[†]	−.91[†]	.02	−.49[†]
	(.02)	(.31)	(.01)	(.10)	(.02)	(.21)
1969/74	.07[†]	−.83[†]	.11[†]	−1.54[†]	****	****
	(.02)	(.29)	(.02)	(.29)	****	****

	1		4		5	
	a	$b-1$	a	$b-1$	a	$b-1$
1961/66	.04	.04	****	****	****	****
	(.08)	(.43)	****	****	****	****
1962/63	.06[†]	−.44	−.04	.63[†]	.03[†]	−.13
	(.02)	(.31)	(.02)	(.23)	(.01)	(.15)
1963/68	.06[†]	−.49	−.04[†]	.54[†]	.03[†]	−.17
	(.02)	(.30)	(.02)	(.23)	(.01)	(.19)
1964/69	.01	−.35	−.01	.39[†]	−.03	.35
	(.02)	(.30)	(.01)	(.19)	(.02)	(.29)
1965/70	−.03[†]	.15	−.05[†]	.21	−.03[†]	−.14
	(.01)	(.18)	(.02)	(.22)	(.01)	(.15)

	7		8		9	
	a	$b-1$	a	$b-1$	a	$b-1$
1961/66	****	****	.06[†]	−.33	****	****
	****	****	(.02)	(.33)	****	****
1962/67	−.02	.54	****	****	****	****
	(.03)	(.44)	****	****	****	****
1963/68	−.01	.33	****	****	****	****
	(.02)	(.36)	****	****	****	****
1964/69	.00	−.16	−.08[†]	1.13[†]	.00	−.19
	(.01)	(.16)	(.03)	(.53)	(.02)	(.26)
1965/70	−.02	−.39[†]	−.10[†]	.85[†]	−.03	−.09
	(.01)	(.16)	(.03)	(.31)	(.02)	(.15)

[†]Significant at the .05 level.

one would not expect a lack of serial correlation between the u_t to be an implication of rational expectations.

The pattern found for the short-term forecasts is rather different from that found for the longer-term ones.[16] Here not only can the null hypothesis ($a = 0$, $b = 1$) be rejected in most cases, but the individual parts can often be rejected. In particular, the coefficients b tended to be significantly less than unity.

With the short-term predictors, we may now look at whether the residuals are serially correlated. More precisely, under the rational-expectations hypothesis, any predictive information contained in the extent to which the last forecast missed should be incorporated in the forecast. To test both of these aspects of the rational-expectations hypothesis, we ran the regression

$$(2.4\text{-}4) \qquad (g_{r,t} - g_{p,t-1}) = a + b g_{p,t-1} \\ + c(g_{r,t-1} - {}_{t-1}g_{p,t-2}) + u_t.$$

Under the rational-expectations hypothesis, all three coefficients should be zero.

Table 2.20 reports the results for 1964–65 and for 1965–66. In the first case, the overall hypothesis can be rejected for all predictions, the column headed "sig" indicating the significance level beyond which the hypothesis can be accepted. While the constant often provides by itself the basis for the rejections, the b coefficients also often did not conform to the hypothesis either. The hypothesis that $c = 0$ could not be rejected in most cases. The overall hypothesis fared a bit better in the next year, which is the one most favorable to it, but rejection still occurs in many instances. Rejection now does occur on account of the c coefficients in several instances.

We cannot perform this same test with the long-term predictions because of the five-year gap between forecast and realization. We may, however, ask whether the extent to which the most recent difference between the actual (one-year) rate of growth and the five-year rate of growth predicted in the previous year actually has predictive content. With only two or three exceptions, the hypothesis that this difference had no predictive power could not be rejected at the 0.05 level. The results for both aspects of this interpretation of the rational-expectations hypothesis jointly paralleled those found in table 2.19.

Another important property of rational expectations is that they efficiently incorporate all available information including the information contained in previously realized outcomes. Although we have seen that previous misses sometimes have (*ex post*) additional predictive informa-

---

16. Unfortunately, the predictors which made forecasts for five consecutive years did not make their forecasts later than 1965.

Table 2.20   Short-Term Predictors' Estimates of Equation (2.4-4) (standard errors adjusted for heteroscedasticity in parentheses)

Pred.	a		b		c		Sig.[‡]
			1964				
A	.07[†]	(.02)	−.36	(.20)	.34[†]	(.08)	.000
B	.05[†]	(.02)	−.24	(.13)	.20	(.15)	.011
C	.06[†]	(.02)	−.43[†]	(.13)	.36[†]	(.13)	.000
D	.08[†]	(.01)	−.40[†]	(.07)	.05	(.09)	.000
E	.03	(.07)	−.22	(.24)	.55	(.30)	.001
F	.04	(.02)	−.17	(.17)	.24	(.20)	.003
G	.13[†]	(.04)	−.34	(.27)	−.09	(.32)	.000
H	.04	(.04)	.12	(.25)	.07	(.07)	.012
I	.14[†]	(.05)	−.25	(.15)	−.06	(.24)	.000
K	−.08[†]	(.02)	.53[†]	(.21)	.15	(.08)	.000
			1965				
A	.03	(.02)	−.53[†]	(.14)	.39[†]	(.13)	.000
B	.00	(.02)	−.22	(.15)	.17	(.19)	.017
C	.23	(.14)	−2.40	(1.32)	−.21	(.30)	.108
D	.07	(.03)	−.70[†]	(.24)	.12	(.20)	.017
E	.02	(.03)	−.32	(.17)	.28	(.29)	.093
F	.02	(.02)	−.25	(.13)	.11	(.13)	.002
G	.09[†]	(.02)	−.86[†]	(.15)	.11[†]	(.05)	.000
H	.01	(.03)	−.25	(.28)	.13	(.16)	.270
I	.19	(.10)	−1.76	(.91)	.18[†]	(.07)	.068
K	.01	(.02)	.10	(.18)	.17	(.11)	.132

[†]Significant at the .05 level.
[‡]Significance level of hypothesis that all coefficients are zero.

tion with the short-term forecasts, we may wonder whether such information will also lead to subsequent revision of forecasts. Under the rational-expectations hypothesis, the change in a forecast made for a given future time should not be related to errors made prior to the current forecast. Any useful information contained in the forecast error during period $t − 2$ should have affected the $t − 1$ forecast and should not affect the change in the forecast from period $t − 1$ to t.

This notion cannot be applied easily to our data, because successive forecasts are for different times. We may, however, consider the hypothesis that for forecast purposes the short-term growth rate can be considered a parameter following a random walk measured with error and so investigate the usual error-learning hypothesis on a cross-sectional basis. Explicitly, this hypothesis states that the *change* in forecast can be considered a linear function only of the difference of the most recent realization from its forecast value and not of previously observed differences. Specifically, we investigate

(2.4-5)
$$_{t+1}g_{p,t} - {}_tg_{p,t-1} = A + B(g_{r,t} - {}_tg_{p,t-1})$$
$$+ C(g_{r,t-1} - {}_{t-1}g_{p,t-2}) + u_t$$

and consider the null hypothesis to be that $C = 0$. In considering this hypothesis, it would not be reasonable to assume that A and B are constant across companies. This would suggest that a random coefficients model may be more appropriate. However, since the major effect of such a specification is to produce heteroscedasticity and since all our inferences already are based on allowing for heteroscedasticity explicitly, our procedures for inference may be considered adequate even in the face of variable coefficients.

Table 2.21 shows the results for the short-term predictors for the three years where it is feasible to pursue the investigation. The estimated coefficient C giving the effect of the error made in the period prior to the previous forecast on the current forecast change generally is not significantly different from zero. Nevertheless, there are many instances in the table, especially in the 1964–65 revision period, where one-period prior forecast errors did appear to influence forecast revisions, a finding inconsistent with the simple error-learning model.[17]

As Table 2.21 also shows, the values of R^2 are generally quite low. Altough part of the variance not accounted for may come from the variation among companies of coefficient B, the general impression is that the error-learning hypothesis is not strong. It remains an open question, however, whether the explanation is that earnings do not follow one of the standard models of expectations formation.

By and large, these results do not seem favorable to the rational-expectations hypothesis. Of course, this may be because of the inappropriateness of testing the hypothesis with cross-section data. To shed further light on this issue, we present, as table 2.22, the average errors of our short-term and long-term forecasters taken as a group. The average errors are measured by the differences between the realization and the average prediction of those forecasters making predictions for the companies in question.

In the early part of our period, both the short- and long-term predictors tended to make forecasts that were too low. Realizations tended to exceed forecasts during most of this early period. This may simply indicate a failure to anticipate the continuation of the extraordinary economic expansion experienced through the period. It may also reflect the underestimation of change frequently found in investigating forecasts and reported by Theil (1966).

In the later period, a similar underestimation of change did not characterize the forecasts. The forecasts were too high in some years, but

---

17. It should also be noted that in some cases the changes in forecast from year to year were correlated.

Table 2.21   **Short-Term Predictors' Estimates of Equation (2.4-5) (standard errors adjusted for heteroscedasticity in parentheses)**

Pred.	B		C		R^2
			1962–63		
A	.11	(.17)	.03	(.09)	.02
B	.02	(.15)	.09	(.10)	.02
C	.25	(.16)	.11	(.08)	.08
D	.02	(.07)	.01	(.07)	.00
E	−.11	(.12)	−.23	(.16)	.10
G	.02	(.12)	.14[†]	(.05)	.18[†]
H	−.13	(.07)	.11[†]	(.12)	.15[†]
I	−.04	(.09)	.08	(.06)	.02
K	−.04	(.12)	.09	(.06)	.03
			1963–64		
A	.17[†]	(.06)	.10	(.05)	.23[†]
B	.17[†]	(.08)	.32	(.23)	.23[†]
C	.46[†]	(.21)	−.09	(.10)	.19
D	.05	(.30)	.04	(.16)	.01
E	−.07	(.09)	.10	(.19)	.02
G	.10	(.07)	.06	(.05)	.05
H	.09	(.14)	.11	(.08)	.05
I	.08	(.08)	.05	(.05)	.03
K	−.07	(.08)	−.08	(.12)	.03
			1964–65		
A	−.07	(.11)	−.15	(.16)	.06
B	.34[†]	(.08)	.01	(.06)	.18[†]
C	.29	(.15)	−.12	(.10)	.15
D	.11	(.10)	−.09	(.09)	.04
E	.09	(.05)	.36[†]	(.07)	.52[†]
G	.15[†]	(.07)	.21[†]	(.07)	.19[†]
H	−.14	(.10)	.13[†]	(.07)	.19
I	.11[†]	(.04)	.18[†]	(.05)	.17[†]
K	−.27	(.19)	.01	(.06)	.10

[†]Significant at the .05 level.

during others they were too low. The only pattern we found consistently was that in years when the forecasts were too high (low), all forecasters tended to be too high (low).

This latter finding is the sort of pattern we might expect from a few common factors throwing off all forecasts. However, insofar as the continuation of the economic expansion lies behind the results, it does not seem to account for the values of *b* that were found. We do not find accentuation of forecast differences, which would produce values of *b* greater than unity in (2.4-2). That is the pattern we might expect if the forecast rankings reflected sensitivity to economic expansion.

Table 2.22   Average Forecast Errors across Sample

Forecast Period	Average Error
Long-Term Forecast	
1966/61	.0450
1967/62	.0321
1968/63	.0300
1969/64	.0014
1970/65	− .0336
1971/66	− .0667
1972/67	− .0308
1973/68	− .0246
1974/69	.0126
Short-Term Forecasts	
1962/61	− .0328
1963/62	.0586
1964/63	.1062
1965/64	.0345
1966/65	.0315
1967/66	− .0841
1968/67	.0441
1969/68	− .0288

A broader, and perhaps the most appropriate, test of expectations rationality is whether forecasters effectively incorporate *all* of the available historical information. To investigate this matter, we asked if there was some combination of historical information and analysts' forecasts that together might be better than using any individual piece of information alone. We asked, *ex post*, how an analyst could have made the best linear one-year prediction for earnings in, say, 1962, given that she had available to her the information now available to us. To deal simply with the problems of missing observations, we concentrate on the average of the available predictions rather than on each individually or some best linear combination of them.

Needless to say, in each year there is some combination of predicted short-term growth, long-term growth, eight- to ten-year historical growth, etc., which would be more highly correlated with realizations than would the predictions of any one forecaster alone. This fact is demonstrated by comparing the seventh column of table 2.23 with the earlier columns. In the earlier columns $\bar{g}_p$ is the average predicted growth and g_{p1} and g_{p2} are the simple historical growth rates defined above. Column 7 shows that using the best linear combination of the predictors plus historical information does improve forecasting ability, although the increase over the average of the predictors is not great. The important question is whether the combination that is calculated to work well in one

Table 2.23   Correlations of Various Predictions with Realizations (1961–65)

Forecast Period (1)	Forecast Date (2)	$\bar{g}_p$ (3)	g_{c1} (4)	g_{p1} (5)	g_{p2} (6)	Best Linear Combination of Forecast and Historical Info.		
						Present Year (7)	Prior Year (8)	P/E (9)
A. Long-Term Forecast								
66/61	61	.5585	.0900	.2436	.3863	.6463	*****	.7129
67/62	62	.5280	.3305	.3511	.3990	.5980	.1409	.5155
68/63	63	.6172	.3802	.4871	.5162	.6533	.5243	.5488
69/64	64	.5814	.1104	.2469	.5026	.6253	.1042	.4829
70/65	65	.4667	−.1099	.1615	.4042	.5797	.4667	.4337
B. Short-Term Forecasts								
62/61	61	.3583	.1886	.1642	.2338	.4694	*****	.5546
63/62	62	.2199	.0028	.0181	.0652	.4407	.2411	.1729
64/63	63	.3197	.3229	.2577	.2638	.5098	.0603	.3598
65/64	64	.3959	−.0823	.1505	.1000	.5403	.0375	.3344
66/65	65	.3773	.1485	.1162	.2042	.4567	.2416	.2524

year will continue to work in a subsequent one. Such is not the case. Instead, the superiority of the linear combination disappears and it is decidedly inferior to the average of the predictors. These correlations are shown in column 8 of table 2.23. Stated differently, there is no combination of analysts' forecasts and historical information that could be used to make better predictions on a consistent basis.[18] This result suggests that there is no systematic relationship between historical and realized growth that is not directly incorporated into the forecasts.[19]

The last column of table 2.23 shows the correlation of the simple price-earnings multiple with the realized growth of earnings. The price-earnings multiple was as good as, and often better than, the average of the analysts' predictions. Since P/E multiples are influenced by more than forecasted growth (as will be shown explicitly in chapter 4), this is a surprising result. It suggests that whatever information there is in the forecasts gets assimilated quickly.

Our investigation of the rationality of the forecasts presents mixed results. We were able to reject the major implications of the narrow interpretation of the hypothesis and can be fairly confident that the standard explicit hypothesis of expectations formation is not correct. We cannot, however, reject the broader interpretation of the rational-expectations hypothesis. We found no consistent or coherent pattern indicating that readily available information is not efficiently incorporated in the forecasts, and it appears that any useful information in the forecasts does get rationally included in share prices. To put the point in a different way, there does not seem to be any more information in the predictions themselves than is already contained in market prices.

18. For a similar analysis of interest-rate forecasts, see Friedman (1980, pp. 8, 9).

19. This analysis was done only for five years because of lack of data for later years for g_{p1} and g_{p2}, which were past growth rates as "perceived" by two of our forecasters.

3 Valuation Models and Earnings Growth

The growth-rate expectations we have been investigating were formed by security analysts to aid them in judging the worth of common stocks. In addition to the questions about the accuracy, agreement, and completeness of the analysts' forecasts that we investigated in chapter 2, these data prompt two further queries: How are expectations of the future growth of earnings related to the value of common stock? Do security analysts' forecasts represent the expectations that actually affect the prices of securities?

Any consideration of these questions requires the use of some theory of the formation of the prices of common stocks in which the expected growth rates of earnings play an important role. The theory should also encompass explicitly major features of the expected growth rates that we uncovered in examining these data. We especially need to recognize in the theory the diversity of expectations that was so evident in our data.

3.1 The Role of Security-Valuation Models

The obvious theory to begin with is the capital-asset pricing model (CAPM) developed initially by Sharpe (1964), Lintner (1965), and Mossin (1966). This theory is now widely used as an approach to security valuation. It provides explicit hypotheses about the relative structure of security prices based on expectations about the returns to investors in securities, and it is now the dominant valuation model.

The CAPM has a number of theoretical and empirical weaknesses. Ross (1976, 1977) has developed a different model based on arbitrage considerations. This arbitrage pricing theory (APT) uses a less general assumption about the nature of security returns than the CAPM, but this limitation is balanced by the less restrictive assumptions about investor behavior adopted by the APT. The key assumption for the APT concerns the nature of returns—an assumption we describe below—and not the arbitrage considerations. We can obtain virtually the same conclusions about valuation as can be obtained with APT by using an alternative argument concerning diversification together with the central assumption of the APT about returns. In our argument, we assume that utility-maximizing behavior leads a number of investors to choose portfolios which are extensively diversified. The occurrence of such diversification then turns out to imply a particular structure of security prices. This alternative argument has the advantage of being somewhat less sensitive than other asset-pricing theories to variations in some other key assumptions. At the same time, if the CAPM should actually be the appropriate theory, then it gives the same results as the diversification theory provided that returns do follow the assumed pattern.

None of these theories explicitly relates expectations of returns to characteristics of the issuers of securities, or to investors' perceptions of them, including the growth rates of their earnings and dividends. Instead, the models concentrate on the returns to be received directly by investors. These returns include payments made by the issuers of securities—in particular, dividends. The returns also include changes in the market values of securities, that is, capital gains. Current market prices are determined in the valuation theories by expectations about future returns. Presumably market prices in the future will also be determined by the expectations that will be held at the time of that valuation as well as by the operation of the valuation process in the future. In order to judge the value of securities today, investors should logically concern themselves with predicting future expectations.

Most models ignore this aspect of the logical structure of valuation. Indeed, they are usually expressed in a rate-of-return form which hides the implicit problems created by the model's requiring expectations of how the model itself will operate later. The major explicit exceptions occur in papers by Stapleton and Subrahmanyam (1978) and by Ohlson and Garman (1980). The valuation model developed in this chapter will wrestle explicitly with the problems of expectations about future market valuation. We relate future expected prices to expectations of the growth of earnings and find that the price-determination process is internally consistent.

3.2 A Diversification Model of Security Valuation

3.2.1 The Basic Model

Heuristically, we start from the insight that prompted Sharpe (1964) to develop the CAPM. Sharpe's insight was that variations in the returns to different securities are related to each other through common dependence on a small number of events or variables.[1] Any risks specific to the security can be removed by diversification. Portfolios typically are diversified, but even investors with very widely diversified portfolios, containing only small holdings of very many securities, do not avoid the risks coming from the common elements. Investors must therefore be receiving appropriate rewards in order for them to be willing to bear these risks. There is no need to reward investors for bearing the risks specific to individual securities since such risks can be "diversified away." Security returns (and so security prices) must exhibit certain patterns in order that the appropriate rewards should exist in the sense that bearing systematic risk does receive a premium but bearing specific risk does not. We will argue that the key element in this description is that investors' portfolios may be considered to be extensively diversified. If this is the case, security prices must exhibit a certain type of pattern.

The situation which we consider may be characterized as follows:

a) There are J types of marketable securities. Associated with each security is a one-period total return of r_j (dollars) per unit of security, which accrues to the holders of the security. The (proportionate) rate of return over the period is π_j, defined as $\pi_j = r_j/p_j - 1$, where p_j is the price of the security.

b) The returns may be treated as random variables. The critical assumption for the diversification argument, as for the Ross APT, is that these random variables have the following structure:

$$(3.2\text{-}1) \qquad r_j = \mu_j + \sum_{k=1}^{K} \gamma_{jk} f_k + e_j.$$

Here μ_j is a fixed parameter giving the expected return of security j, $j = 1, \ldots, J$. The f_k are K random variables, each with mean zero.[2] It is assumed that $k < J$. In fact, we would expect there to be very few factors while there are a large number of securities. The γ_{jk} are coefficients. The e_j are random variables, independent of the f_k and of the other e_m, $m \neq j$. In statistical terms, this is the factor-analysis model, which we used for other purposes in chapter 2; but here we are not assuming that the f_k are normally distributed or necessarily that they are independent of each other.

---

1. It is easy to overlook the fact that Sharpe's model does not really conform to this insight since he does not assume any particular structure for the covariance matrix of returns. The insight is also suggested in Myers (1968), from which the diversification model might be derived.

2. Insofar as the factors do not have mean zero, their expectations multiplied by the coefficients γ_{jk} are incorporated in the expected returns μ_j.

Use of this structure in the present context is intended to capture the hypothesis that returns are related only through a limited number of common factors and are otherwise independent of each other. These factors may be considered to include movements in the general stock market, in economic activity, in the rate of inflation, and so on. Equation (3.2-1) also embodies the highly restrictive assumption that the dependence of returns on the common factors is linear.[3] As we shall see, this restrictive and rather arbitrary aspect of the assumption is important to the results to be obtained and can be relaxed only to a limited extent. Note that (3.2-1) is expressed for returns rather than rates of return. We consider the alternative in section 3.2.2.

c) There are a number of investors, indexed by i, who choose their holdings of securities v_{ji}, $j = 1, \ldots, J$, so as to maximize the expected utility of end-of-period returns $R_i = \Sigma_{j=1}^{J} r_j v_{ji}$. In doing so, they are aware of the process by which returns are generated, given by (3.2-1). Each investor takes the prices of securities as given, unaffected by his own decisions. In carrying out the maximization, the investor is constrained by his initial holdings of securities $\bar{v}_{ji}$; that is, his budget constraint is

$$(3.2\text{-}2) \qquad \sum_{j=1}^{J} p_j v_{ji} = \sum_{j=1}^{J} p_j \bar{v}_{ji}.$$

Thus, letting U_i represent the investor's utility function, the investor's portfolio choice can be considered to maximize

$$(3.2\text{-}3) \qquad E(U_i(R_i)) = E\left[U_i\left(\sum_{j=1}^{J} r_j v_{ji}\right)\right]$$

$$= E\left[U_i\left(\sum_{j=1}^{J}\left(\mu_j + \sum_{k=1}^{K} \gamma_{jk} f_k + e_j\right) v_{ji}\right)\right]$$

subject to constraint (3.2-2). As usual, the investor's utility function U_i is assumed to be monotonically increasing, with continuous first derivatives, and concave (so that the investor is risk-averse).

d) As a result of maximizing their utility functions given the prices that they observe in the market, at least some of these utility-maximizing investors hold extensively diversified portfolios in the sense that the holding of each of these investors of a number of securities is sufficiently small that each one regards his exposure to the specific risks of each of these securities—that is, to the risks coming from the random variations in their e_j's—as being trivial. Explicitly, we shall consider a portfolio to be extensively diversified with respect to a security when the investor's marginal disutility of the exposure to the specific risk of the security can be considered negligible relative to the marginal disutility of the system-

---

3. A discussion of the nature of the factors can be found in Roll and Ross (1980). The common-factor structure (3.2-1) was earlier used in a valuation model by Fama (1971), though he assumed all random quantities had stable distributions.

atic risk exposure to the common factors. We shall correspondingly define his holding of such a security as being extensively diversified.

The investor's choice can be characterized by the first-order conditions for maximization of (3.2-3) subject to (3.2-2), namely,

$$(3.2\text{-}4) \qquad E(r_j U_i') - \lambda_i p_j = \mu_j E(U_i') + \sum_{k=1}^{K} \gamma_{jk} E(f_k U_i') + E(e_j U_i')$$

$$- \lambda_i p_j = 0,$$

where $U_i' = dU_i(R_i)/dR_i$; λ_i is the Lagrange multiplier of the constrained maximization problem, and it has the standard interpretation of being the marginal utility of wealth. Dividing (3.2-4) by λ_i yields

$$(3.2\text{-}5) \qquad p_j = \mu_j a_{0i} + \sum_{k=1}^{K} \gamma_{jk} a_{ki} + E(e_j U_i')/\lambda_i.$$

Note that the coefficients a_{ki} are the same for all securities j.

All terms of (3.2-5) depend on the overall variability of return since they arise from taking the expectations of U_i' and its covariances with other random variables. Within this overall dependence, we may regard the first term on the right-hand side of (3.2-5) as giving the marginal effect of variation in the holding of security j through the expected return of this security. The second term reflects the marginal effect arising through variation with the various common factors of the return of the jth security. The final term reflects the marginal specific risk being introduced into the portfolio through security j. These last two terms reflect the effect of security j on the risk of the portfolio since they arise only from the concavity of the utility function and from the stochastic nature of returns.

If we denote the distribution of the random variables as $G(\cdot)$, the numerator of the last term in (3.2-5) can be written as

$$(3.2\text{-}6) \qquad E(e_j U_i') = \int e_j \left\{ dU_i \left[\sum_{j=1}^{J} \left(\mu_j + \sum_{k=1}^{K} \gamma_{jk} f_{jk} + e_j \right) v_{ji} \right]/dR_i \right\}$$
$$\times \, dG(f_1, \ldots, f_k, e_1, \ldots, e_j).$$

Since U_i is concave, for any given values of the other random variables U_i' is monotonically decreasing (increasing) in e_j as v_{ji} is positive (negative). Since we assume that e_j is independent of other random variables and has mean zero, the expectation in (3.2-6) therefore has a sign opposite to that of v_{ji}. The continuity of U_i' in R_i ensures that (3.2-6) is continuous in v_{ji}. The last term of (3.2-6) can thus be made arbitrarily small by choosing v_{ji} small enough.

One might also presume that the concavity of the utility function would mean that the absolute size of (3.2-6) increases with the absolute value of v_{ji}. This ignores the effect of changes in v_{ji} on (3.2-6) through changes in exposure to other factors. In other words,

$$(3.2\text{-}7) \qquad \partial(e_j U_i')/\partial v_{ji} = U_i'' e_j^2 + U_i'' e_j \mu_j + U_i'' e_j \sum_{k=1}^{K} \gamma_{jk} f_k,$$

and the intuitive argument applies strictly to the first term. Suitable additional assumptions would need to be made if it were to apply to the expectation of (3.2-7). The argument does apply to $\partial^2 E(U_i)/\partial v_{ji}^2 = E(U_i'' r_j^2)$.

In contrast to the final terms of (3.2-6), the coefficients a_{ki} of the γ_{jk} do not depend primarily on the amount of jth security chosen. Instead, $a_{ki} = E(f_k U_i')/\lambda_i$ depends on how $U_i'(R_i)$ varies with f_k. If we assume that the f_k are independent of each other,[4] this correlation depends primarily on $\Sigma_{h=1}^{J} \gamma_{jk} v_{hi}$, which may be regarded as the total exposure of the portfolio to f_k, and not just on the exposure coming from the jth security $\gamma_{jk} v_{ji}$. Indeed, continuing to assume that the f_k are independent of each other, if $\Sigma_{h=1}^{J} \gamma_{hk} v_{hi} = 0$, then U_i' does not vary with f_k and a_{ki} is zero in (3.2-5) even though $\gamma_{jk} v_{ji}$ may be nonzero. This contrast between the last two terms of (3.2-5) reflects the assumption that the investor is only vulnerable to fluctuations in e_j through his holding of security j while he is vulnerable to the common factors through all his holdings.

Our central hypothesis about the extent of diversification states that the first of the risk terms in (3.2-5), $\Sigma_{k=1}^{K} \gamma_{jk} a_{ki}$, is large relative to the last term. Indeed, we assume that v_{ji} is so small that the last term can be ignored, but that the exposures to risk from the common factors, $\Sigma_{j=1}^{J} \gamma_{jk} v_{ji}$, are not so small that the a_{ki} can be overlooked. With such diversification, equation (3.2-5) can be approximated by

$$(3.2\text{-}8) \qquad p_j = \mu_j a_{0i} + \sum_{k=1}^{K} \gamma_{jk} a_{ki}.$$

The price of the security may be treated as a linear function of its expected return and its own coefficients for each of the common factors. As expressed in equation (3.2-8), it might seem that the coefficients of the linear function are specific to the investor i, but this cannot be the case if diversification is widespread.

Suppose that the number of securities being held by some investor i for which (3.2-8) holds exceeds $(K + 1)$, the number of factors plus one. Then the price of these securities must be determined in such a way that they obey approximately a linear equation, namely, (3.2-8). Similarly, suppose that another investor, say, h, has extensively diversified holdings (that is, values of v_{jh} which are sufficiently small that [3.2-8] gives a close

---

4. The specification does not require independence of the f_k, and this assumption is used here only to aid heuristic interpretation of the model. Note that if the f_k are not independent, the a_{ki} will not necessarily be zero when $\Sigma_{h=1}^{J} \gamma_{hk} v_{hi} = 0$. The assumption is usually made in the statistical factor-analysis model to obtain identifiability of the γ_{jk}; but as we explain in section 3.4, our empirical implementation of the model will be along somewhat different lines.

approximation to [3.2-5]) of at least $(K + 1)$ of these securities. Then the coefficients for investor h, a_{kh} $(k = 0, \ldots, K)$, must be the same as those for investor i, and the prices of all the securities of which his holdings are extensively diversified must also obey the same linear equation (3.2-8). Furthermore, if a third investor has extensively diversified holdings of at least $(K + 1)$ securities of which at least one of the other two investors has extensively diversified holdings (even if neither holds $[K + 1]$ of these securities himself), then the coefficients for the third investor must be the same as those for the other two, and any other securities of which his holdings are extensively diversified will have prices which exhibit the same linear structure.

More generally, then, if investors diversify extensively and if there is sufficient overlap among investors in the securities of which their holdings are extensively diversified, we can proceed sequentially in the way outlined to build up a set of securities found in the extensively diversified parts of some portfolios, all of which must (approximately) obey equations of the form

$$(3.2\text{-}9) \qquad p_j = \mu_j a_0 + \sum_{k=1}^{K} \gamma_{jk} a_k .$$

Equation (3.2-9) expresses the main conclusion of the diversification model about security prices. Implicitly it claims that the market determines prices for the characteristics of expected return and association with the common factors but gives a zero value to specific risk. That this pattern of prices must exist is inferred from the "stylized fact" of reasonably wide diversification by some investors, given the other assumptions. It is worth noting that the argument inferring the pattern of prices does not turn on the process of equilibrium price determination, but on the pattern of demand of some investors that is assumed to be observed.

Returning to equation (3.2-5), we can say that it will be the case that any investor having extensively diversified holdings of $(K + 1)$ securities to which (3.2-9) applies must have extensively diversified holdings of all of them because the final terms of (3.2-5) must be negligible for all these securities. Therefore the argument concerning the overlapping sequences of diversified holdings may seem needlessly complicated. However, the argument remains applicable even when other considerations prevent investors from having extensively diversified but nonzero holdings of all securities to which (3.2-9) might apply. It is indeed the ability of this theory to withstand changes of asumptions and restrictions that makes it appealing.

3.2.2 Variations in Investors' Opportunities

The diversification argument is insensitive to many institutional considerations to which other valuation arguments are vulnerable. It holds up well to a prohibition on negative holdings of securities, to significant costs of short-selling, or to costs that limit the number of securities that it is practical or desirable to hold.

It is highly questionable whether allowing negative holdings on the same terms as positive ones well approximates the situation that investors do face. Although short-selling goes part way to providing for the assumed opportunities, it does not really offer them fully. As Miller (1977) and Jarrow (1980) point out, there are significant costs and foregone opportunities in short-selling as well as institutional impediments that are not trivial.

A prohibition of negative holdings does not alter the form of the first-order conditions for securities of which a positive amount is held. Formally the investor may be regarded as maximizing (3.2-3) subject to (3.2-2) and the constraint

$$(3.2\text{-}10) \qquad v_{ji} \geq 0; \qquad j = 1, \ldots, J.$$

The first-order conditions (3.2-4) now become

$$(3.2\text{-}11) \qquad \mu_j E(U_i') + \sum_{k=1}^{K} \gamma_{jk} E(f_k U_i') + E(e_j U_i)$$
$$+ \psi_{ji} - \lambda_i p_j = 0.$$

The additional term ψ_{ji} is the non-negative Kuhn-Tucker multiplier arising from constraint (3.2-10). It has the usual property that $\psi_{ji} v_{ji} = 0$. Hence, for securities for which $v_{ji} > 0$, (3.2-10) reduces to (3.2-4) and the diversification argument continues to hold for small positive holdings. The prices of these securities therefore conform with the relationship (3.2-9). Thus, if utility-maximizing decisions yield diversified portfolios when negative holdings are not allowed, the earlier conclusion about prices applies: the prices of securities which investors do hold in diversified portfolios must exhibit the linear structure shown in (3.2-9).

We saw earlier that $E(e_j U_i') = 0$ when $v_{ji} = 0$. For securities for which (3.2-10) is binding, we can rewrite (3.2-11) as

$$(3.2\text{-}12) \qquad \mu_j a_{0i} + \sum_{k=1}^{K} \gamma_{jk} a_{ki} = p_j - \psi_{ji}/\lambda_i \leq p_j;$$

that is, securities which are not held by investor i are considered to be overvalued by him. If the investor does have extensively diversified holdings of at least $(K + 1)$ securities for which (3.2-9) holds, then his values of a_{ki} equal the a_k for these prices and ψ_{ji} will be zero for all securities to which the diversification argument applies. Constraint (3.2-10) therefore only becomes interesting when other changes in the model are made.

A similar argument to the one advanced when short sales are prohibited applies when they are allowed but involve additional costs not incurred with positive holdings. Equation (3.2-5) remains appropriate for securities of which the investor holds positive amounts. If these amounts are also small, the final term is again insignificant, and so (3.2-9) still must hold approximately.

Costs of various sorts may be associated with the number of different types of securities held. If these diversification costs are sufficiently small, the investor will be able to diversify extensively enough to eliminate virtually all systematic risk. Given the list of securities held by a utility-maximizing investor, the first-order conditions (3.2-4) apply to these securities and the structure of prices (3.2-9) must also obtain approximately if extensive diversification occurs. The argument developed in the previous section about overlapping sets of securities becomes particularly pertinent in this situation. With costs for the number of securities held, we would not expect investors actually to hold all securities for which (3.2-9) might hold. Instead, they will only proceed to the point where the specific risk of securities held can be regarded as small. Nevertheless, securities connected to each other through some sequence of extensively diversified holdings of the sort described in section 3.2-1 will all obey the same equation even though any particular portfolio may include only a small proportion of them. As diversification costs become important, however, the specific-risk terms will also increase in importance in (3.2-5) as diversification becomes less extensive and so the appropriateness of the approximation (3.2-9) becomes less apparent.

We have been considering investors' utility functions to be defined over end-of-period return. Investors undoubtedly do have wider concerns. It is hard to believe that investors' investment horizons are not multiperiod or that their utility functions depend only on the returns of their portfolio of securities. Fortunately, our conclusions are not sensitive to allowing the utility function also to depend on other circumstances or variables that may be correlated with the values taken on by "systematic" factors. In this respect, the model easily overcomes the difficulties that Fama (1970) showed could arise for valuation models from their being embedded in a wider and multiperiod context. We may indeed think of the factors as representing the general economic conditions that will affect investors' investment and consumption opportunity sets and their other income opportunities as well as the returns to securities.

We can readily expand the investor's utility function in (3.2-3) to include other choice variables and dependence on other random aspects of the state of the world. What matters is that the utility function depends on security selection only through the effect that the amount of the security held has on R_i, because the argument relies on assuming that $\partial E(U_i)/\partial v_{ji} = E[r_j \partial U_i/\partial R_i]$. Similarly the budget constraint may be a great deal more complicated than (3.2-2) provided that v_{ji} only enters it linearly, multiplied by p_j. When these conditions are met, equations (3.2-4) continue to express the first-order conditions for the security choices of a utility-maximizing investor. The other critical assumption needed for the diversification theory is that for some investors e_j is correlated with U'_j only through its inclusion in R_i so that the final term of (3.2-5) is zero when v_{ji} is zero for such investors who do include security j in the extensively diversified part of their portfolios. In other words, the second critical condition is that

(3.2-13) $E(e_j U'_i) = 0$ when $v_{ji} = 0$.

This condition will hold if e_j is independent of the other random variables that affect the investor since the $E(U'_i | v_{ji} = 0)$ does not depend on e_j and hence (3.2-13) will hold. Such a condition seems a reasonable interpretation of the model, with the f_k capturing correlations of returns not only among themselves but also with other things that generally affect investors. The model does not preclude some investors' being affected by variations in e_j directly, but it would then predict that such investors would not include security j in the extensively diversified part of their portfolios.

The diversification model is not insensitive to variations in the assumption (3.2-1) made about returns, though some alterations of this assumption can be made. While the assumption in (3.2-1) concerns the levels of return per share, the model could easily be expressed in terms of rates of return. Indeed, formally, if we divide equation (3.2-9) by $p_j a_0$ and rearrange, we obtain

(3.2-14) $\mu_j / p_j = 1/a_0 - \sum_{k=1}^{K} (a_k / a_0)(\gamma_{jk}/p_j)$.

Letting $\rho_j = \mu_j / p_j - 1 = E(\pi_j)$ and defining α_{jk} as (γ_{jk}/p_j), we can rewrite this equation as

(3.2-15) $\rho_j = b_0 + \sum_{k=1}^{K} b_k \alpha_{jk}$.

The parameter $b_0 = 1/a_0 - 1$ could be considered to be the risk-free rate of interest, $\bar{\rho}$. Stated differently, $a_0 = 1/(1 + \bar{\rho})$. With the prices p_j being treated as fixed, either way of writing the model is appropriate.

We might have assumed from the outset that, instead of equation (3.2-1), the appropriate specification is

(3.2-16) $\pi_j = \rho_j + \sum_{k=1}^{K} \alpha_{jk} f_k + e_j$.

Equation (3.2-15) might then appear to be a more appealing way of writing the valuation conclusion of the model than equation (3.2-9). Equation (3.2-14) can now be used to translate the model to equations (3.2-1) and (3.2-9). Specification (3.2-1) has the advantage over (3.2-16) that with it one can think readily of the determination of current prices by expected further return. Moreover, it makes clear that prices, rather than investors' expectations, can adjust to bring about the structure of prices and expected rates of return that is characteristic of the model. However, over time equation (3.2-16) may show more stability than expression (3.2-1) because, for example, unexpected capital gains might tend to arise primarily through proportional changes in μ_j and γ_{jk}. Equation (3.2-16) may therefore be a better basis for empirical work than assumption (3.2-1), and will be so used later.

The assumption we cannot easily relax is the linear structure assumed in (3.2-1) or (3.2-16). For instance, if r_j depends on a few factors through some nonlinear function, say, $r_j(f_1, \ldots, f_K, e_j)$, then the first-order conditions corresponding to (3.2-4) are

$$(3.2\text{-}17) \qquad \int r_j(f_1, \ldots, f_k, e_j) U_i'(R_i) dG(f_1, \ldots, f_K, e_1, \ldots, e_j)$$
$$- \lambda p_j = 0.$$

These conditions do not in general seem to impose a useful structure on prices even though diversification does occur.

This limitation of the model may seem unfortunate. Valuation, as section 3.3 examines at more length, involves discounting returns over time. This discounting will tend to introduce rather complicated non-linearities into returns even though the underlying stochastic structure of more basic elements is linear. The presumption of the diversification model is that a linear structure still yields an adequate approximation, or at least that investors act as if they believe it does.

The model can accommodate some forms of nonlinearity in (3.2-1). For example, a polynomial dependence of returns on the factors would simply introduce the coefficients of the polynomial separately into the vaulation equation (3.2-9). A more interesting case arises when the relationship is bilinear.

As we shall find in section 3.3, systematic variability of returns can be considered to arise from two sources. The dividends that the investor can expect will vary with general economic conditions as will the general market appreciation of the company, which may produce capital gains. We might consider the γ_{jk} to reflect this sensitivity. The second source of variability is that the market may change the value it places on these characteristics. Such changes would result in price changes and produce capital gains. That is, the a_k coefficients in (3.2-9) may change, and there is nothing in the diversification model to prevent such change. We might then assume two sets of K factors (now without mean zero), f_k and m_k, with means $\bar{f}_k$ and $\bar{m}_k$, respectively, where the second set of factors represents potential random changes in market valuation. Then we might replace (3.2-1) with

(3.2-18)
$$r_j = \mu_j + \sum_{k=1}^{K} \gamma_{jk} f_k m_k + e_j$$

$$= \mu_j + \sum_{k=1}^{K} \gamma_{jk} \bar{f}_k \bar{m}_k + \sum_{k=1}^{K} \gamma_{jk}(f_k - \bar{f}_k)(m_k - \bar{m}_k)$$

$$- \sum_{k=1}^{K} \gamma_{jk}(f_k - \bar{f}_k)\bar{m}_k - \sum_{k=1}^{K} \gamma_{jk}(m_k - \bar{m}_k)\bar{f}_k + e_j.$$

The first-order conditions corresponding to (3.2-4) yield

(3.2-19)
$$p_j = (\mu_j + \sum_{k=1}^{K} \gamma_{jk} \bar{f}_k \bar{m}_k) a_{0i}$$

$$+ \sum_{k=1}^{K} \gamma_{jk}\{E[(f_k - \bar{f}_k)\bar{m}_k U_i'] + E[(m_k - \bar{m}_k)\bar{f}_k U_i']$$

$$+ E[(f_k - \bar{f})(m_k - \bar{m})U_i']\}/\lambda_i + E(e_j U_i')/\lambda_i$$

$$= \mu_j' a_{0i}' + \sum_{k=1}^{K} \gamma_{jk} a_{ki}' + E(e_j U_i')/\lambda_i.$$

This is of the same form as (3.2-5), and diversification has the same implications for the final term as it had in (3.2-5). Therefore, while the exact interpretation of the a_{ki}' coefficients has changed, the structure (3.2-18) implies the same sort of price structure as does (3.2-1) when there is diversification. Equations (3.2-18) and (3.2-19) might suggest that we should be able to detect $2K$ factors in returns but that only K factor coefficients enter valuation. However, the factors are actually the $f_k m_k$, of which there are only K. The general form of (3.2-9) is also preserved when some factors in (3.2-18) enter in a bilinear way and other linearly, which would happen if some factors were not random, or if the same m factor applied to more than one of the γ_{jk} coefficients.

3.2.3 Diversity of Expectations among Investors

We have presumed in developing the diversification model that all investors know the values of the key parameters μ_j and γ_{jk}, or at least that they are all in agreement about what these values are.[5] This may not be a good approximation, especially when the model is to be used with data such as we examined earlier where differences among individual predictors were prominent. Diversity of perceptions about the values of μ_j and γ_{jk} would seem to strike at the basis of the theory, which has relied on there being a few common values for these parameters in order to obtain the structure of prices. However, diversity of expectations causes us difficulties mainly when negative holdings are prohibited or costly.

5. This assumption plays the role of the homogeneous expectations assumption in the usual CAPM. It is not strictly speaking necessary that all investors have the same subjective distribution of returns, as long as they do agree on the expected return and on the coefficients of the common factors in each security's return.

Suppose that each investor's perception of the process generating returns corresponds to equation (3.2-1), but that different investors do not use the same parameters so that investor i perceives return to be generated by

$$(3.2\text{-}20) \qquad r_j = \mu_{ji} + \sum_{k=1}^{K} \gamma_{jki} f_k + e_{ji}.$$

The individual first-order conditions now give rise to

$$(3.2\text{-}21) \qquad p_j = \mu_{ji} a_{0i} + \sum_{k=1}^{K} \gamma_{jki} a_{ki} + E(e_{ji} U_i') / \lambda_i.$$

If the portfolio is extensively diversified—again in the sense that the investor's holdings of at least some securities are sufficiently small that for these securities the last term of (3.2-21) is negligible—then the prices of such securities must obey a linear relationship in the parameters that the investor perceives.

Suppose another investor, m, also has extensively diversified holdings of more than $(K + 1)$ of the securities that investor i holds in small quantities. Then the last term of (3.2-21) is negligible, and also for this investor we obtain

$$(3.2\text{-}22) \qquad \mu_{ji} a_{0i} + \sum_{k=1}^{K} \gamma_{jki} a_{ki} = \mu_{jm} a_{0m} + \sum_{k=1}^{K} \gamma_{jkm} a_{km} = p_j.$$

By hypothesis, equation (3.2-22) applies to more than $(K + 1)$ securities so that the relationship in (3.2-22) cannot come about simply by adjustment of the marginal utility coefficients a_{ki}. The investors' expectations must themselves be related to each other through their approximately obeying a linear relationship. To illustrate, if there is agreement on the γ_{jk}, equation (3.2-22) becomes

$$(3.2\text{-}23) \qquad \mu_{jm} = \mu_{ji} a_{0i} / a_{0m} + \sum_{k=1}^{K} \gamma_{jk} (a_{km} - a_{ki}) / a_{0m}$$

for all securities for which the holdings of both investors are well diversified. This restriction on the μ_{jm} was not part of our original hypothesis about investors' expectations. What we have found is that the hypothesis of diversification across the same securities imposes a strong restriction on the extent to which the expectations of different investors can differ, at least with respect to the securities they hold.

The difficulty produced by diversification and diversity of expectations can also be expressed in terms of prices. Suppose that two investors have extensively diversified holdings of $(K + 1)$ of the same securities. Then we can express the prices of any securities of which the second investor has an extensively diversified holding in terms of his expectations for that security and the valuation coefficients of the first investor. To see this, let V_i and V_m be the $(K + 1) \times (K + 1)$ matrices with rows made up of vectors

$\{\mu_{ji}, \gamma_{j1i}, \ldots, \gamma_{jKi}\}$ and $\{\mu_{jm}, \gamma_{j1m}, \ldots, \gamma_{jKm}\}$, for any $(K+1)$ securities held in extensively diversified portfolios by each. We can then solve (3.2-22) to obtain

$$(3.2\text{-}24) \qquad \{a_{0m}, \ldots, a_{Km}\}' = V_m^{-1}V_i\{a_{0i}, \ldots, a_{Ki}\}'$$
$$= D_{mi}\{a_{0i}, \ldots, a_{Ki}\}'.$$

The difficulty we noted is that D_{mi} must be the same no matter which securities are selected for the V matrices provided both investors do have extensively diversified holdings of them. Then we can write (3.2-21) as

$$(3.2\text{-}25) \qquad p_j = \{\mu_{jm}, \gamma_{j1m}, \ldots, \gamma_{jKm}\}D_{mi}\{a_{0i}, \ldots, a_{Ki}\}'.$$

The overlapping portfolios argument is also applicable in this situation. If there is a matrix D_{nm} connecting investors n and m as in (3.2-24), then we can let $D_{ni} = D_{nm}D_{mi}$ even though n and i do not have diversified holdings of the same securities. Similarly, partial overlap of n with i and m could produce the constraint.

The problem we now face is to account for diversification in the face of diverse expectations. To do so, let us suppose that diversity of expectations among investors is captured by

$$(3.2\text{-}26) \qquad \mu_{ji} = \mu_j + \epsilon_{ji} \quad \text{and}$$
$$\gamma_{jki} = \gamma_{jk} + \eta_{jki},$$

where the additional terms ϵ_{ji} and η_{jki} can be treated as random variables having mean zero and being independent across investors. Condition (3.2-22) now becomes

$$(3.2\text{-}27) \qquad (\mu_j + \epsilon_{ji})a_{0i} + \sum_{k=1}^{K}(\gamma_{jk} + \eta_{jki})a_{ki}$$
$$= (\mu_j + \epsilon_{jm})a_{0m} + \sum_{k=1}^{K}(\gamma_{jk} + \eta_{jkm})a_{km}.$$

The parameters μ_j and γ_{jk} may represent the true parameters of the process that is generating returns, but need only be the average of the investors' perceptions. The most straightforward way for (3.2-27) to hold is for the random terms to be equal to each other so that diversity of expectations between investors about security parameters is actually negligible for the diversified parts of their portfolios. The most reasonable way for this to occur is for the random quantities to be zero. With random differences among investors which have mean zero, we can presume that an investor's expectations for many securities will be close to the mean expectation and that these securities will be the ones of which his holdings will be extensively diversified. In that case, the coefficients a_{0i} and a_{ki} must also be the same for all investors. In turn, prices will then have to obey (3.2-9).

To develop the argument more fully, rewrite (3.2-21) as

$$(3.2\text{-}28) \qquad E(e_j U_i')/\lambda_i = p_j - (\mu_j + \epsilon_{ji})a_{0i}$$

$$- \sum_{k=1}^{K} (\gamma_{jk} + \eta_{jki})a_{ki}.$$

As noted earlier, the left-hand side of this equation is zero when $v_{ji} = 0$ and otherwise has sign opposite to v_{ji}. If diversification is expected to occur in typical investors' portfolios so that the expected value (taken across investors) of the left-hand side of (3.2-28) is zero, then

$$(3.2\text{-}29) \qquad p_j = E(\mu_j + \epsilon_{ji})a_{0i} + \sum_{k=1}^{K} [E(\gamma_{jk} + \eta_{jki})a_{ki}]$$

$$= \mu_j a_{0i} + \sum_{k=1}^{K} \gamma_{jk} a_{ki},$$

for all i. Equation (3.2-29) is the same as (3.2-8), which produced the valuation formula developed earlier.[6] Hence, even in the face of diverse expectations among investors, the model of price determination continues to be valid if diversification is a good approximation to observed behavior. The additional argument is that, because diversification implies that investors' expectations obey restriction (3.2-22), we may safely treat an investor's having extensively diversified holdings of securities as indicating that his expectations about them are typical.

The diversification model with heterogeneous expectations does predict that investors will have certain holdings that are not small because each investor's opinions may not be typical for some stocks. Investors will have relatively large holdings of the securities they deem especially attractive, involving them in a nontrivial exposure to the specific risks they perceive these securities to bear. One would also expect that some atypical holdings would be negative.[7]

This consideration suggests that the argument for the diversification model may not stand up well to a prohibition on negative holdings (or substantial costs of short-selling). The weakness is especially pressing if most portfolios, even extensively diversified ones, do not contain most securities. This pattern of investor behavior implies, given the other assumptions, that most investors perceive most securities to be over-

6. If ϵ_{ji} and η_{jki} are such that their medians and modes are the same as their means, then the assumption that "typical" behavior in these senses is diversification produces the same result.

7. Extensive short-selling does not occur, but we would attribute this phenomenon to the significant transactions costs involved rather than to investors' having homogeneous expectations. It is probably also the case that professional investment managers concentrate their efforts on finding securities that appear especially attractive. They do not seek out securities that may be overpriced.

valued or, at least, not more attractive than the securities in their portfolios. Restriction (3.2-27) still must hold for the expectations of any pair of investors with respect to securities in which each has extensively diversified holdings. It is now less reasonable, however, to suppose that this occurs because these expectations represent typical opinions and that one can infer from diversification that the coefficients a_{ki} need to be the same for all securities involved.

Suppose that, with negative holdings prohibited, investors hold only a scattering of securities. These holdings represent the few securities that they do not perceive to be overvalued. The Kuhn-Tucker conditions (3.2-12) can be written for securities of which the investor has a zero holding as

$$(3.2\text{-}30) \qquad (\mu_{ji}a_{0i} + \sum_{k=1}^{K} \gamma_{jki}a_{ki})/p_j \leq 1.$$

The inequality is reversed for ones he does hold.

The values of $(\mu_{ji}a_{0i} + \Sigma_{k=1}^{K}\gamma_{jki}a_{ki})$, which represent the marginal values of securities to investors ignoring specific risk, are random variables. Since, by assumption, most investors do not hold any particular security, the value of this quantity for an investor who does hold the security must be unusually high. It must therefore be in the upper part of the distribution of this random variable. If we assume in the usual way that the density function is smooth and unimodal, the density decreases as this quantity increases.

For securities that an investor does hold,

$$(3.2\text{-}31) \qquad -E(e_{ji}U_i')/\lambda_i p_j = (\mu_{ji}a_{0i} + \sum_{k=1}^{K} \gamma_{jki}a_{ki})/p_j - 1.$$

Diversification corresponds to small values of the right-hand side of (3.2-31). But these values, being in the upper tail of a unimodal distribution, are more likely to fall in an interval of given width with lower bound zero than to fall in any other positive interval of the same width. We may therefore conclude that an extensively diversified holding of any particular security is more probable than a larger one. The diversification argument used the observation of diversification to conclude that prices must exhibit certain patterns. Now, however, observing diversification only arises from the random nature of expectations and the observation that any positive holding is unusual. Hence the apparently systematic tendency to diversification may have no implication for security prices.

We have seen that equations (3.2-27) could happen to describe many of the securities that the opinions and utilities of each investor lead him to select without there being any systematic connection between the opinions of different investors or between prices and the μ_j and γ_{jk} parameters. Any nondiversification tendencies that would arise from prices not following the linear relationship specified earlier are hidden and frustrated by the non-negativity constraint which prevents the typical (and less optimistic) opinion from finding expression in the market. While we may properly conclude that all investors who do hold small quantities of security j have the same value of the sum in (3.2-27), this in turn does not directly tell us about valuation relationships expressed in terms of more objective—or agreed upon—parameters.

Nevertheless, this argument against the diversification theory may not be as devastating as it may first appear. To be sure, the costs of short-selling are substantial (if not strictly speaking prohibitive), and some major market participants are directly prohibited from selling short. However, failure to hold most securities may arise from other sources.

There are several good reasons for portfolio managers to limit the number of securities they hold. As is well known, adequate diversification may easily be achieved with holdings of as few as twenty or thirty securities and the addition of further securities to the portfolio will probably reduce specific risk to an insignificant degree. Thus, for all practical purposes, there is little additional benefit from full diversification. On the other hand, there may be significant costs to increased numbers of holdings. "Prudent man" rules are often interpreted as requiring that someone from the investment company staff periodically visit the managements and facilities of all companies held in the portfolio. At the very least, these rules would require that periodic reports be prepared for review by an investment committee. In addition, custodial fees and audit charges, as well as the fees of collecting dividends and other distributions, are partly a function of the number of types of securities held. Thus there may be small but significant costs to more extensive diversification, which after some point has only very small or indeed negligible benefits. These costs may provide the reason for any particular investor not holding most securities.

An investor contemplating adding another security to his portfolio has to balance the advantages of the added holding against the increased costs. The advantages come as increased expected returns or decreased risk exposure. With extensive diversification, further decreases in risk coming from still smaller holdings of those securities already included are negligible. Against this decreased risk must be set the increase in risk coming from the positive holding of the new security. The risk from the new security increases with the size of the holding. Even if an unusually high rate of return is expected, investment will occur only if the quantity held can be large enough for the increased return to overcome the transactions costs without so increasing specific risk that no advantage accrues to the investor. Although we have treated the investor as certain about his own appreciation of the parameters of the distributions of return, it would be more reasonable to presume that he also treats them as random and so as giving rise to risk. Without (costly) investigation by the investor, we might suppose that the dispersion of his subjective distribution is such that it rules out pursuing any small perceived above-normal return. At the same time, we may assume that the expected return from investigation to bring the posterior dispersion down is less than the cost. If all this is the case, failure by most investors to hold a particular security cannot be taken to indicate that only those with unusually favorable opinions of the security do hold it. Any investor's not holding a particular security suggests only that she does not perceive it to offer very unusually favorable opportunities, not necessarily that she considers it a poor investment.

These arguments make it reasonable to suppose that an investor's opinions about the securities he does hold in small quantities represent average or typical opinion rather than extreme ones. Given that an investor may hold a fairly large fraction of the securities about which he has well-informed opinions, it is then the case that many of these opinions will tend to be near the means of their distributions. For securities for which his opinions are unusually favorable, an investor will, of course, have a large holding while he will hold none of the securities he judges a relatively poor investment.

This behavior does not upset the basic pricing of the diversification model, although its derivation does rely on an investor's small holdings tending to represent an average opinion. That this condition may obtain is rendered more likely by the model's being potentially self-fulfilling. Suppose that the diversification model does apply to the expected values across investors of the parameters. Suppose also, as we have been arguing, that a large part of an investor's beliefs and portfolio holdings correspond reasonably closely to these values (so that his values of the parameters a_{ki} correspond to the market coefficients). Then this investor may reasonably assume that any security which he has not investigated in detail will be found on investigation to offer only an expected return and coefficients for the factors that would not make it a clearly compelling candidate for inclusion or exclusion in a portfolio. That is, he can base his expectations about securities about which he does not have reliable, independent information on the market's valuation. As a result, the market parameters do represent the average of informed opinion, which is then joined by the typical uninformed opinions of those who do not hold the security. Such expectations are exactly what we need to preserve the validity of the diversification model.

When we consider whether heterogeneous expectations and prohibition (or large costs) of short-selling destroy the validity of the diversification argument, the crucial question is why a typical investor does not hold a particular security. If the reason is that she does not really know much about the security, or that she thinks its value is about right but that it offers only opportunities roughly equivalent to ones available from securities she already holds, no problems arise. If the omission can be explained only by her perceiving that the security offers a poor return relative to the ones she holds, then diversity of expectations and restrictions on short-selling would destroy the basis of the argument.

Our discussion has concentrated on diversity of evaluations of the firm-specific parameters μ_{ji} and γ_{jki}. Another cause of diverse expectations raises far less difficulty, as Ross (1977) has noted. We have treated the common factors f_k as having mean zero—with μ_j absorbing any nonzero means that actual factors may have. Instead, we may regard the factors as quantities requiring forecast, such as economic activity, interest rates, inflation, or even "regulatory climate." Differences of opinion might result from different forecasts of these quantities. Specifically we might assume that

$$(3.2\text{-}32) \qquad \mu_j = \gamma_{j0} + \sum_{k=1}^{K} \gamma_{jk}\mu_k .$$

Suppose that diversity of expectations arises from investors' having different values for μ_k, say, μ_{ki}, so that

$$(3.2\text{-}33) \qquad \mu_{ji} = \gamma_{j0} + \sum_{k=1}^{K} \gamma_{jk}\mu_{ki} .$$

Equation (3.2-5) now becomes

$$(3.2\text{-}34) \qquad p_j = (\gamma_{j0} + \sum_{k=1}^{K} \gamma_{jk}\mu_{ki})a_{0i} + \sum_{k=1}^{K} \gamma_{jk}a_{ki}$$
$$+ E(e_jU_i')/\lambda_i$$
$$= \mu_j a_{0i} + \sum_{k=1}^{K} \gamma_{jk}[(\mu_{ki} - \mu_k)a_{0i} + a_{ki}]$$
$$+ E(e_iU_i')/\lambda_i$$
$$= \mu_j a_{0i} + \sum_{k=1}^{K} \gamma_{jk}a_{ki}' + E(e_iU_i')\lambda_i .$$

This is of the same form as (3.2-5). Investors adjust their exposure to the f_k so as to alter their marginal utilities to offset forecast differences with the result that the linear objective structure of valuation is preserved.

3.2.4 Differential Tax Treatment of Investors

This discussion has centered around random differences in the perceived returns. There may also be systematic differences among individual investors arising from different tax treatments of various parts of return streams. The tax laws do make distinctions among different types of returns associated with a particular security. Specifically, the dividend and capital gains components of total returns may be taxed differently. In addition, different investors are taxed at different rates on the two components. Incorporating this feature of actual investment situations in the model introduces some serious empirical implications about the extent to which diversification does occur.

Suppose two types of returns are associated with a security, r_j^1 and r_j^2, taxed in the case of investor i at the rates t_i^1 and t_i^2, respectively. Let $s_i^1 = (1 - t_i^1)$ and $s_i^2 = (1 - t_i^2)$ be the after-tax proportions of returns that come to investor i from the two sources. Equation (3.2-1) now becomes

$$(3.2\text{-}35) \qquad r_j = r_j^1 + r_j^2$$

$$= \mu_i^1 + \mu_j^2 + \sum_{k=1}^{K} (\gamma_{jk}^1 + \gamma_{jk}^2) f_k + e_j^1 + e_j^2.$$

The relevant return for investor i is

$$(3.2\text{-}36) \qquad r_{ji} = s_i^1 r_j^1 + s_i^2 r_j^2$$

$$= s_i^1 \mu_j^1 + s_i^2 \mu_j^2 + \sum_{k=1}^{K} (\gamma_{jk}^1 s_i^1 + \gamma_{jk}^2 s_i^2) f_k$$

$$+ e_j^1 s_i^1 + e_j^2 s_i^2.$$

The equation to be derived from the first-order conditions, corresponding to (3.2-5), is

$$(3.2\text{-}37) \qquad p_j = (s_i^1 \mu_j^1 + s_i^2 \mu_j^2) a_{0i} + \sum_{k=1}^{K} (s_i^1 \gamma_{jk}^1 + s_i^2 \gamma_{jk}^2) a_{ki}$$

$$+ E(e_j^1 s_i^1 U_i' + e_j^2 s_i^2 U_i') / \lambda_i.$$

Extensive diversification would imply that the p_j obey the linear equations obtained by dropping the last term in equation (3.2-37). In general, this will not be possible when there are many investors unless tax rates do not vary across them or the proportions of the two types of returns are constant across securities. Neither condition seems very plausible. For example, extensive diversification would require inter alia that $(\mu_j^1 s_i^1 + \mu_j^2 s_i^2) a_{0i}$ be the same for all investors. This will not be the case unless we can write the term $(\mu_j^1 s_i^1 + \mu_j^2 s_i^2)$ as the product of parameters ϕ_j and θ_i in the form

$$(3.2\text{-}38) \qquad \phi_j \theta_i = (\mu_j^1 s_i^1 + \mu_j^2 s_i^2)$$

for all j and i. The same type of requirement applies to other terms in (3.2-37).

Differential tax treatments raise a very serious problem for the diversification theory if it is presumed that the diversified portfolios contain securities with significantly different splits between the dividend and the capital-gain components of return and are held by individuals with different rates of taxation. Whether this presumption is justified is less clear. There are many major institutional investors, such as pension funds and endowment funds, for which the distinction between income and capital gains is immaterial because no differences arise in their tax treatment. Such investors dominate the market for many securities in the sense that they are between them the principal holders. If these investors have extensively diversified portfolios, then the model will be applicable for the securities that they do hold in small quantities. Insofar as other investors receive different returns due to taxes, one would expect them to diversify over other securities, especially if restrictions on negative holdings[8] apply or there are costs associated with the number of securities held. The diversification argument does not preclude different valuation equations for securities held in different portfolios provided that they are not connected through portfolios in which there are diversified holdings of the different types of securities.

The existence of differential tax treatments of dividends and capital gains raises problems for other valuation theories, including the CAPM. It also raises a fundamental question concerning the justification for a firm's paying dividends at all. Our argument may account for dividend-paying behavior. If common-stock valuation is dominated by institutional investors not affected by tax differences, then the valuation formula of the diversification model holds without distinguishing the forms that returns may take. The possibility of dividend policy significantly affecting valuation through tax effects is therefore removed and only other reasons for retaining earnings (including their effects on expected returns) remain relevant.

3.2.5 Comparison with Other Valuation Models

The arguments for the applicability of the diversification model are hardly conclusive when heterogeneity of expectations is recognized. The validity of the other main candidates is unfortunately no more clear. These are the CAPM and Ross's (1976, 1977) strikingly original APT.

Like Ross's argument, our reasoning relies on diversification to eliminate risks specific to the security and produces the same conclusions. Ross's original argument is easily summarized. Provided that negative holdings are permitted on the same terms as positive ones, an investor can hold a portfolio with zero net cost to himself. That is, he can form a portfolio with holdings v_{ja} such that

$$(3.2\text{-}39) \qquad \sum_{j=1}^{J} v_{ja} p_j = 0.$$

---

8. Negative holdings—that is, short sales—in which the different types of return receive the same tax treatment as positive holdings certainly are not feasible. It may be worth noting that Blume and Friend (1975) found that the portfolios of individuals are not extensively diversified.

Second, he can choose this portfolio in such a way that the effects of each systematic factor cancel out and the portfolio return is not affected by the values taken on by these factors; that is, the portfolio is such that

$$(3.2\text{-}40) \qquad \sum_{j=1}^{J} v_{ja}\gamma_{jk} = 0, \qquad k = 1, \ldots, K.$$

If there are many securities, then the portfolio can also be diversified so that the holding of any one security is small. The return to the portfolio is $(\sum_{j=1}^{J} \mu_j v_{ja} + \sum_{j=1}^{J} e_j v_{ja})$. With adequate diversification, the second term can be treated as zero. The first term then can be taken as yielding the certain return on a costless portfolio. It "should" be zero since otherwise profitable opportunities would exist to invest costlessly and receive a riskless, positive return. The condition that $\sum_{j=1}^{J} \mu_j v_{ja} = 0$ for all v_{ja} obeying both (3.2-39) and (3.2-40) implies that there are coefficients a_k, $k = 0, \ldots, K$, such that

$$(3.2\text{-}41) \qquad p_j = \mu_j a_0 + \sum_{k=1}^{K} \gamma_{jk} a_k.$$

This is also the conclusion of the diversification argument.

Arbitrage in the sense used in this argument clearly requires that negative holdings be possible costlessly. The relevance of a pure arbitrage argument when this is not the case may seem slim.[9] The advantage of the diversification argument is that it is not vulnerable to a constraint against negative holdings. The nature of the argument is also different. The APT relies on a property of market equilibrium and the law of large numbers to infer the structure of equilibrium prices. The diversification argument uses a stylized "fact" about utility-maximizing investors to infer the structure of security prices they face.

Diversity of expectations about expected return or factor coefficients also makes a pure arbitrage argument implausible. Different investors presumably would perceive different arbitrage possibilities, and it would

9. Surprisingly, Roll and Ross (1980) try to argue that negative holdings are not needed for the model because it must also "work" in differential form around the investors' (positive) holdings. However, this requires diversification to be valid. Specifically, consider a differential portfolio change, $dv_{ji}, i = 1, \ldots, J$ such that $\sum_{j=1}^{J} p_j dv_{ji} = 0$ and $\sum_{j=1}^{J} \gamma_{jk} dv_{ji} = 0$, $k = 1, \ldots, K$ (so that the change has the properties of an arbitrage portfolio). The argument then appears to be that $\sum_{j=1}^{J} \mu_{ji} dv_{ji} = 0$ because no increase in risk will be introduced into the portfolio by the change. But this argument does require diversification. Let σ_j^2 be the variance of e_j. Then the differential change in portfolio variance will be $\sum_{j=1}^{J} v_{ji}\sigma_j^2 dv_{ji}$. This will be of the same order of magnitude as $\sum_{j=1}^{J} \mu_j dv_{ji}$ unless the $v_{ji}\sigma_j^2$ for which dv_{ji} are nonzero are themselves infinitesimal. Thus the portfolio's holdings of these securities must be extensively diversified. While this differential argument does not itself support the arbitrage argument, it does indicate that if diversification occurs in the portfolios of investors who would exploit potential arbitrage opportunities, then the APT pricing must exist even if these investors are not expected utility maximizers.

not be possible for the market to eliminate them for all investors. Hence, with diverse expectations within the context of the model (3.2-1), investors must be presumed to perceive arbitrage possibilities that they are not able to exploit extensively for some reason. As Ross (1977) noted, however, the arbitrage argument is robust to diversity of expectations over the expected value of the factors of the sort we considered in (3.2-32), just as is the diversification argument.

The other alternative to the diversification model is the CAPM. The CAPM is a general-equilibrium theory based on the hypothesis that all investors' utility functions can be defined over the means and variances of their portfolios. Letting ω_{jh} be the covariance of return j with return h, the first-order conditions yield

$$(3.2\text{-}42) \qquad p_j = \mu_j \theta_i + \psi_i \sum_{h=1}^{J} \omega_{jh} v_{hi}.$$

Aggregation and the imposition of the equilibrium condition $\sum_{i=1}^{I} v_{ji} = n_j$, with n_j being the total number of shares of security j outstanding and I the number of investors, produce

$$(3.2\text{-}43) \qquad p_j = \mu_j \theta + \psi \sum_{h=1}^{J} \omega_{jh} n_h.$$

Equation (3.2-43) indicates that the market adjusts prices so that the market portfolio—that is, a portfolio with holdings proportional to n_j—is mean-variance efficient. Equation (3.2-43) can be manipulated to give the standard expression for the CAPM:

$$(3.2\text{-}44) \qquad \rho_j = \bar{\rho} + (\rho_m - \bar{\rho})\beta_j,$$

where β_j is the regression coefficient of the jth rate of return on the rate of return of the market portfolio, ρ_m is the expected rate of return on the market portfolio, and $\bar{\rho}$ is the expected rate of return on a portfolio uncorrelated with the market and is the rate of return on the risk-free security if it exists. Equation (3.2-44) corresponds to (3.2-15). However, as Roll (1977) emphasized, it is a direct implication of (3.2-43) and can only be tested using exactly the market portfolio.

The impracticality of the CAPM disappears when the return assumption (3.2-1) is also made. Letting ξ_{km} be the covariance of the factors f_k and f_m, the variances and covariances can be expressed as

$$(3.2\text{-}45) \qquad \omega_{jj} = \sum_{k=1}^{K} \sum_{m=1}^{K} \gamma_{jk} \gamma_{jm} \xi_{km} + \sigma_j^2,$$

$$\omega_{jh} = \sum_{k=1}^{K} \sum_{m=1}^{K} \gamma_{jk} \gamma_{hm} \xi_{km}, \qquad j \neq h.$$

Here σ_j^2 is the variance of the specific factor e_j. The price equation (3.2-42) can now be written

$$(3.2\text{-}46) \qquad p_j = \mu_j/(1 + \overline{\rho}) + \psi \sum_{k=1}^{K} \gamma_{jk} \sum_{m=1}^{K} \sum_{h=1}^{I} \xi_{km}\gamma_{hm}n_h + \psi\sigma_j^2 n_j$$

$$= \mu_j/(1 + \overline{\rho}) + \sum_{k=1}^{K} \gamma_{jk}\phi_k + \psi\sigma_j^2 n_j.$$

If $\sigma_j^2 n_j$ is small relative to the middle terms (which arise from the covariances of return j with the common factors), then we can safely approximate (3.2-46) by (3.2-9), the valuation equation that is implied by diversification. If this is the case, it will also be the case that the portfolios chosen by investors can be considered extensively diversified in the sense used in section 3.2.1. Similarly, (3.2-15) approximates (3.2-44) when the specific risk term in (3.2-46) is small. In other words, when the return assumption (3.2-1) is made and when specific risks are small in the economy relative to systematic risks, the prices arising from the CAPM are well approximated by the APT formula.

When (3.2-1) does not hold, the CAPM encounters what is at present the insurmountable problem of measuring β_j in a way which would make the approach valid, since the market portfolio cannot be measured in the appropriate way. This removes a large part of the attraction of the theory since the mean-variance utility-maximizing hypothesis and the uniform nature of all investors' behavior are not very appealing. While the CAPM can be widened to allow nonmarketable returns as Mayers (1972) showed, the sum of these nonmarketable incomes would also need to be measured accurately. The conditions needed to obtain the CAPM in a multiperiod setting are very strong as Fama (1970) and Merton (1971) showed, and it is questionable if a wider model can be given empirical content without a factor type specification. As we shall see in section 3.4, the assumption (3.2-1) is very convenient for giving empirical content to the valuation theory, quite apart from its allowing conclusions to be drawn from the weaker assumptions about investor behavior of the diversification model.

The CAPM is quite robust to some forms of diversity of expectations if short-selling is costless. However, it is vulnerable to restrictions on short-selling and to other restrictions on investors' holdings when there are heterogeneous expectations or when other conditions prevent investors' optimal risky portfolios from being proportional to the market portfolio. Analysis then becomes difficult as Levy (1978) and Jarrow (1980) demonstrated, and useful valuation formulae cannot be derived. The measurement difficulties and the implications of the CAPM about portfolio holdings that are contrary to observation make the diversification model appear a more promising valuation approach on which to base empirical work.

The tests we shall conduct later will use the sort of regression coefficients that are normally considered to test the CAPM. However, our justification for their use does not require the validity of the CAPM and the corresponding appropriateness of market indexes. As we explain in section 3.4, these coefficients can be treated as reliable proxies for the factor coefficients.

3.3 Expected Returns and Earnings Growth

A number of tests of the diversification model are possible. The main prediction of the theory is that the prices of securities will be linearly related to their (*ex ante*) expected returns and their coefficients, γ_{jk}, of the factors in equation (3.2-1). Equivalently, expected rates of return will be linear functions of these coefficients. When *ex ante* expectations are equated to the mathematical expectations of the returns that can be observed, the most direct approach would be to estimate the model (3.2-1), expressed in rate of return form, using factor analysis, and test the hypothesis of the diversification model as a restriction on the parameters. Similarly, using data on r_j, μ_j, and γ_{jk} might be estimated and related to price data.

Such investigations are largely beyond the capabilities of the data set being used in this study. Furthermore, by concentrating on *ex post* returns, this approach presumes that expectations held by the investors correspond to the actual parameters of the distribution of returns. In consequence, it would throw no light on the role and nature of expectations of the sort we have been studying. Our objective in the present section is to express the expectations of returns in terms of the growth rates we have collected and to consider to what extent the return structure of the diversification model remains reasonable within this framework. The hypothesis about investors' expectations is very simple because of the fact that the useful expectations we were able to collect concerned only growth rates of earnings per share.

The quantity about which expectations are formed in the valuation model is the total return to a security, denoted by r_j. Presumably, the gross return to the holder of a share is the dividend paid in the period plus the price of the share at the end of the period. Let t represent the time subscript, which will always be the last subscript. The current period is denoted by zero. Let d_{jt} be the dividend paid in the period immediately preceding t so that the prices p_{jt} are ex dividend. For simplicity, we assume that dividends are paid at the ends of periods. Then the presumption is that

(3.3-1) $\qquad r_{jt} = d_{jt+1} + p_{jt+1},$

so that

(3.3-2) $\qquad \mu_{jt} = E(r_{jt}) = E(d_{jt+1}) + E(p_{jt+1}).$

Expression (3.3-2) depends on the price of the security in the next period. It does not take a very perceptive investor to realize that next period's price is relevant to his returns or that other investors' attitudes (even irrational ones) toward the securities in the next period will affect the prices in that period. But it is not clear what the investor should assume about these matters. Indeed, the problems involved in Keynes's (1936) celebrated beauty contest may easily manifest themselves in the market. Self-fulfilling forecasts, based on no sensible valuation of the assets of a company, could in some periods even dominate the determination of the price of its shares. The history of speculative bubbles or the problems involved with the valuation of assets such as Picasso paintings must cause some doubts about formulations which tie the expectations of investors to features of securities in which they invest. But some such formulation must be used if the theory is not to be an empty bit of logic.

Suppose that utility-maximizing investors with extensively diversified portfolios believe that prices in the future will be formed in the manner suggested by the diversification theory in equation (3.2-9). That is, assume investors believe that

$$(3.3\text{-}3) \qquad p_{jt} = \mu_{jt}a_{0t} + \sum_{k=1}^{K} \gamma_{jkt}\alpha_{kt},$$

where the time subscripts recognize that, in principle, all quantities in (3.3-3) may change over time. We may then presume that investors form their expectations of p_{jt} by taking expectations of the right-hand side of (3.3-3) so that (3.3-2) becomes

$$(3.3\text{-}4) \qquad \mu_{jt} = E(d_{j,t+1}) + E(\mu_{j,t+1}a_{0,t+1} \\ + \sum_{k=1}^{K} \gamma_{jk,t+1}a_{k,t+1}).$$

We can see from this expression that risk arises from two sources. First, the valuation coefficients a_{kt} may change; second, the evaluation of the firm-specific parameters μ_{jt} and γ_{jkt} may change. In the latter case, probably the most important source of change is a potential reevaluation of the earnings (and hence dividend) prospects of the company.

Repeated substitution of (3.2-4) for μ_{jt} in itself yields

$$(3.3\text{-}5) \qquad \mu_{j0} = E(d_{j1}) + E\left[\sum_{t=2}^{\infty} \left(\prod_{s=1}^{t-1} a_{0s}\right)d_{jt}\right] \\ + E\left(\sum_{k=1}^{K} a_{k1}\gamma_{jk1}\right) \\ + E\left[\sum_{t=2}^{\infty} \left(\prod_{s=1}^{t-1} a_{0s}\right)\sum_{k=1}^{K} a_{kt}\gamma_{jkt}\right].$$

This involves a formidable number of terms and expectations, including the products of the a_{0s} coefficients. Considerable simplification is needed if anything useful is to be said about valuation. This can be achieved by assuming that the expected values of the valuation coefficients formed at time zero (conditional on any intervening terms) are all equal in the sense that

(3.3-6) $E(a_{kt}) = a_{k0}, \qquad k = 1, \ldots, K,$

(3.3-7) $\gamma_{jkt} = \gamma_{jk},$

and

(3.3-8) $E\left(\prod_{s=1}^{t} a_{0s}\right) = a_{00}^{t}.$

Assumption (3.3-6) is needed mainly for notational convenience and can be easily relaxed. The same is less true for (3.3-7) only in the sense that we shall need constant values to give empirical content to the model. Assumption (3.3-8) can be relaxed less readily and only partially without the danger of introducing possibly serious nonlinearities into the diversification model. Assumptions (3.3-6) to (3.3-8) and the additional assumption that the a_{0s} are independent of d_{jt}, of γ_{jkt}, and of a_{kt} allow us to write (3.3-5) as

(3.3-9) $\mu_{j0} = \sum_{t=0}^{\infty} a_0^t E(d_{jt+1}) = \sum_{t=1}^{\infty} a_0^t \sum_{k=1}^{K} a_k \gamma_{jk}.$

Determination of μ_{j0} now depends on the future path of dividends. The easiest assumption to make about dividends is that they are expected to grow (indefinitely) at a constant rate g_j so that $E(d_{jt}) = d_{j0}(1 + g_j)^t$. When it is recalled that we can express a_0 as $1/(1 + \bar{\rho})$, where $\bar{\rho}$ is the risk-free interest rate, (3.2-9) becomes

(3.3-10) $p_{j0} = d_{j0} \sum_{t=1}^{\infty} (1 + g_j)^t / (1 + \bar{\rho})^t$

$+ \sum_{k=1}^{K} \sum_{t=0}^{\infty} a_k \gamma_{jk} / (1 + \bar{\rho})^t$

$= d_{j0}(1 + g_j)/(\bar{\rho} - g_j) + \sum_{k=1}^{K} a_k \gamma_{jk}(1 + \bar{\rho})/\bar{\rho}.$

This equation can be written as

(3.3-11) $g_j + (1 + g_j)d_{j0}/p_{j0} = \bar{\rho} - (1 + \bar{\rho}) \sum_{k=1}^{K} a_k \gamma_{jk}$

$\times (g_j - \bar{\rho})/(p_{j0}\bar{\rho})$

$= \bar{\rho} - \sum_{k=1}^{K} b_k \beta_{jk}.$

The expression on the left-hand side of (3.3-11) can be interpreted by supposing for the moment that the price of a security can be expressed as the present value of the expected stream of dividends discounted at the (constant) expected rate of return to the security, ρ_j. That is, if we assume that

(3.3-12) $p_{j0} = \sum\limits_{t=1}^{\infty} E(d_{jt})/(1+\rho_j)^t$

$= d_{j0} \sum\limits_{t=1}^{\infty} (1+g_j)^t/(1+\rho_j)^t$

$= d_{j0}(1+g_j)/(\rho_j-g_j)$,

then we can solve for ρ_j as

(3.3-13) $\rho_j = g_j + (1+g_j) d_{j0}/p_{j0}$.

We can therefore interpret (3.3-11) as being an equation for the expected rate of return to security j, and so it corresponds to the expected rate of return equation (3.2-15). If dividends in the next period, or their expected values, are known, then equation (3.3-13) becomes

(3.3-14) $\rho_j = g_j + d_{j1}/p_{j0}$,

which also becomes the expression in (3.3-11). With d_{j0} in place of d_{j1}, (3.3-14) gives the formula when a continuous time model is used.

Instead of expressing the model in terms of expected rates of return in (3.3-11), we could divide (3.3-10) by earnings to obtain

(3.3-15) $p_{j0}/e_{j0} = [(1+g_j)/(\bar{\rho}-g_j)] d_{j0}/e_{j0}$

$+ \sum\limits_{k=1}^{K} (a_k\gamma_{jk}/e_{j0})(1+\bar{\rho})/\bar{\rho}$.

This formulation brings out the relationship between our valuation model and more traditional approaches based on earnings multiples such as that by Williams (1938). There the risk term is ignored so that the valuation expression is given by only the first term of the right-hand side of (3.3-15).

These traditional formulations have a number of formidable drawbacks which apply here too. Their derivations are inapplicable in cases where no dividends are paid. They lead to an infinite value for the security when $g_j \geq \bar{\rho}$. They require projecting differential growth rates from here to kingdom-come at a constant rate. This last drawback would seem to render the model particularly inappropriate for use with growth-rate projections such as ours that were specifically made for limited periods of time.

Such difficulties have led several writers to formulate finite-horizon models for share prices. The basic idea is that dividends and earnings are assumed to grow at rate g_j for T periods. They then either stop growing or else proceed to grow only at some normal rate, such as the general rate of growth of the economy. In some models, the growth rate is assumed to revert to the final growth rate in stages, or according to a smooth decay function. Correspondingly, dividends may return in any one of several ways to some standard payout ratio consistent with a continuation of normal growth corresponding to that of the economy as a whole.

There is a large family of explicit models that can be developed from these approaches. They tend to share two features. First, they are apt to be nonlinear in the important quantities. Second, they all depend on the same rather limited list of variables. Thus the various formulations based on the discounted-dividends approach all suggest that there is an implicit function of the form

$$(3.3\text{-}16) \qquad f(\rho_j, g_j, d_{j0}, e_{j0}) = 0.$$

In the context of the diversification model, ρ_j includes μ_{j0}, p_{j0}, and also the terms $\Sigma_{k=1}^{K} \gamma_{jk} a_k$ which enter μ_j by being logically part of future prices. In principle we can solve (3.3-16) for μ_{j0}. Suppose that we can write this solution as

$$(3.3\text{-}17) \qquad \mu_{j0} = e_{j0}\mu(g_j, d_{j0}/e_{j0}, \sum_{k=1}^{K} \gamma_{jk} a_k / e_{j0}).$$

Then, dividing (3.2-9) by e_{j0} and assuming a linear approximation for μ in (3.3-17), we obtain

$$(3.3\text{-}18) \qquad p_{j0}/e_{j0} = c_0 + c_1 g_j + c_2 d_{j0}/e_{j0}$$
$$+ \sum_{k=1}^{K} c_{k+2} \gamma_{jk}/e_{j0}.$$

A still better approximation might arise from using quadratic terms from (3.3-17) as well. However, some experiments using the explicit limited-horizon model of Malkiel (1963) indicated that a linear equation such as (3.3-18) fitted very well over a wide range of parameter values and growth rates and was a good approximation for the true nonlinear model. These same formulations also arise as approximations when the price-formation equations are taken as the starting point for the derivation of expected return ρ_j.

The conclusion of these arguments is that, although the constant growth-rate and constant expected-return models may seem implausible, they may serve as an adequate linear approximation. The specific formulation we use is geared to the data available, concentrating on the growth rates of earnings. However, we do have both short- and long-term growth rates available, and we found that they were not closely related. There is a large variety of two-parameter models for earnings that could be expressed in terms of long- and short-term growth rates. Rather than adopt any specific such model, we shall assume that the short-term growth rate may appear as another argument in (3.3-17) and so as an additional variable in (3.3-18).

Our subsequent empirical work is based on relying on the adequacy of this linear approximation without explicitly assuming a particular process for earnings growth and retention. In addition, however, we shall investigate one explicit formulation for ρ_j based on the simple model (3.3-14) to which the valuation model (3.3-11) is supposed to apply.

Having adopted a more specific (though approximate) hypothesis about expected returns, we now need to examine to what extent the critical aspects of (3.2-1) needed for the diversification model seem reasonable. The question is whether the assumptions that prices follow (3.2-9), that expectations are formed in the way discussed, and that diversification is observed are all internally consistent.

Equations (3.2-9) and (3.3-1) allow us to write the actual return as

$$(3.3\text{-}19) \qquad r_{j0} = d_{j1} + p_{j1}$$

$$= d_{j1} + \mu_{j1}a_{01} + \sum_{k=1}^{K} \gamma_{jk1}a_{k1}.$$

Assume that the γ_{jk} are constant. Then using (3.3-4) we obtain

$$(3.3\text{-}20) \qquad r_{j0} - \mu_{j0} = d_{j1} - E_0(d_{j1}) + \mu_{j1}a_{01} - E_0(\mu_{j1})a_{00}$$

$$+ \sum_{k=1}^{K} \gamma_{jk}(a_{k1} - a_{k0}),$$

where E_0 indicates the expectation as of time zero. Now assume that the factor model applies to unexpected changes in dividends and expected returns (or capital gains if a_0 is constant) in the sense that

$$(3.3\text{-}21) \qquad d_{j1} - E_0(d_{j1}) = \sum_{k=1}^{K} \delta_{jk}f_{k1} + \epsilon_{j1}$$

and

$$(3.3\text{-}22) \qquad \mu_{j1} - E_0(\mu_{j1}) = \sum_{k=1}^{K} \phi_{jk}f_{k1} + \eta_{j1}.$$

Using specification (3.3-17) for μ_j, equation (3.3-22) suggests that the factors reflect any systematic influences that affect dividends or earnings of firms and their growth prospects as well as future discount rates. If we assume temporarily that the a_k coefficients are all constant, we obtain

$$(3.3\text{-}23) \qquad r_{j0} - \mu_{j0} = \sum_{k=1}^{K} (\delta_{jk} + a_0\phi_{jk})f_k + \epsilon_{j1} + a_0\eta_{j1}.$$

It is natural then to equate the coefficients $(\delta_{jk} + a_0\phi_{jk})$ with γ_{jk} and $(\epsilon_{j1} + a_0\eta_{j1})$ with e_1. The main difficulty here is that a_0 may well change so that the γ_{jk} would also change and do so by more than a factor of proportion constant across companies. Although the model could be developed without further difficulty using the coefficients δ_{jk} and ϕ_{jk} as (separate) γ_{jk} coefficients, we would then need separate ways of obtaining estimates of these coefficients. This would require development of models for dividends and earnings growth going far beyond the scope of the present study. Furthermore, we have already suggested that simple formulations provide adequate approximations to the more complicated (and unknown) specific models. In order to achieve empirical simplicity therefore we shall assume that $(\delta_{jk} + a_0\phi_{jk}) = \gamma_{jk}$. We can then express (3.3-20) as

(3.3-24)
$$r_{j0} - \mu_{j0} = a_{00} \sum_{k=1}^{K} \gamma_{jk} f_k + (a_{01} - a_{00})E_0(\mu_{j1})$$

$$+ (a_{01} - a_{00}) \sum_{k=1}^{K} \gamma_{jk} f_k$$

$$+ \sum_{k=1}^{K} \gamma_{jk}(a_{k1} - a_{k0}) + e_{j0}.$$

This specification is close to the bilinear form hypothesized in section 3.2.2 which, though nonlinear in factors, does give rise to the valuation model in equation (3.2-9). This valuation equation itself was used in obtaining equation (3.3-23) so that the formulation we have adopted is self-consistent, given the various approximations assumed. The key one among them is that γ_{jk} can be regarded as constant.[10] This might be relaxed while maintaining the spirit of the diversification model, but only by producing major additional programs to obtain useful empirical measures of risk.

3.4 Specification of Risk Measures

Our problem in the previous section concerned relating the data on expected earnings growth to the valuation model. Relevant data are not available on the perceptions of market participants about risk, and we shall have to presume that parameters estimated from *ex post* data correspond to investors' perceptions. The resulting variables of necessity are mainly *ex post* measures derived from realized data rather than true *ex ante* data representing the views actually expressed by investors. We shall find, however, that our data do permit the development of one *ex ante* risk measure that proves quite serviceable.

The approach we take to obtain risk measures is more easily explained by considering the coefficients γ_{jk} in (3.2-1) than those in the more complicated equation (3.3-23). We shall, however, assume that over time the coefficients are more stable if we estimate in rate of return form. That is, we shall assume that (3.2-16) holds over time and consider estimating the parameters α_{jk}. This choice was made partly to increase comparability with other valuation studies.

The data set available to us makes estimation of the α_{jk} coefficients by factor analysis impractical. We therefore adopt a different procedure,

10. As equation (3.3-23) makes clear, one of the γ_{jk} coefficients should be $E_0(\mu_{j1})$. Like the problem encountered with combining (3.3-19) and (3.3-20), this raises the problem that the γ_{jk} are not likely to be constant over time rather than directly attacking the valuation formulation. The assumption might be made more palatable by presuming something like (3.2-32).

which may not be inferior and which bears an immediate connection to most recent investigations of valuation models. This involves regressing experienced rates of return of each company on various market or economy-wide indexes. The standard empirical approach to the CAPM uses such regression coefficients; but if (3.2-1) is not correct, this procedure is subject to the criticism of Roll (1977) that the market portfolio must be correctly specified before useful measures can be derived. Fortunately, the assumptions of the diversification model permit use of such regression coefficients, though not without some econometric difficulties.

To bring out the essence of the argument, assume for a moment that there is only one factor so that we can write (3.2-16) as

$$(3.4\text{-}1) \qquad \pi_{jt} = \rho_j + \alpha_j f_t + e_{jt}.$$

Since f is unobservable, we can normalize it by assuming that $E(f_t^2) = 1$. Let $\sigma_j^2 = E(e_{jt}^2)$. We can try to represent f_t by an "index" g_t, a weighted sum of individual security returns with weights consisting of v_{jg} ($j = 1, \ldots, J$) units of each security. (With actual indexes, many v_{jg} are zero.) The rate of return to this index is

$$(3.4\text{-}2) \qquad \pi_{gt} = \sum_{j=1}^{J} \rho_j v_{jg} = \sum_{j=1}^{J} f_t \alpha_j v_{jg} = \sum_{j=1}^{J} e_{jt} v_{jg}$$
$$= \rho_g + f_t \alpha_g + e_{gt}.$$

Thus the index also is a linear function of the common factor f_t and of a random term. The covariance of this index with the return to security j is given by

$$(3.4\text{-}3) \qquad E(\pi_{gt} - \rho_g)(\pi_{jt} - \rho_j) = E(f_t \alpha_g + e_{gt})(f_t \alpha_j + e_{jt})$$
$$= \alpha_g \alpha_j + \sigma_j^2 v_{jg},$$

since, by assumption, f_t not only has unit variance but also is independent of all e_{jt}, which are assumed to be independent of each other. If the returns are normally distributed,[11] the regression of the rate of return of each security, π_{jt}, on the rate of return of the index, π_{gt}, has population regression coefficient

$$(3.4\text{-}4) \qquad \beta_{gj} = E[(\pi_{gt} - \rho_g)(\pi_{jt} - \rho_j)] / E[(\pi_{gt} - \rho_g)^2]$$
$$= (\alpha_g \alpha_j + \sigma_j^2 v_{jg}) / (\alpha_g^2 + \sigma_g^2)$$
$$= \theta_1 \alpha_j + \theta_2 \sigma_j^2 v_{jg}.$$

---

11. The normality assumption is required to ease expression of the expected value of the regression coefficients. Without it, analogous expressions hold for the expectations though with different explicit interpretations of some coefficients and all formulae hold asymptotically when we take the limits in probability.

Equation (3.4-4) indicates that the regression coefficient is a linear combination of the systematic risk and of the specific risk associated with security j. The second term depends on the size of v_{jg} relative to the total holdings of securities incorporated in the index and on the variance of σ_j^2 of the specific risk of the security. If v_{jg} can be considered to be small, β_{gj} may be taken to be proportional to the coefficient α_j needed for specifying the valuation equation. The factor of proportion θ_1 is the same for all securities. As a result, this measure would be quite adequate for investigations of the valuation model since that model does not provide hypotheses about the numerical values of the coefficients a_k in (3.2-9) or b_k in (3.2-15).

Whether one can safely ignore the specific-risk term in equation (3.4-4) depends partly on the index being used. Major indexes are heavily weighted with precisely the leading securities that we have been studying. Indeed, one might feel that an index which included none of these securities was a rather odd construction. However, if the index can be taken to represent a fairly extensively diversified portfolio, then the reasoning that suggests that the security's own variation can be considered trivial for purposes of valuation also suggests that the term $\sigma_j^2 v_{jg}$ in (3.4-4) may be ignored. Thus, if the diversification argument is appropriate, the use of the regression coefficient β_{gj} calculated from a broadly based index is appropriate. It is not required, as it would be if only the general CAPM were valid, that the index represent the true "market."

The essence of the argument is that the index may itself be regarded as a measure of f_t which is subject to an error of observation. However, with an adequately diversified index, the measurement error does not produce a serious bias since, with the second term in (3.4-4) negligible, $\beta_{gj} = \theta_1 \alpha_j$ with θ_1 having the same value for each security.

The variables on which the regressions are run need not be limited to one index, or indeed even to market indexes. Instead, we can also use other quantities such as national income or inflation with which we expect earnings or dividends to be correlated or with which the market-valuation parameters might vary. We can also use rates of return of other securities or other common factors. Extension to more variables may cause some problems of interpretation, however.

Suppose that an H-element vector of variables x_t is available on which we can regress the rate of return of each security. Let these variables be such that we can describe them as

(3.4-5) $\qquad x_t' = \phi_0' + f_t'\Phi + \eta_t',$

where f_t is now the K-element vector of true factor values, Φ is the $K \times H$ matrix of (population) coefficients for the (hypothetical) regression of x_t on f_t, and η_t is the vector of residuals from this regression. We shall treat these residuals as random variables with the usual regression assumptions, namely, that they have mean zero and variance/covariance matrix S. The assumption that (3.2-1) fully describes all relevant correlations of returns with other quantities, which is the key to the diversification model, leads to the assumption that all residuals of the equations (3.4-1) for the rates of return of the individual securities, e_{jt}, are independent of the vector η_t.

Our suggested procedure is to regress the separate rates of return π_{jt} on the variables x_t (augmented by a constant). The regression is thus of the form

$$(3.4-6) \qquad \pi_{jt} = \hat{\delta}_{j0} + x_t'\hat{\delta}_j + \hat{w}_{jt},$$

where $\hat{\delta}_j$ is the vector of estimated regression coefficients and $\hat{w}_{jt}$ are the residuals. Since we will want to use $\hat{\delta}_j$ in place of α_j, the K-element vector of factor loadings α_{jk} from (3.2-16), we are concerned with the relationship of $\hat{\delta}_j$ to α_j.

Suppose that X is the $T \times H$ matrix whose rows are the observations on $(x_t - \bar{x})$ to be used in calculating the regression, $\bar{x}$ being the vector of average observations of x_t. Let F be the $T \times K$ matrix whose rows are the corresponding f_t' vectors and π_j be the corresponding $T \times 1$ vector with typical element $(\pi_{jt} - \Sigma_{t=1}^{T}\pi_{jt}/T)$. For the moment let e_j designate the $T \times 1$ vector with typical element e_{jt}. Then the estimates of $\hat{\delta}_j$ of (3.4-6) can be taken as estimating δ_j, given by

$$(3.4-7) \qquad \delta_j = E(\hat{\delta}_j)$$
$$= E(X'X)^{-1}X'\pi_j$$
$$= E[(X'X)^{-1}X'F]\alpha_j + E[(X'X)^{-1}X'e_j]$$
$$= \Xi\alpha_j.$$

The last equality in (3.4-7) arises from assuming that e_j is independent of X. Note that Ξ is the expected value of the regression coefficients in the (multivariate) reverse regression of F on X. The supplementary specification (3.4-5) was not used in obtaining (3.4-7), and it serves only to make it reasonable to assume that the estimates $\hat{\delta}_j$ have the usual properties. With (3.4-5), the "true" residual of (3.4-6) becomes

$$(3.4-8) \qquad w_{jt} = \pi_{jt} - x_t'\delta$$
$$= e_{jt} + (f_t' - x_t'\Xi)\alpha_j$$
$$= e_{jt} + f_t'[I - \Phi\Xi]\alpha_j + \eta_t'\Xi\alpha_j.$$

While this is not necessarily independent of x_t, it can be considered orthogonal to it since e_{jt} is and the remaining terms are the (population) residuals of the reverse regression.[12]

---

12. The difficulties here are overcome if we assume that all variables are normally distributed. Then the reverse regression is as appropriate as (3.4-5). If we let $E(f_t f_t') = M$, a

Equation (3.4-7) expresses δ_j as a linear transformation of the coefficients α_j, with the same transformation being used for each company. Several aspects of this transformation are worth noting. First, even if there are as many variables as factors, i.e., if $H = K$, and there is a one-to-one correspondence of factors to variables in the sense that $\Phi = I$, δ_j is a biased estimate of α_j. This bias results in each element of δ_j being a linear combination of all the elements of α_j. To avoid this, we would need $E(F'F)$ and S as well as Φ to be diagonal, so that $X'X$ could also be expected to be diagonal. This does not happen to be a condition that appears to be met in our data. Without these conditions, Ξ will not be diagonal so that any one δ_j coefficient will combine the effects of several factors. One must therefore be cautious in interpreting the elements of δ_j as giving the effects of the factors to which the corresponding elements of x_t correspond most directly.

More thorny, but still tractable, problems arise when the number of x-variables is not the same as the number of factors. In the event that there are more x-variables than factors, i.e., if $H > K$, it will not be the case that only K of the δ_j coefficients will be nonzero; instead, normally all these population coefficients will differ from zero. One can therefore expect their estimates also to be nonzero. What will be the case is that there will be a linear relationship among the population coefficients. When a set of J companies is considered, with the δ_j vector for each being estimated, then the cross-product matrix of the true regression coefficients would be singular in the sense that

$$(3.4\text{-}9) \qquad \sum_{j=1}^{J} (\delta_j \delta_j') = \Xi \sum_{j=1}^{J} (\alpha_j \alpha_j') \Xi',$$

and so the matrix in (3.4-9) is of (at most) rank K. Thus, if we were able to use the true coefficients δ_j in place of α_j (or γ_j) to estimate the valuation model, we would be confronted with perfect multicollinearity if we had more δ_j coefficients than there were α_j coefficients. This problem would also arise if there were fewer α_{jk} coefficients than factors, as (3.2-18) suggests might be the case, and we had as many δ_j as there were factors.

The true values of δ_j are no more available than are the true α_j coefficients. All we can use are estimated coefficients $\hat{\delta}_j$, and these coefficients do not share the property of the population parameters revealed in (3.4-9). These estimated coefficients, of course, differ from the true population parameters by the usual estimation error, say, u_j. That is, what we have available are

---

little manipulation gives us that $\Xi = [\Phi'M\Phi + S]^{-1}\Phi'M$ and w_{jt} is both independent of x_t and normally distributed. Similarly, if we have a large sample and if $M = p \lim F'F/T$, then again we can express $p \lim \Xi = [\Phi M'\phi + S]^{-1}\Phi'M$, and the orthogonality of w_j to X raises no difficulties for large samples since $p \lim w_j' X/T = 0$.

(3.4-10) $\hat{\delta}_j = \delta_j + u_j$

$\qquad\qquad = \Xi\,\alpha_j + u_j.$

Let $h_j = E(w_{jt}^2)$, with w_{jt} being the residual in (3.4-8). Presuming that it does have the usual regression properties yields the usual formula

(3.4-11) $E(u_j u_j') = E(\hat{\delta}_j - \delta_j)(\hat{\delta}_j - \delta_j)'$

$\qquad\qquad\qquad = h_j(X'X)^{-1}.$

As a result, corresponding to (3.4-9), we obtain

(3.4-12) $E\left[\sum\limits_{j=1}^{J}(\hat{\delta}_j\hat{\delta}_j')/J\right] = \Xi\sum\limits_{j=1}^{J}\alpha_j\alpha_j'/J\Xi'$

$\qquad\qquad\qquad + \left(\sum\limits_{j=1}^{J}h_j/J\right)(X'X)^{-1},$

which is of full rank. We would then apparently be able to use all $\hat{\delta}_j$ coefficients in estimating a valuation equation even though there are more of them than factors.

The estimation errors present in the $\hat{\delta}_j$ coefficients act as measurement errors when we turn to estimation of the valuation equation. The major consequence of this is that all $\hat{\delta}_j$ coefficients can be expected to have nonzero estimated effects in the valuation equation even though there are more of them than of the α_j coefficients. More disconcerting, other risk variables, provided they do have some correlation with the α_j, will appear to enter the valuation equations even though (3.4-5) is correct and $H \geq K$. The reason is the same as the reason why the δ_j coefficients can all be nonzero even when $H > K$. Indeed, expression (3.4-10) relates δ_j to α_j in the same sort of way that (3.4-5) related to x_t to f_t. This would also be the case for having still other risk measures. It is therefore fortunate that solutions are available to the problems caused by $\hat{\delta}_j$ being subject to estimation error.

The structure of the cross-product matrix of $\hat{\delta}_j$ given in (3.4-12) corresponds closely to the one assumed by the model used in statistical factor analysis. However, $\Sigma_{j=1}^{J}(h_j/J)(X'X)^{-1}$ is not a diagonal matrix, as is usually required for factor analysis. Balanced against this difficulty is the fact that $(X'X)$ is known. As a result, the applicability of the factor-analysis model can be investigated (through using a different metric for δ_j) and we are able to investigate from the regression coefficients, all of which may differ significantly from zero, how many underlying common-factor coefficients are actually present in security returns.

Determining the number of linearly independent δ_j coefficients indicates the number of γ_j coefficients that the diversification model suggests should be present in the valuation equation, but it does not solve the errors-in-variables problem also presented by the δ_j. The structure of the cross-product matrix shown in (3.4-12) and the fact that h_j can be estimated along with δ_j mean that we can correct for the estimation errors in $\hat{\delta}_j$. The procedure, developed in Cragg (1982), yields consistent estimates not of the a_k coefficients of (3.2-9) since α_j or γ_j are not estimated directly, but it will consistently estimate the vector $a'\Phi^{-1}$, where a is the vector of valuation coefficients. More important, other coefficients, including those of other possible explanatory variables, will now be estimated consistently. Thus, testing whether these coefficients are zero does test whether additional variables affect valuation and not simply whether they may help to proxy the inaccurately measured α_{jk} coefficients. This is fortunate since two further measures of risk suggest themselves from the data we shall be using.

The first additional risk variable is the variance of the individual predictions of long-term growth for each company, referred to as s_g^2. This variance may be taken to indicate the extent of uncertainty about the future rate of growth of the company, which may well be related to the uncertainty about the future returns of the company's securities. The variable s_g^2 may capture some combination of both specific and systematic risk, since disagreement about the future growth of earnings may come from different perceptions about the individual companies, or it may arise from different opinions about the values to be taken on by variables that affect all companies, such as economic activity or interest rates.

This common-variable interpretation of the variance of the predictions would conform with our earlier discussion of these forecasts. We found when examining the forecasts in section 2.2.4 that a common-factor model might well be appropriate. In section 3.2.3 we noted that differences of opinion might stem from two sources, one of which has a common-factor interpretation. Combining the specifications considered in section 3.2.3 might suggest that

$$(3.4\text{-}13) \qquad \mu_{ji} - \mu_j = \gamma_{j0i} - \gamma_{j0} + \sum_{k=1}^{K} (\gamma_{jki} - \gamma_{jk})(\mu_{ki} - \mu_k)$$

$$+ \sum_{k=1}^{K} \gamma_{jk}(\mu_{ki} - \mu_k) + \sum_{k=1}^{K} \mu_k(\gamma_{jki} - \gamma_{jk}).$$

For simplicity in describing the possible nature of s_g^2, assume that all individual differences in (3.4-13) are independent of each other so that we can consider s_g^2 to measure

$$(3.4\text{-}14) \qquad E(s_{gj}^2) = E\left[\sum_{i=1}^{I} (\mu_{ji} - \mu_j)^2 / I \right]$$

$$= E\left\{ \left[\sum_{i=1}^{I} (\gamma_{j0i} - \gamma_{j0})^2 + \sum_{k=1}^{K} \mu_k^2(\gamma_{jki} - \gamma_{kj})^2 \right. \right.$$

$$\left. \left. + \sum_{k=1}^{K} \gamma_{jk}^2(\mu_{ki} - \mu_k)^2 \right] / I \right\},$$

where I is the number of predictors. Variation in this quantity across firms arises partly from the variations in the evaluation of the individual firms but also partly from the differences in the values of the vectors of predicted values captured in the last term of equation (3.4-14). If this latter source of disagreement dominates the expression, then the variance (or the standard deviation) of the predictions of growth might be considered a measure of systematic risk. If differences of opinion about individual firms dominate, then it is more a measure of a type of specific risk. If only systematic risk in the sense of the γ_{jk} coefficients matters as the diversification theory suggests, then s_g^2 would only be important if the x_t variables used in estimating $\hat{\delta}_j$ failed to catch some type of common factor.

The second risk measure we consider is the estimated residual variances from the regressions of π_{jt} on x_t used to calculate the coefficients $\hat{\delta}_j$. More than the previous measures, this one could be taken to be a measure of specific risk. However, as shown in expression (3.4-8), systematic risk also enters this variable through the errors-in-variables problem. Nevertheless, if we first deal with the estimation errors in $\hat{\delta}_j$ coefficients, we might then consider use of this residual variance with these coefficients as a test indicating whether specific risk matters.

Arguments developed in this chapter allow us now to proceed to investigate the relationships between the predictions of earnings growth which we collected and the valuation of securities. The approach taken by the APT, especially using our diversification argument, to establish share prices provides a valuation equation which is robust to many variations in the specific assumptions used in its derivation. Given the hypothesis that many portfolios can be considered extensively diversified, a particular type of relationship should exist that relates security prices to expected returns and to risk measures. Reasonable arguments suggest that the predicted growth rates which we collected are closely related to and can be used to derive expected returns. Finally, in the present section, we have indicated how variables corresponding to the relevant risk measures may be obtained.

4 Empirical Connection of the Growth Forecasts with Share-Valuation Models

We suggested in chapter 3 that a relationship should exist between the earnings growth expectations we have collected and the market values of the corresponding shares. The present chapter reports on our empirical investigation of this relationship. This investigation may be regarded in one of two ways. Assuming that growth-rate expectations are a major input used by investors to form expected security returns, our empirical work tests the validity of the valuation models. Conversely, if we maintain the validity of the valuation models, we may be regarded as testing the hypothesis that earnings growth expectations do play a major role, along with the other specified variables, in investors' evaluations of expected security returns.

We begin by investigating the expected rate of return measure suggested by equation (3.3-14) and obtained by using the averages of the long-term expected growth rates. We are particularly concerned with whether the relationship between expected return and the systematic risk variables represented by various regression coefficients holds when expected return is measured with our analysts' forecasts. First, in section 4.1 we specify more precisely exactly what measures of risk will be employed. Next, in section 4.2, we examine the prima facie evidence in favor of hypotheses suggested by the diversification model. Section 4.3 then adopts a more structural approach, which takes into account some econometric problems that were discussed in section 3.4. We switch in section 4.4 to the alternative specification (3.3-15), which we suggested might also give a good representation of the model. This price-earnings ratio formulation allows us to enquire whether other growth forecasts might give a closer explanation of valuation relationships than the expectations data we collected. Failure to find such improvement allows us to conclude that our growth measures are closest to the actual expectations that enter market valuation.

Having a model for prices also allows us to investigate whether knowledge of the model and access to the expectations data would have allowed superior stock selection. The fact that they would not comes as no surprise, but the reasons are of considerable interest. These are the subject of section 4.5. The various findings of these investigations are summarized in section 4.6.

4.1 The Risk Measures Used

It is not clear from the diversification model exactly what measures of risk would be most appropriate. We did provide, in section 3.4, a theoretical justification for the general approach that we shall take. Nevertheless, some empirical investigation is needed before we can ascertain what specific measures are most appropriate; that is, we need to select the exact form of the regression equation whose estimated coefficients will stand for the factor coefficients. We begin by exploring relationships between security returns and some economic variables that are of interest whatever valuation model is appropriate. Once we have established the variables to be used, we proceed to explore the valuation relationships suggested by the theory.

The first set of variables employed are measures of so-called market risk derived from the regressions of the realized rates of return on various market-wide variables.[1] We experimented with several market indicators including the Standard & Poor's 500 Stock Index, the Dow Jones Industrial Average (of 30 stocks), and the (value) weighted and unweighted indexes made available by the University of Chicago's Center for Research in Security Prices (CRSP). The realized rates of return were obtained from the CRSP. Our results turned out not to be sensitive to use of the alternative market indexes, so we report here only the results for the CRSP weighted index. This index tended to give results as strong as any in terms of r^2 for the regressions of company returns on the index and provided coefficients which were marginally stronger for the subsequent simple regressions reported in section 4.2.

Correlation with other types of variables may also yield needed risk measures whether the extended CAPM (involving nonmarketable income streams) or the diversification model is assumed. We selected three such additional variables. They are the rate of change of National Income (NI), the short-term interest rate measured by the ninety-day Treasury Bill rate, and the rate of inflation measured by the increase of the Consumer Price Index.[2] These may be considered typical measures of

1. These are the "beta" coefficients often calculated allegedly to give content to the CAPM.
2. We used alternatively the rate of change of GNP as opposed to NI; the long rate as opposed to the short; and the GNP deflator as opposed to the CPI. The alternative series were so highly correlated that it made little difference which we employed.

some risks to which investors are subject, stemming from variation in other sources of income, from changes in interest rates, and from changes in inflation.

The period over which the regression coefficients should be calculated is not clear a priori. It is not even clear that only past values should be used. The theory involves the covariances of returns with various quantities in the future. These parameters could safely be estimated from past data if they did not change or if investors did not perceive change. Such stability is unlikely. Changes in the nature and type of activities that corporations pursue and alterations in the structure of the economy make it likely that the appropriate regression coefficients change through time. Insofar as investors can perceive and even anticipate these changes, they are unlikely simply to extrapolate past betas into the future. Indeed, many of the popular "beta services" in the financial community explicitly adjust the betas calculated from past data, on the basis of changes that are known to have occurred in the structure of the business. Thus, in calculating the relevant betas at any time, it might be sensible to use values estimated with data following the time at which the valuation took place. Fortunately, our expectations data are not based on calculations using the realizations over the forecast period so we do not have to worry about spurious correlations being found between the expected return and these future values.

We adopted a compromise approach after some experimentation. The regression coefficients are calculated using quarterly observations over ten-year periods. The periods used covered the three years prior to the valuation date and the seven years following it. The results reported in the next section are not very sensitive to variations in the details of this procedure. Almost the same results were obtained, for example, when we took five years before and after the valuation date. Nevertheless, we did find that use of data entirely from past periods gave less satisfactory results than those obtained by including some future data. Extending the estimation period into the future improved the values of r^2 and was particularly important for obtaining some precision in evaluating the effect of inflation.

We also tried monthly rather than quarterly observations and shorter time periods over which to make the calculations of covariances with the market index. Again we found that the results improved when future data were included in the calculations, i.e., when some foresight regarding the future was assumed. However, the use of the shorter period made no substantial difference to the results. Since it is desirable to calculate all the regression coefficients over the same period so that the variance-covariance matrices of these estimates can be easily obtained for use in testing certain hypotheses, and since National Income is available only quarterly, we pursued the quarterly calculations.

4.2 Association of Expected Return and Risk

4.2.1 Strength of Individual Measures

The first question we investigate is the relationship between expected return and each of the various risk measures. The critical questions are whether the regression coefficients specified in the previous section are related to expected return and whether other types of risk measures (not suggested by the CAPM) are more important.

The expected return variable we use is suggested by equation (3.3-14). Let $\bar{g}_{jt}$ be the average of the long-term predicted (percentage) rates of growth available for company j at time t, D_{jt+1} be the dividends expected to be paid per share in the course of the next year (as estimated by the predictor which furnished data in all years), and P_{jt} be the end-of-year closing price (ex dividend where appropriate) for the shares of company j. Then the expected percentage rate of return, $\bar{\rho}_{jt}$, is calculated as

$$(4.2\text{-}1) \qquad \bar{\rho}_{jt} = \bar{g}_{jt} + 100(D_{jt+1}/P_{jt}).$$

Simple regressions of this expected return measure on the various risk proxies are summarized in table 4.1. The sort of cross-sectional data we are using makes us vulnerable to heteroscedasticity, which can produce some seriously misleading results from our data if the problem is ignored. To avoid the difficulties produced by heteroscedasticity, we calculated the standard errors of the coefficients in the way advocated by White (1980) that allows for any heteroscedasticity that may be present. We report in table 4.1 the asymptotic t-values for the regression coefficients calculated in this way. Because of the adjustment for heteroscedasticity, the coefficient of determination r^2 is not a monotonic transformation of these t-values. The values of r^2 did nevertheless tend to parallel the t-values.

The first risk measure is the regression coefficient of the (excess) rate of return of each security on the (excess) rate of return to the CRSP value-weighted market index. It is denoted by $\hat{\beta}_{Mj}$ and was obtained by estimating the equation

$$(4.2\text{-}2) \qquad \pi_{jt} - \rho_t = \beta_{Mj}(\pi_{Mt} - \rho_t) + u_{jt}$$

for each company j over forty quarters, that is, forty values of t. Here π_{jt} is the ex post return to company j, ρ_t is the short-term (ninety-day) Treasury Bill rate taken to represent the risk-free rate of interest, and π_{Mt} is the rate of return of the CRSP index. This β_{Mj} coefficient is, of course, the measure suggested by the CAPM if one ignores the problem that the market index must provide complete coverage of marketable securities. We then proceed to estimate the equation

$$(4.2\text{-}3) \qquad \bar{\rho}_{jt} = a_0 + a_1 \hat{\beta}_{Mj} + v_{jt}.$$

Table 4.1 **Risk Measures and Naive Expected Return (asymptotic *t*-values adjusted for heteroscedasticity)**

A. Using Regression Coefficients

Year	$\hat{\beta}_M$	$\hat{\beta}_Y$	$\hat{\beta}_r$	$\hat{\beta}_p$
1961	4.04	2.37	− .59	− 1.13
1962	2.01	1.82	.92	− .54
1963	1.74	.96	− .33	− .59
1964	2.21	.77	− 1.45	− 1.08
1965	1.92	1.48	− 1.52	− 1.40
1966	3.99	2.48	− 4.04	− 4.33
1967	3.11	2.93	− 4.44	− 3.83
1968	3.91	1.98	− 4.27	− 4.02

B. Using Variance Measures

Year	s_g^2	s_g	s_e	s_s^2
1961	1.90	.99	2.89	1.68
1962	3.63	3.63	1.56	− .32
1963	2.39	2.09	.52	1.51
1964	6.47	2.42	.83	− 3.14
1965	4.76	3.30	1.21	− .91
1966	2.21	2.76	1.60	
1967	2.82	3.91	1.35	
1968	8.21	6.98	2.68	

$\hat{\beta}_M$ = coefficient of the CRSP value weighted index.
$\hat{\beta}_Y$ = coefficient of the rate of change of National Income.
$\hat{\beta}_r$ = coefficient of the Treasury Bill rate.
$\hat{\beta}_p$ = coefficient of the rate of change of prices.
s_g^2 = variance of the long-term growth predictions.
s_g = standard deviations of the long-term growth predictions.
s_e = standard error of regression of return on four variables.
s_s^2 = variance of the short-term growth predictions.

This equation is estimated separately for each year *t* on the basis of all companies *j* for which we had data in that year. The resulting *t*-values for a_1 appear in table 4.1.

The *t*-values obtained from estimating equation (4.2-3) are positive and usually significant. The strength of the association is not great, however: the value of r^2 corresponding to the highest *t*-value is only 0.16. The weakness of these associations could arise from the particular market index and periods used. However, as noted above, the results did not vary substantially if alternative indexes were used in place of the CRSP weighted index, and seemed more apt to be weaker than stronger. They also were not substantially changed by using the coefficient obtained by regressing individual returns on the market return rather than using excess returns in each case. Moreover, the results were not very sensitive to changing the period over which the coefficients were estimated, provided that at least some observations following the date at which the growth forecasts were made were included.

Although the regression coefficients with the CRSP index give significant results, strong t-values (and coefficients of determination) are sometimes obtained from using the regression coefficients of the securities' returns on the rate of change of National Income, indicated by $\hat{\beta}_Y$ in table 4.1, in place of $\hat{\beta}_M$ in estimating equation (4.2-3). These t-values are not, however, as strong as those for the coefficient of the CRSP index.

Our next risk measures come from estimating the regression of each security's rate of return on the rate of inflation ($\hat{\beta}_p$) and on the Treasury Bill rate ($\hat{\beta}_r$). Systematic relationships between security returns and inflation and interest rates are consistent with the wider specification of returns being associated with a variety of factors, as we argued in chapter 3. Table 4.1 indicates that these alternative risk measures do not do as well as the standard $\hat{\beta}_M$ measure during the early years. They do, however, tend to have a much stronger influence later in the 1960s when inflation rates and interest rates begin to soar. The signs of β_r and β_p can be expected to be negative if they do not also stand as proxies for other risk measures. A higher value of β_p indicates that a stock provides a better inflation hedge, which is a desirable attribute. Similarly, a positive value of β_r indicates that the stock does well when interest rates rise and hence is negatively correlated with realized returns from fixed income securities.

These results clearly indicate that the various regression coefficients are indeed related to expected return. The next question is whether other types of risk measure have still closer associations. Part B of table 4.1 summarizes the results obtained by using various variance measures for risk instead of regression coefficients.

The first of these alternative risk measures is the variance of the predictions of long-term growth, s_g^2. This quantity may possibly be interpreted as a measure of own variance and thus of specific risk. Nevertheless, the decomposition shown in equation (3.4-14) suggests that it may instead be a particularly good expectational proxy for systematic risk. For the years 1962 through 1965, when our sample was widest, s_g^2 gives stronger results than any of the regression risk measures. It also shows positive associations with expected rates of return in other years, which are clearly significant except in 1961.

Equation (3.4-14), which provides the basis for the possible interpretation of s_g^2 as representing systematic risk, also indicates that s_g^2 would be a quadratic rather than a linear combination of the factor coefficients γ_{jk}. This might suggest that the standard deviations of growth forecasts might be stronger measures of systematic risk than the variances. However, as the column of table 4.1 headed s_g shows, there was no reliable tendency for this to be the case.

If s_g^2 should represent specific risk rather than systematic risk, one might expect a better measure to be provided by the residual variances or standard errors of estimate of the regressions of the rates of return on the various systematic variables. Our findings do not, however, support this supposition. The standard errors from the regression of return on the four variables used to calculate the β coefficients produced weaker results than did s_g^2. They are shown in the column of table 4.1 headed s_e. The residual variances, that is, s_e^2, gave no stronger results.

The success of the variance of the long-term predictors makes one wonder whether the variance of the short-term growth predictions could also be used to provide a useful measure. This did not prove to be the case. The results, given in the final column of table 4.1, show mixed signs and are generally not significant. This risk measure quite clearly is weaker than the variance of the long-term predictions.

4.2.2 Use of Several Risk Measures

These results already have some interesting implications despite the simplistic approach used. There is, however, no reason to limit ourselves to only one risk measure. We now turn to the wider specification where in the first step the realized rate of return is regressed on all the suggested variables.[3] Before looking in the next section at the more structural aspects of this specification, we examine the prima facie case that all these variables are relevant to valuation, even though these inferences may turn out to be influenced by errors-in-variables difficulties.

The coefficients were obtained from the multiple regression of the rate of return of each security on the CRSP value-weighted index (M), on the rate of change of National Income (DY), on the Treasury Bill rate (r), and on the rate of inflation (DP). The equation fitted for each company is

$$(4.2\text{-}4) \qquad \pi_{jt} = \delta_{0j} + \delta_{Mj}M_t + \delta_{Yj}DY_t$$
$$+ \delta_{rj}r_t + \delta_{pj}DP_t + u_{jt},$$

and the estimated regression coefficient $\hat{\delta}_{ij}$ serves as risk measures. The cross-section specification for $\bar{\rho}_{jt}$ is expanded from (4.2-3) to

$$(4.2\text{-}5) \qquad \bar{\rho}_{jt} = a_0 + a_1\hat{\delta}_{Mj} + a_2\hat{\delta}_{Yj} + a_3\hat{\delta}_{rj} + a_4\hat{\delta}_{pj}.$$

Estimates of this equation are given in table 4.2.

A number of findings indicated by table 4.2 are worth emphasizing. Of most importance, each type of coefficient is significant in some years. In the first part of the period only the market coefficient is significant. However, toward the end of the period other coefficients tend to be important, especially those measuring systematic relationships with inflation and interest rates. When these results are taken at face value, two

---

3. These are the regressions from which the standard errors of estimate referred to in table 4.1 were obtained.

| Table 4.2 | | | Regression Estimates for Extended Model for the Expected Rate of Return (asymptotic t-ratios adjusted for heteroscedasticity) | | | |

Year	Constant	$\hat{\delta}_M$	$\hat{\delta}_Y$	$\hat{\delta}_r$	$\hat{\delta}_p$	R^2
1961	7.01	1.58	.23	$-.02$	$-.03$	.15
	(12.75)	(2.78)	(1.47)	$(-.73)$	$(-.59)$	
1962	7.82	1.19	.20	.02	$-.02$	.10
	(10.82)	(1.59)	(1.61)	(.54)	$(-.29)$	
1963	6.94	1.63	.05	$-.03$	$-.01$	.07
	(14.85)	(3.04)	(.44)	$(-.46)$	$(-.12)$	
1964	6.00	2.58	$-.06$	$-.08$	$-.06$	.12
	(10.22)	(3.80)	$(-.74)$	(-1.27)	$(-.68)$	
1965	8.31	.79	.11	$-.07$	$-.10$	.07
	(18.31)	(1.57)	(1.14)	(-1.25)	(-1.04)	
1966	9.85	.90	.17	$-.09$	$-.19$	.19
	(21.18)	(2.11)	(1.92)	(-3.25)	(-3.60)	
1967	9.82	1.26	.25	$-.15$	$-.30$	.26
	(17.46)	(2.11)	(2.55)	(-4.19)	(-3.67)	
1968	8.83	3.98	.42	$-.24$	$-.52$	.28
	(11.70)	(4.69)	(3.28)	(-4.19)	(-3.77)	

explanations for them come to mind. First, in the more stable early part of the period, estimates of the δ coefficients may be sufficiently imprecise that in the subsequent estimation of equation (4.2-5) the relatively greater errors of measurement lead to lack of significance. Second, investors may have become more concerned about the other sources of risk, such as inflation and interest-rate instability, as the decade proceeded.[4] Overall, the results suggest strongly that all influences play a role, though it is an open question whether this is because they act as proxies for other variables.

The signs of the coefficients tend to be the same across the different equations. Although with errors in variables we must be cautious in attaching much importance to the signs of particular coefficients, the patterns obtained do usually conform to the signs suggested by intuition. Positive association with either the market return or income raises the expected rate of return. Correspondingly, positive partial correlation with the rate of inflation, indicating that the stock tends to act as a hedge against inflation, lowers the expected rate of return. Finally, the coefficient for the Treasury Bill rate usually has the expected negative sign. There is, however, a good deal of correlation across securities (roughly about 0.6) between the coefficients for the Treasury Bill rate and for the rate of inflation so that one may be partly serving as an additional proxy for the other. This correlation is sufficiently low, however, that one cannot legitimately presume that variations in the rate of change of prices and in the short-term rate of interest necessarily represent the same

4. Inflation, as measured by the annual rate of change in the Consumer Price Index, remained below the 2 percent level through 1965. Later in the decade, inflation increased to the 6 percent level.

variable. Except for this fairly mild correlation, multicollinearity problems are small, making it less plausible that all the different measures serve as proxies for some single variable.

Inclusion of all these different regression coefficients does not account for the strength we found earlier for the variance of the predictions. When that variable was included in (4.2-5) along with the four $\hat{\delta}$ variables measuring various systematic risks, it usually was highly significant with a positive coefficient. The a coefficients for the four $\hat{\delta}$ variables tended to retain the same signs, though with lessened significance. The apparent importance of s_g^2 may in part result from errors-in-variables problems or misspecification. Nevertheless, it may also indicate that s_g^2 is a particularly useful expectational proxy for several of the systematic risk measures. What is important is that the values of R^2 are sufficiently high and so very highly significant that there is no question about there being some underlying systematic association among the variables included in the specification.

4.3 Structural Relations between Expected Return and Risk Coefficients

The results reported in the previous section may arise because the market actually takes a multifaceted approach to risk. In contrast, they may simply be the outcome of using poor data. To investigate this question, we proceed in two stages. First, we examine the extent to which our risk coefficients exhibit the linear structure that we indicated in section 3.4 would be found if there were fewer factors than the number of independent variables used in the regressions in which the $\hat{\delta}_j$ coefficients were calculated. Establishment of the number of factor coefficients is also needed in order to proceed to take account of the errors of estimation of the $\hat{\delta}$ coefficients. The second stage involves estimating the valuation model allowing for the presence of these errors.

4.3.1 The Number of Factor Coefficients

We showed in equation (3.4-12) that the variance-covariance matrix of the regression coefficients has a particular structure under the common-factor model for rates of return. Let $\hat{\delta}$ be the average of the $\hat{\delta}_j$ vectors, and let $\bar{\alpha}$ be the average of the α_j vectors whose elements α_{jk} are the coefficients of the common K factors in the (true) rate-of-return equation (3.2-16). Letting $\bar{h} = \Sigma_{j=1}^{J} h_j/J$, where h_j is the residual variance, we can rewrite equation (3.4-12) as

$$(4.3\text{-}1) \qquad V = E\left[\sum_{j=1}^{J} (\hat{\delta}_j - \bar{\delta})(\hat{\delta}_j - \bar{\delta})'/J \right]$$

$$= \Xi'\left[\sum_{j=1}^{J} (\alpha_j - \bar{\alpha})(\alpha_j - \bar{\alpha})'/J \right]\Xi + \bar{h}(X'X)^{-1}.$$

Table 4.3   Significance Levels for the Hypothesis That More Than Specified
Numbers of Factors Are Present in the Regression Coefficients

	Number of Factors			
Years	0	1	2	3
1959–68	.000	.816	.594	.174
1960–69	.000	.134	.266	.126
1961–70	.000	.890	.784	.303
1962–71	.000	.935	.839	.951
1963–72	.000	.767	.789	.305
1964–73	.000	.001	.059	.694
1965–74	.000	.068	.196	.992
1966–75	.000	.005	.065	.398
1967–76	.000	.006	.053	.317

Since $(X'X)$, the cross-product matrix of the variables used to estimate the coefficients, is known,[5] we can investigate the hypothesis that this common-factor structure does apply[6] to the variance-covariance matrix of the estimated coefficients calculated for the different companies. Assuming that the coefficients are normally distributed across companies, we performed likelihood-ratio tests of a variety of hypotheses. In doing so we used the value of $\bar{h}$, the average of the estimates coming from the estimates of the individual regressions, rather than jointly estimating this parameter in the factor analysis. No substantial differences in results occur when instead $\bar{h}$ is estimated from the $\hat{\delta}$ data.

The regression coefficients used for different years are far from being independent, since thirty-six of the quarterly observations are the same in regressions for adjacent years. Nevertheless, the patterns that occur over time are of interest. When we tested the hypothesis that there are less than four factors represented by the four regression coefficients, the data strongly supported the hypothesis that there are fewer factors. These tests are summarized in table 4.3 in terms of the smallest significance levels at which one could reject the (null) hypothesis of only zero, one, two, and three factors over the alternative hypothesis of at least four different factors being present.[7]

The hypothesis of only one factor is very strongly indicated in the early part of the period. However, when observations from the 1970s begin to

5. Of course, when the $\hat{\delta}$ vector being investigated does not contain the constant term, the appropriate row and column are first removed from $(X'X)^{-1}$.

6. Specifically, the procedure involves the principal components of $\Sigma_{j=1}^{J} (\hat{\delta}_j - \bar{\delta}) (\hat{\delta}_j - \bar{\delta})'/J$ in the metric of $(X'X)^{-1}$. See Anderson and Rubin (1956) for a discussion of maximum likelihood estimates of the model. The fact that $\bar{h}(X'X)^{-1}$ is known makes more factors identifiable than would usually be the case.

7. Qualitatively similar results are obtained when we test three versus four factors, two versus three, etc.

play an important part, the data indicate that at least two factors are present and would reject at the 0.10 level the hypothesis of two factors in favor of three factors for some of the estimations.

The reason for the success of a one common-factor model in the early estimates was not that the correlations of different quantities, which themselves all varied significantly, could be fully attributed to a single factor. Rather, it was the case that some of the estimated coefficients varied so little across companies, relative to their errors of estimation, that both the variances across companies of their true values, δ_{jk}, and their correlations with other coefficients could be treated as zero.

This problem is illustrated by the data from the 1960s shown in table 4.4. There we present the matrices

$$\sum_{j=1}^{J} (\hat{\delta}_j - \bar{\delta})(\hat{\delta}_j - \bar{\delta})'/J$$

and

$$\left[\sum_{j=1}^{J} (\hat{\delta}_j - \bar{\delta})(\hat{\delta}_j - \bar{\delta})'/J - \bar{h}(X'X)^{-1} \right].$$

All the variances of the $\hat{\delta}_r$ and $\hat{\delta}_p$ coefficients can be attributed to estimation errors, and the hypothesis that the variance across companies in the true coefficients was zero could not be rejected. Indeed, all the variance can be so attributed for $\hat{\delta}_p$, the coefficients of inflation. Later, as interest rates and inflation rates themselves showed more variation, this ceased to be the case and all coefficients showed variation across companies significant beyond the 0.05 level. As noted earlier, while short-term interest rates and inflation may primarily reflect the same factor (as might be the case if the real rate of interest is constant), the magnitude of measurement errors in each variable must then be very substantial since collinearity problems in the data were mild and do not clearly account for the

Table 4.4   **Covariance Matrices of the Regression Coefficients Fitted for 1960–69**

	$\hat{\delta}_M$	$\hat{\delta}_Y$	$\hat{\delta}_r$	$\hat{\delta}_p$
	A. Unadjusted			
$\hat{\delta}_M$	.09			
$\hat{\delta}_Y$	.17	4.46		
$\hat{\delta}_r$	.47	−3.78	58.9	
$\hat{\delta}_p$	−.03	1.27	−22.9	19.3
	B. After Subtraction of Estimation Error			
$\hat{\delta}_M$	.05			
$\hat{\delta}_Y$	.13	1.08		
$\hat{\delta}_r$	.61	1.63	5.13	
$\hat{\delta}_p$	−.28	−1.21	4.73	−4.25

difficulties. Furthermore, the results about the number of factors were repeated when we dropped the interest-rate variable from the original regressions. The 1964–73 period and later ones indicated the presence of at least two and possibly three factors. Prior to that period, the variance-covariance matrices suggest only a single factor.

Earlier investigations of the appropriateness of the common-factor model to security returns suggested that several factors would be found. King (1966) as well as Roll and Ross (1980) each found support for such a hypothesis. Hence one may suspect that our results for the early years reflect the peculiarities of the data on some of the independent variables in that period.

These tests have involved the variance-covariance matrices of the regression coefficients. This was appropriate in view of our desire to use the adjusted matrices subsequently in estimation where it is necessary to avoid using singular matrices. However, the original hypothesis applies also to the averages (across companies) of the coefficients, that is, to

$$E\left[\sum_{j=1}^{J} \hat{\delta}_j \hat{\delta}_j'/J - \bar{h}(X'X)^{-1}\right].$$

When we investigated the number of factors, recognizing that the means of the regression coefficients should have the same factor structure, we found evidence for two factors rather than only one in the early years. That is, the hypothesis of only one factor can be rejected well beyond the 0.05 level, but not that of there being only two factors. The results for the later years did not change appreciably. We can still conclude that there are certainly two, and possibly three, common factors.

4.3.2 Results Allowing for Estimation Error

The previous findings about the number of factor coefficients present in the rate of return regressions pose a dilemma for the next part of our investigation. We suspect that the reason for finding only one factor in the early years is that the other factors happened to have very little variation in the 1960s. However, if the risk was still present that they would vary, then their coefficients should still enter the valuation equation. Using a one-factor model would then involve misspecification. Testing the hypothesis that more than one factor is actually present does require that the data clearly involve more than one factor. A procedure developed in Cragg (1982) that allows for estimation errors in $\hat{\delta}$ involves the use of

$$\left[\sum_{j=1}^{J} (\hat{\delta}_j - \bar{\delta})(\hat{\delta}_j - \bar{\delta})'/J - h(X'X)^{-1}\right]^{-1}.$$

The procedure makes sense only if the matrix is clearly positive definite. When this is the case, we can allow for the estimation error to see what inferences stand up even when its effects are recognized. In doing so, we shall use the simplification, discussed in Cragg (1982), in which the u_{jt} of equation (4.2-4) are assumed to be normally distributed.

We resolve the dilemma posed by our findings about the structure of the $\hat{\delta}_j$ coefficients by fitting two types of model, allowing in each case for the estimation errors of the regression coefficients. First, we estimate the equations for the expected rate of return using only the regression coefficient for the market and the variance of the long-term predictors; i.e., we fit the equation

$$(4.3\text{-}2) \qquad \bar{\rho}_{jt} = a_0 + a_1\beta_{Mj} + a_2s_{gj}^2.$$

Here, the β_{Mj} are based on the three years before and the seven years after the valuation. Second, we use the coefficients for the 1966–75 period, estimated without the interest-rate variable; that is, we estimate

$$(4.3\text{-}3) \qquad \bar{\rho}_{jt} = b_0 + b_1\gamma_{Mj} + b_2\gamma_{Yj} + b_3\gamma_{pj} + b_4s_{gj}^2,$$

where the γ_j are calculated from the regression

$$(4.3\text{-}4) \qquad \pi_{jt} = \gamma_{0j} + \gamma_{Mj}\pi_M + \gamma_{Yj}DY + \gamma_{pj}DP + v_{jt}$$

for the period 1966–75. As we noted, there γ coefficients do support (though not strongly) the conclusion that a three-factor model is appropriate.

The first approach does little to resolve the puzzle. In the early part of the period, β_M was not significant while s_g^2 was always stronger and usually significant. For 1966 and subsequent years, when the number of predictors available on which to base s_g^2 becomes small, β_M is highly significant, and positive, as is s_g^2 in the last two years. These results suggest that s_g^2 is not simply another proxy for the systematic risk measured with considerable estimation error by β_M. Instead, it suggests that a model with two or more factors is appropriate—or that there is another relevant risk concept proxied by s_g^2.

The results of the second approach shed quite a bit more light on the matter. When adjustment was made for errors in variables and allowance was made for heteroscedasticity, it usually turned out that none of the coefficients was significantly different from zero. At best, but one would be, and then only just at the 0.05 level. This was true whether s_g^2 was included or not. Overall, however, when s_g^2 was included in the equation, the hypothesis that all γ_j parameters had zero coefficients in equation (4.3-3) could be rejected beyond the 0.01 level, except in 1963 and 1965. When s_g^2 was not included, the hypothesis could sometimes be rejected at the 0.10 level and sometimes not.

Part of the difficulty stems from multicollinearity. As lack of certainty about the number of underlying factors indicated, the "corrected" $\hat{\gamma}_j$ coefficients are correlated with each other. Moreover, there is some correlation with s_g^2, though it is small. The technique used involves much more complicated standard errors than ordinary regression, and for a given covariance matrix of explanatory variables these standard errors are considerably larger. More coherent results were obtained when the γ_Y coefficient for National Income was eliminated from (4.3-3). A pattern then emerged in which the coefficient of inflation and the variance of the predictors were significant, but the coefficient for the market index was not. Eliminating this coefficient as well as the one for national income then produced the results shown in table 4.5.

The results shown in table 4.5 are similar in nature for the different years. The risk variable s_g^2 has a positive and usually significant effect. The notable change in its magnitude in 1966 corresponds to the change in the number of predictors from which the forecast data were collected. The sensitivity of the security's rate of return to the rate of inflation as measured by γ_p had a negative effect as we would expect.

These results suggest that at least two factors are relevant in valuation. One may be equated broadly to inflation and its associated effects. The other, possibly representing market risk, seems to be better represented by the variance of the predictions of long-term growth than by any of the regression coefficients. Its exact nature therefore remains a bit of a puzzle. The first factor has a negative sign and is usually significant at the 0.10 level. This was true even in the early years when the experienced variations in the inflation rate were very small. The second factor is very strongly positive and highly significant.

Table 4.5   **Equation for Expected Rates of Return Allowing for Estimation Error in $\hat{\gamma}_1$ (asymptotic t-values adjusted for heteroscedasticity)**

Year	Constant	γ_p	s_g^2	"r^2"*	r_ϵ†
1961	9.26	−1.13	.63	.56	—
	(12.62)	(−1.72)	(6.30)		
1962	8.40	−.46	.67	.38	.88
	(30.87)	(−1.70)	(4.96)		
1963	8.18	−.61	.72	.34	.89
	(32.30)	(−1.58)	(2.98)		
1964	8.55	−.74	.63	.54	.84
	(21.17)	(−1.92)	(18.77)		
1965	9.01	−.74	.62	.61	.90
	(24.20)	(−1.99)	(29.39)		
1966	10.72	−.20	.05	.08	.68
	(28.48)	(−.73)	(1.48)		
1967	11.35	−.53	.03	.25	.67
	(24.88)	(−1.65)	(2.05)		
1968	11.93	−.75	.05	.70	.48
	(17.74)	(−1.82)	(7.44)		

*"r^2" is $1 -$ (estimated residual variance)/(variance of ρ_{jt}).

†r_ϵ is correlation of residuals with previous year's residuals.

These results have been corrected for the errors of measurement in the regression coefficients, but errors in s_g^2 have been ignored. The interpretation we have been giving to that variable means that we cannot calculate the variance of errors in its measurement by assuming that it is simply the sampling variance of predictions which all have the same mean for each firm. We did, however, attempt to deal with this measurement error by the use of instrumental variables while continuing to allow for the estimation errors in the regression coefficients. To do so, we used as instruments the regression coefficients γ_M and γ_Y and the residual variances s_e^2, whose usefulness we explored earlier, in table 4.1.

The main difficulty with the instrumental-variable approach in this case was that the proposed instruments are not closely associated with s_g^2. The value of R^2 obtained from regressing s_g^2 on all the instruments and γ_p varied from 0.05 to 0.31. The main effect of this weakness on the estimates of the equations for expected return was to reduce the standard errors of the coefficients of s_g^2 sharply. These findings strengthen the impression that s_g^2 contains relevant information about risk not readily available in other forms. However, the significance levels of γ_p were not affected by the use of instrumental variables, and the results were qualitatively much the same as those shown in table 4.5 in terms of the signs and magnitudes of the coefficients.

4.3.3 Constancy over Time

One of the interesting questions about valuation equations is whether the coefficients remain the same each year or whether they change. There is nothing in the valuation theory to suggest that they should be constant. The opportunity sets faced by investors, extending beyond simply the financial securities available to them, probably change and so may their preferences and concerns about various types of risk. The results of tables 4.2 and 4.5 give an impression of considerable variation. We now test for variability explicitly.

The residuals from the equations shown in table 4.5 for different years are correlated even after allowance is made for the effects of estimation errors of $\hat{\gamma}_p$. Problems of missing observations mean that we can simultaneously calculate the equations for a common set of companies in all years only at the expense of losing a large number of companies. Pairwise comparisons indicated that the residuals for adjacent years are quite highly correlated. The correlations of these residuals are recorded in table 4.5 in the column headed r_e. It gives the correlations of the residuals in one year with those of the year immediately preceding. The quantities tabulated are the correlations of residuals using a common set of companies to estimate the regression coefficients in the two years. The exact values of the coefficients used differ slightly from those shown in table 4.5 because of the reduced number of observations used in their calculation.

The correlations of residuals, which are highly significant, complicate the problem of inquiring into the stability of the regression coefficients over time. Zellner's (1962) "seemingly unrelated regression technique" can be adapted in a straightforward way to the estimation of our equations even when allowing for estimation error of the original regression coefficients as well as for heteroscedasticity. To avoid the extensive loss of observations involved when all equations are fitted simultaneously, only pairs of equations were fitted.

Pairwise estimation of the equations usually produced significant differences in the coefficients of the valuation equation for different years. The main exceptions, where rejection did not occur even at the 0.10 level, are the 1964–65 comparison and the 1962–63 one. The coefficient for 1963 did differ from that for 1964 significantly at the 0.01 level even though the values shown in table 4.5 indicate the same qualitative findings in the sense that the coefficients are of similar magnitude.

The different estimation procedure used in these tests, which involve estimating the coefficients of each of two years jointly, did not change the conclusions about risk that were derived from our regressions in section 4.3.2 for the individual years. Indeed, these estimates indicated stronger support than the ones in table 4.5 for the hypothesis that two types of risk measures are indicated by the data.

4.3.4 Average Realized Return and Risk

The constant term $\hat{\delta}_{0j}$ obtained when equation (4.2-4) was fitted to obtain the other $\hat{\delta}$ coefficient contains implicitly another estimate of the expected rate of return. It is the average rate of return realized over the period, which many empirical studies of valuation presume corresponds to the return expected *ex ante* by investors. We can use this estimate to investigate the *ex post* validity of the APT, or diversification model, which suggests that we should find the same number of factors in the $\hat{\delta}_j$ vector when $\hat{\delta}_{0j}$ is included as when it is not. This consideration induces us to repeat the investigations carried out in section 4.3.1 with the other coefficients, but now including the constant $\hat{\delta}_{0j}$ as well.[8]

The estimates for the earlier periods included in our investigation tend to confirm the model fully in the sense that exactly the same number of factors is significantly present in the covariance matrix including the constant as we found when only the regression coefficients were used. This support for the model is less than might appear to be the case, however. As was the case for some of the coefficients, significant variation across companies was not present in the average rates of return in the

---

8. All independent variables are measured as deviations from their averages, so the constant term is also the average quarterly rate of return in the period over which the regression coefficients are calculated.

early years. In the final two years, the wider covariance matrix indicated that at least five factors were needed to account for the covariances of the constants with the other coefficients.

With the companies altering their natures over time and with the market valuation of risk quite possibly changing substantially over the decade of the seventies, such a finding should not be surprising even if the common-factor model is a correct description of security returns. However, it does not seem feasible to use these "objective," *ex post* measures of returns to obtain comparisons with the very successful results obtained from the *ex ante* measures we have employed. These estimated average *ex post* returns are not closely correlated with the *ex ante* measures derived from using the long-term growth predictions. The strong and interesting results we have obtained with these *ex ante* measures of expected returns and the fact that the *ex post* ones are not closely related to them emphasize the importance of using genuinely *ex ante* expectations of returns for studying security valuation.

4.4 An Alternative Valuation Specification

The derivation of the valuation model in chapter 3 suggested that the expected return formulation we have been investigating is only one approximation to the underlying model and that an alternative model may also be usefully estimated. The alternative approximation produces a more traditional formulation in which the price-earnings ratio is the dependent variable and earnings (dividend) growth, the payout ratio, and our various risk measures are treated as explanatory variables. The expected return formulation is particularly convenient for focusing on the risk structure suggested by the diversification model. The alternative allows us to ask whether growth-rate expectations are more relevant for valuation than other measures. It also allows us to investigate the role of the short-term growth predictions as well as to examine again which risk measures appear to be strongest.

An empirical analysis of the price-earnings model is also desirable because of an ambiguity of interpretation of the expected return models we have been studying. The results of the return model indicate partly that predicted earnings growth is connected with the regression coefficients giving the associations of rates of return to various economic indicators. Recall, however, that we found evidence in chapter 2 that a common-factor model may fit the growth predictions of security analysts. Our findings for the expected rates of return may reflect this feature of the data, even though the expected rate of return includes the dividend yield as well as the expected growth rate. Thus it is not entirely clear that we have actually been investigating a valuation relationship.

Implementation of the alternative model involved dividing both end-

Table 4.6   **Risk Measures in Stock Price Regressions (asymptotic *t*-values for alternative risk variables in equation [4.4-1])**

Year	β_M	β_Y	β_r	β_p	s_g^2
1961	− .32	1.10	1.25	.01	− .41
1962	− 4.54	− .71	.59	2.58	− 5.79
1963	− .33	.74	− .43	.28	− 2.37
1964	− 2.38	− 2.76	− .88	1.65	− 9.75
1965	1.43	1.32	− .70	− .43	− 1.24
1966	− 1.49	− .87	.14	.33	− .19
1967	1.34	.74	− 2.29	− 2.34	− 8.67
1968	2.29	− .22	− 1.41	− 2.74	− 1.12

of-year prices (P) and the dividends projected to be paid (D) by average normalized earnings[9] $(\overline{NE})$ to give the equation

$$(4.4\text{-}1) \qquad P/\overline{NE} = a_0 + a_1 \bar{g}_p + a_2 D/\overline{NE} + a_3 RISK,$$

where *RISK* stands for the various risk variables used.

4.4.1 Risk Measures

We begin our investigation of equation (4.4-1) by treating each of the risk measures we have been using as alternatives, just as we did when considering equation (4.2-1). In these regressions, both the average expected five-year growth rate and the dividend payout ratio almost always had positive and significant coefficients throughout the sample period.

The pattern for the risk measures is more complicated than earlier. Table 4.6 corresponds to table 4.1. In these regressions, a negative sign should be expected for the risk measures based on covariance with the market index and with national income, since higher risk should, ceteris paribus, lower price-earnings multiples. Although both $\hat{\beta}$ measures have the correct negative values more often than not, the *t*-values indicate that they are only occasionally significant. Positive signs should be expected for the risk measures based on reported inflation and interest rates. As was found in the regressions in table 4.1, these risk measures are only significant toward the end of the period studied, but their signs are often incorrect in these valuation regressions.

These findings indicate the difficulties of using the simple regression coefficients as risk measures in a specification also containing several other variables. In contrast to these ambiguous results, the variance of

9. The "normalized" earnings were furnished by two of the forecasters and were described in chapter 1. When more than one forecaster's estimates of "normalized" earnings were available for a company, the estimates were averaged. The results are little different (but a bit poorer) if reported earnings over the most recent twelve-month period are substituted for "normalized" earnings.

Table 4.7   *P/NE* **Regression Estimates of Equation (4.4-1) (asymptotic *t*-ratios adjusted for heteroscedasticity)**

Year	Constant	$\bar{g}_p$	$D/\overline{NE}$	s_g^2	R^2
1961	1.88	3.91	1.22	$-.57$	.81
	(.64)	(7.51)	(.24)	$(-.41)$	
1962	3.30	2.23	8.41	-1.17	.75
	(1.75)	(16.69)	(2.91)	(-5.79)	
1963	2.85	2.70	6.71	$-.59$	.77
	(.94)	(11.20)	(1.75)	(-2.37)	
1964	2.53	2.15	13.16	-1.09	.77
	(1.73)	(23.94)	(6.13)	(-9.71)	
1965	1.76	2.82	4.73	$-.66$	.67
	(.62)	(6.98)	(1.14)	(-1.24)	
1966	.22	1.74	7.42	$-.01$	.57
	(.09)	(9.62)	(2.79)	$(-.19)$	
1967	1.88	2.35	-1.05	$-.09$	.69
	(.67)	(13.28)	$(-.35)$	(-8.67)	
1968	2.18	1.78	5.13	$-.04$	.52
	(.56)	(8.10)	(.99)	(-1.12)	

the predictions always has a negative sign. Its significance does vary considerably across years, primarily reflecting variation in the magnitude of its coefficient. The important point, which agrees with our previous results with the expected return measures, is that s_g^2 provided a better single risk proxy than the regression coefficients based on more objective calculations. It also provided a more significant and consistent measure than the residual variances of the regressions, s_e^2.

Table 4.7 shows the full estimates of equation (4.4-1) using s_g^2 as the risk variable. The growth-rate variable is highly significant in each of the years covered. The payout ratio has the expected sign except in one year but is usually insignificant.[10] As we have already noted, the risk variable always has the correct negative sign and is often significant.

4.4.2 Alternative Growth Measures

The extent to which using truly expectational data is important for valuation models is indicated in table 4.8. Here we show the values of R^2

10. The positive sign of the dividend coefficient should not be interpreted as evidence that dividend policy can affect the value of the shares. This coefficient indicates only that a ceteris paribus change in dividend payout will increase the price of the shares. Among the things held constant in this equation is the growth rate of earnings and dividends per share. A positive dividend coefficient thus indicates only that *given* the future growth rate in earnings and dividends, the price of a share should be higher, the higher is the current percentage of earnings that can be paid out. The famous "dividend irrelevancy" theorem of Miller and Modigliani (1961) says that an increase in dividend payout will tend to reduce the growth rate of earnings per share since new shares will now have to be sold to make up for the extra funds paid out in dividends. A positive dividend coefficient is thus in no way inconsistent with the dividend irrelevancy theorem.

Table 4.8   Values of R^2 for Alternative Specifications
                   of the Valuation Equation

| | Specification | | |
Year	1	2	3
1961	.42	.45	.81
1962	.50	.53	.75
1963	.49	.50	.77
1964	.37	.43	.77
1965	.29	.31	.67
1966	.31	.44	.57
1967	.32	.36	.69
1968	.33	.41	.52

NOTE. See text for specifications.

for various combinations of historical and expectational data. The first specification (column 2) involved regressing the price-earnings multiple on three historic figures: the past ten-year growth rate of cash earnings, the average (over the preceding seven years) historic dividend-payout rate, and β_M, estimated using only previous data. The third column substitutes the expectational variable s_g^2 for the β_M coefficient. The fourth column repeats the specification of equation (4.4-1) with s_g^2 as the risk variables, $\overline{g}_p$ and $D/\overline{NE}$ in place of historic growth and payout, and $P/\overline{NE}$ as the dependent variable in place of P/E. These r^2 values are the same as in table 4.7.

The dramatic change in the value of r^2 for the valuation equation occurs when $\overline{g}_p$ is used for the growth rate. Other variations have comparatively minor effects. There are, of course, a large number of ways of calculating past growth. Our findings hold up for the wide variety of historical growth rate we tried as well as the one reported in table 4.8. Using the average predicted growth rates substantially improves the fit of the regression. It is therefore safe to conclude that insofar as the market does value growth, the growth rates involved are far better represented by actual predictions made by security analysts than by any mechanically calculated rate.

One may wonder whether we would have done better to use only one forecaster rather than the average we have employed. Problems of missing observations again hinder this investigation. One of the advantages of using the average is that it allows us to include most of the companies in the regressions. However, it is also the case that closer fits tended to be obtained by using the average growth rates of all predictors than by employing the forecasts of any single firm. This suggests that our survey was useful in getting closer to what might be considered the expectations of a "representative" investor.

4.4.3 Role of Short-Term Predictions

In addition to the long-term growth estimates, which have played such an important role in our empirical valuation work thus far, we also collected short-term predictions for earnings in the next year. These were described and analyzed in chapters 1 and 2. Given the long-term growth rate, a stock should sell for a higher price if more of that growth is expected to be realized earlier in the period. Therefore we augmented our valuation equation (4.4-1) to include the term $\widetilde{E}_{t+1}/\overline{NE}$, the ratio of next year's average predicted earnings $(\widetilde{E}_{t+1})$ to average normalized earnings (for the present period). Equation (4.4-1) then becomes

$$(4.4\text{-}2) \qquad P/\overline{NE} = a_0 + a_1 g_p + a_2 \widetilde{E}_{t+1}/\overline{NE} + a_3 D/\overline{NE} + a_4 s_g^2.$$

The results obtained with this specification are presented in table 4.9. The addition of a term for short-term growth does add some explanatory power to the regression, although the significant t-statistic for the coefficient of $\widetilde{E}_{t+1}/\overline{NE}$ comes partly at the expense of the long-term growth coefficient. The dividend and risk terms generally retain their usual signs, though they are often not significant.

4.4.4 Variations of Specification

The success of the short-term growth variable raises the question whether more generally a nonlinear specification might be appropriate. As we noted in section 3.4, the linear form of the equation is only an approximation to some more complicated true form. To investigate this

Table 4.9 $P/\overline{NE}$ **Regression Estimates of Equation (4.4-2) (asymptotic t-values adjusted for heteroscedasticity)**

Year	Constant	$\bar{g}_p$	$\widetilde{E}_{t+1}/\overline{NE}$	$D/\overline{NE}$	s_g^2	R^2
1961	−35.02	3.07	41.31	−1.58	−.71	.88
	(−4.16)	(11.94)	(4.78)	(−.35)	(−.75)	
1962	−3.36	1.99	8.57	6.96	−1.00	.75
	(−.82)	(14.05)	(2.15)	(1.97)	(−4.20)	
1963	−11.43	2.58	13.66	7.22	−.53	.81
	(−2.61)	(12.25)	(4.33)	(1.57)	(−2.16)	
1964	−7.21	2.13	8.56	13.19	−.84	.81
	(−2.46)	(18.67)	(3.80)	(5.41)	(−2.52)	
1965	−14.53	2.82	10.53	8.20	−1.09	.78
	(−1.89)	(7.12)	(1.73)	(1.82)	(.99)	
1966	−7.67	1.83	6.51	8.94	−.02	.58
	(−1.94)	(10.41)	(2.00)	(3.59)	(−.28)	
1967	−8.55	2.31	9.33	1.15	−.08	.72
	(−1.41)	(12.70)	(1.67)	(.33)	(−7.18)	
1968	−15.77	1.57	18.20	4.66	−.03	.55
	(2.54)	(6.74)	(3.12)	(.96)	(−.86)	

possibility, we used a quadratic specification for the growth and dividend-payout variables. That is, we added the squares of $\bar{g}_p$ and of $D/\overline{NE}$ and their cross-product to the specification (4.4-2).

Use of these nonlinear terms did little to improve the explanatory power of the equation, though in some instances they did have significant coefficients. Stability was found neither in which variables were significant nor in their signs. Since undoubtedly our variables have substantial measurement errors, these findings may well represent little more than the problems such errors produce.

It is not surprising in view of these findings that we sometimes found that breaking the sample into various groups produced significant differences between the groups. Thus, when the equation was run separately for low-dividend/high-growth and high-dividend/low-growth companies, (where the dividing lines are the medians of the variables), we did find some significant differences in coefficients. Similarly, fitting the equation for different industry groups produced some significant differences across industries in the coefficients (e.g., dividends were more highly valued in public utility companies). Since in each case the classifications tended to reduce the variances of the independent variables, the significant differences may arise simply from the changed importance of the variances of the measurement errors relative to the variances of the true underlying variables.

4.4.5 Measurement and Estimation Error

Allowing for errors of estimation in calculating the regression coefficients did not relieve the problems we encountered when we introduced the risk measures (based on regression coefficients) directly in estimating equation (4.4-1). Using either $\hat{\beta}_M$ or the $\hat{\gamma}$ coefficients defined in equation (4.3-4), whether alone or in conjunction with s_g^2, produced neither stable nor significant coefficients for these variables when they were added to (4.4-2). It is far from clear that the reason for this finding was that such risk terms do not also play a role in valuation; in other words, we cannot conclude that a model with only one factor is appropriate. Instead, we may ascribe the findings, at least partially, to multicollinearity, particularly with the payout ratio. When these regression coefficients were added to the specification, the coefficient of $D/\overline{NE}$ usually became completely insignificant and it was highly correlated with the coefficients for β_M or for the $\hat{\gamma}_j$ coefficients. As we noted earlier, the growth variable $\bar{g}_p$ is also somewhat correlated with these risk proxies. In this connection, it is interesting to note that Rosenberg and Guy (1976) have suggested that both dividend payout and growth potential are important systematic risk variables.

Measurement errors are far from being confined to the risk variables. Clearly our growth variables are subject to error and the payout variable also is only an approximation to what the market could perceive to be the payout rate. These errors may account for some of the problems we have encountered.

As was also the case when we sought instruments for s_g^2, finding good instruments for the growth rate and the payout variables was not easy. We have already seen that $\bar{g}_p$ contains useful information not available from mechanically calculated growth rates. As a result, satisfactory instruments for it are unlikely to be found. We tried using past four- and ten-year calculated growth rates as instruments for $\bar{g}_p$ and the lagged value of $D/\overline{NE}$ for the current value of this variable. When we used the specification (4.4-1), we also included $\tilde{E}_{t+1}/\overline{NE}$ as an instrumental variable. We could also take advantage of some of the correlations of risk with growth and payout by treating $\hat{\gamma}_m$ and $\hat{\gamma}_Y$ as additional instruments when only $\hat{\gamma}_p$ and s_g^2 were used as risk measures.

Using instrumental variables to deal with these measurement errors did not substantially alter our findings. What we obtained were equations qualitatively similar to those shown in tables 4.7 and 4.9, but with much larger standard errors for the coefficients. This finding may be taken to indicate, at least, that errors in variables have not produced seriously misleading results in those tables. When the problems of multicollinearity of the growth and dividend variables with the risk ones were combined with the complicated variances of the coefficients that were the result of making allowance for the estimation error of the risk parameters, it is small wonder that more precise results could not be obtained about the precise specification of risk.

4.4.6 Stability over Time

We found earlier that the coefficients of the expected return model varied over time. The question of the constancy of the valuation equation is particularly interesting in the present form, where prices are the dependent variable. Stability of the coefficients is also important to those who wish to make practical use of valuation equations in connection with assigned values of the independent variables to estimate the "intrinsic worth" of a security. Furthermore, constancy of the relationship is important if a firm is to seek to follow policies that will maximize the values of its shares, since it will find it hard to please investors if their desires are changing.

An inspection of tables 4.7 and 4.9 indicates that the coefficients of our equations do change considerably from year to year, and in a manner that is consistent with the changing standards of value in vogue at the different times. We may illustrate this finding by the regression results of table 4.9. At the end of 1961, "growth stocks" were in high favor, and it is not surprising to find that the coefficient of the growth rate (3.07) is highest in this year. During 1962, however, there was a conspicuous change in the structure of share prices that was popularly called "the revaluation of growth stocks." This revaluation is reflected in the decline of the growth-rate coefficient for 1962 to 1.99. At the same time, dividend payout became more highly valued in 1962 than it had been in 1961, the dividend coefficient rising from -1.58 to 6.96. Nineteen sixty-two was also the year when the coefficient of the risk measure was most strongly negative.

In order to test formally whether the coefficients of the valuation equation were the same over time, we again had to recognize that the residuals in different years were not independent. The correlations, which are shown in table 4.10, are somewhat smaller than those found in section 4.3 when we were investigating the expected rates of return, but they are significantly different from zero. They again raise the need to use an appropriate technique for assessing the stability of the coefficients and the problem that calculating all the equations simultaneously for a common set of companies entails the loss of a large proportion of the observations.

Using the seemingly unrelated regression technique for a pair of years, we could reject the hypothesis of equality of the coefficients in each pair of years at least at the 0.01 level. When all years were considered simultaneously, rejection occurred beyond the 0.0001 level despite the large loss of observations. Thus it seems clear that valuation relationships do change over time. While this finding may, of course, be due to problems with the data being used, it certainly lends no credence to the proposition that the parameters do not change.

4.5 Use of the Valuation Model for Security Selection

One of the most intriguing questions concerning empirical valuation models is whether they can be used to aid investors in security selection. The estimated valuation equation shows us, at a moment in time, the average way in which variables, such as growth, payout, and risk, influence market price-earnings multiples. Given the value of these vari-

Table 4.10	Correlations of Residuals in Adjacent Years and with Subsequent Returns		
Year	Residuals from (4.4-1)	Residuals from (4.4-2)	Residuals of (4.4-2) with Future Returns
1961/62	.52	.62	$-.20$
1962/63	.56	.57	.09
1963/64	.41	.46	$-.25$
1964/65	.30	.39	$-.06$
1965/66	.37	.32	.06
1966/67	.50	.48	$-.03$
1967/68	.60	.64	$-.10$
1968/69	—	—	.20

ables applicable to any specific security, we can compute an estimated price-earnings ratio based on the empirical valuation equation. The next step is to compare the actual price-earnings multiple with that predicted by the valuation equation. If the actual multiple is greater than the predicted one, we might suppose that the security is temporarily overpriced and recommend sale. If the actual price-earnings multiple is less than the predicted multiple, we might designate the security as temporarily underpriced and recommend its purchase.

Even on a priori grounds, it is possible to think of many reasons why such a procedure would prove fruitless. For example, if high growth-rate stocks tended to be overpriced during one particular period, the estimated growth-rate coefficient would be larger (by assumption) than that which is warranted. However, the recommended procedure will not indicate that these stocks are overpriced because "normal" market-determined earnings multiples for these securities will be higher than is warranted. Nevertheless, in view of the popularity of these techniques with some practitioners, it seems worthwhile to try some experiments using our data.

The results of some of our experiments are shown in table 4.10. We measured the degree of "over-" or "underpricing" as the predicted ratio of the residual from the valuation equation (4.4-2) to the predicted earnings multiple, that is, as $(P/\overline{NE} - \hat{P}/\overline{NE})/(\hat{P}/\overline{NE})$. A percentage measure was chosen in view of the considerable variance in actual earnings multiples. If the model is useful in measuring underpricing, then underpriced securities, determined according to this criterion, ought to outperform overpriced issues over some subsequent period. We picked one year as the appropriate horizon and measured subsequent returns in the usual manner as

$$(4.5\text{-}1) \qquad P_{t+1} = (P_{t+1} - P_t + D_{t+1})/P_t.$$

If the empirical valuation model is successful in selecting securities for purchase, the percentage residual (degree of overvaluation) from the valuation equation ought to be negatively related to these subsequent returns. As the fourth column of table 4.10 indicates, in only five of the eight years for which this experiment was performed was the relationship negative, and the degree of association was low. There was a positive relationship for the other three years.[11] Two of these correlations are significant at the 0.05 level: the negative one in 1963/64 and the positive one for 1968/69. The 1961/62 correlation just misses significance at this level. We would not consider these significant correlations as representing forecasting success. As we argue below, we suspect strongly that we

---

11. We were no more successful at finding wrongly priced securities using expectations data for the individual predictors rather than the average expectations of the particular group.

have left out some common factors and that this omission could lead to correlations over particular periods of time. Unless one can forecast these changes in a way not already available to the general market participant, one can hardly exploit these changes. It is therefore particularly indicative that one of the significant correlations had the "wrong" sign.

Supplementary tests conducted by the type of equation or industry and other groupings produced similar results. For example, subsequent returns were still unrelated to the residuals when we first split the sample into high and low growth and dividend groupings. Similar results were obtained when the experiment was attempted for separate industries. We also found that the residuals from the equations employing historical data in place of our expectational data were no more successful in predicting subsequent performance. Moreover, these results were unaltered when the subsequent returns were measured over alternative time periods such as one-quarter ahead or two or more years ahead. The technique simply did not produce excess returns in any consistent or reliable fashion over any time period in the future. These findings are what we should expect in a reasonably efficient market.

Some statistics are presented in table 4.11 that may be helpful in interpreting the reason for our predictive failures. We note, using the 1963 valuation equation as an example, that the percentage degree of under- or overpricing is not highly correlated with subsequent returns, the coefficient of determination being only 0.06. It is possible to isolate four reasons for our lack of forecasting success.

1. The first reason is that the valuation relationship changes over time. We might be unable to select truly underpriced securities because by the next year the norms of valuation have been significantly altered. Thus what was cheap on the basis of the 1963 relationship may no longer represent good value on the basis of the 1964 equation. To test how important this change might be, we performed the following experiment: We assumed that investors knew at the end of 1963 exactly what the

Table 4.11   Analysis of Lack of Forecasting Success

Year	Description	r^{2*}
1963	Valuation equation with 1963 predictions	.06
1964	Valuation equation with 1963 data (assumes next year's valuation relationship is known)	.10
1963	Valuation equation with realized growth rates (assumes perfect foresight regarding future long-term growth and next year's earnings)	.14
1963	Valuation equation with 1964 predictions (assumes perfect foresight regarding market expectations next year)	.27

*Percent residuals versus 1964 return.

market valuation relationship would be for the end of 1964; that is, we assumed perfect foresight regarding next year's valuation equation. Then, on the basis of the 1964 valuation equation, we used the 1963 data to calculate warranted $P/\overline{NE}$ multiples, which could then be compared with actual multiples to determine whether each security was appropriately priced. Correlating the percentage residuals with subsequent returns, we found that the coefficient of determination nearly doubled, 10 percent of the variance in subsequent returns now being explained.

2. A second reason for lack of success might be the quality of the expectations data employed. As indicated in chapter 2, the growth-rate forecasts used in the present study were not accurate predictors of realized growth. To determine how much better off we would have been with more accurate forecasts, we assumed perfect foresight regarding the future long-term growth rate of the company. Thus the 1963 empirical valuation equation was used to determine "normal" value, but in place of $\overline{g}_p$ we substituted the realized long-term growth rate through 1968. Using these realized data to determine warranted price-earnings multiples, we correlated the percentage residuals therefrom with future returns. As expected, an even greater improvement in forecasting future returns was found. The r^2 rises to 0.14.

3. As a further experiment, perfect foresight was assumed not about the actual rate of growth of earnings but rather regarding what the market expectations of growth would be next year, that is, about $\overline{g}_p$ next year. Calculating the degree of overpricing as before, we find a much greater improvement in prediction of future returns. Twenty-seven percent of the variability of future returns is now explained, compared with only 6 percent in the original experiment. We conclude that if one wants to explain returns over a one-year horizon, it is far more important to know what the market will think the growth rate of earnings will be next year rather than to know the realized long-term growth rate. This observation brings us back to Keynes's celebrated newspaper contest. What matters is not one's personal criteria of beauty but what the average opinion will expect average opinion to think is beautiful at the close of the contest.

4. A final source of error is that the valuation model does not capture all the significant determinants of value for each individual company. Despite our success in accounting for approximately three-quarters of the variance in market price-earnings multiples, there are likely to be special features applicable to many individual companies that cannot be captured quantitatively. For example, it turned out that the stock of many tobacco companies always appeared to be underpriced. The reason for this is not difficult to conjecture. There is a risk of government sanctions against the tobacco industry that weighs heavily in the minds of investors, but that is not related to the risk measures we have employed. Such an explanation is not at variance with the underlying approach to risk

valuation that we have been using. The common susceptibility of the tobacco companies to an identifiable but ignored hazard is simply an important factor which we have omitted from our data.

This problem of omitted variables may account for the correlations of residuals which we found in the equations. If certain factors specific to individual companies were consistently missing, the residuals from the valuation equations could be expected to be positively correlated over time. This is exactly what we found in table 4.10. Thus, despite our success in using expectations data to estimate a valuation equation which has far more explanatory ability than those based on historic information, it is still quite clear that certain systematic valuation factors are missing from the analysis. Consequently, it cannot be said that all deviations of actual from predicted price-earnings ratios are simply manifestations of temporary over- or underpricing.

4.6 Conclusion

Our investigations of valuation models, while not without some ambiguous results, suggest several notable conclusions. These conclusions concern the role in market valuation of the sort of earnings forecasts we have collected, the nature of risk valuation, and the efficiency of the market.

4.6.1 Valuation of Expected Growth

One of our major findings is that the average of the expected long-term growth rates, together with the risk measure provided by the variance of the growth-rate predictions, gives a closer account of the valuation of common stocks than do alternatives. These growth rates were clearly superior in accounting for prices to any of the simple alternatives we considered. More closely fitting equations are the results that one would expect from smaller errors of measurement or from using data that contain more relevant information in place of less germane measures. Hence one can safely presume that our data are more similar to the expectations being valued in the market than are measures based on *ex post* realized growth or regression coefficients. This conclusion, based on the ability to "explain" prices, is buttressed by noticing that the overall risk-free expected rates of return suggested by the estimates of the expected return regressions are of plausible orders of magnitude.

The finding that prices reflect expected growth occurred in spite of the difficulties we encountered from the large variations in which companies were covered by each of the various predictors. Earlier we saw that there is a great deal of diversity of expectations among forecasters, an aspect of reality with which valuation models do not usually cope. We also found that, while hardly being strong predictions, the expectations data appear to yield forecasts at least as accurate as, and often better than, naive forecasts based on *ex post* realizations. Furthermore, we found that we could not calculate a linear combination of different types of forecasts whose superior forecasting performance continued over time.

Efficient market hypotheses suggest that valuation should reflect the information available to investors. Insofar as analysts' forecasts are more precise than other types we should therefore expect their differences from other measures to be reflected in the market. It is therefore noteworthy that our regression results do support the hypothesis that analysts' forecasts are needed even when calculated growth rates are available. As we noted when we described the data, security analysts do not use simple mechanical methods to obtain their evaluations of companies. The growth-rate figures we obtained were distilled from careful examination of all aspects of the companies' records, evaluation of contingencies to which they might be subject, and whatever information about their prospects the analysts could glean from the companies themselves or from other sources. It is therefore notable that the results of their efforts are found to be so much more relevant to the valuation than the various simpler and more "objective" alternatives that we tried.

We saw in section 3.2.3 that diversity of expectations together with market imperfections might invalidate the valuation model. However, we also argued that there were theoretical grounds for supposing that the model would still hold for the average of investors' expectations. It is therefore of particular interest that our empirical results do support the hypothesis that prices reflect average expectations.

It is no surprise that we found roles for both short- and long-term expected rates of growth. Models of valuation using only long-term growth rates are clearly only simplifications of the more complicated processes that earnings and dividends follow over time, and we would expect market valuation to reflect the more complicated processes.

4.6.2 Risk Measures and Valuation

The results did not provide wholly unambiguous support for the specific valuation models developed here. A number of aspects of our results about risk are particularly intriguing. It is clear from our results that expected returns do seem to be related to various systematic risk factors. Equally clearly, our results do not give straightforward support to the simple form of the CAPM. It would appear that systematic risk is not entirely captured by single measures of covariance with the market index. This has important implications for those who attempt to use the modern investment technology in practical problems of portfolio selection. One such suggestion, which had attracted a considerable following in the investment community by the 1980s, was the proposal for a yield-tilted index fund.

The reasoning behind the yield-tilted index fund seems appealingly plausible. Since dividends are generally taxed more highly than capital gains and since the market equilibrium is presumably achieved on the basis of after-tax returns, the equilibrium pretax returns for stocks that pay high dividends ought to be higher than for securities that produce lower dividends and correspondingly higher capital gains. Hence the tax-exempt investor is advised to buy a diversified portfolio of high-dividend-paying stocks. In order to avoid the assumption of any greater risk than is involved in buying the market index, the tax-exempt investor is also advised to purchase a yield-tilted index fund, that is, a very broadly diversified portfolio of high-dividend-paying stocks that mirrors the market index in the sense that it has a beta coefficient β_M precisely equal to unity.

Even on a priori grounds one might question the logic of the yield-tilted index fund. Many of the largest investors in the market are tax-exempt (such as pension and endowment funds) and others (such as corporations) actually pay a lower tax on capital gains than on dividend income.[12] Thus it is far from clear that the marginal investor in the stock market prefers to receive income through capital gains rather than through dividend payments. Our theoretical arguments in chapter 3 also indicated that great care must be taken with arguments involving "marginal" investors and pointed out that the diversification theory gives no presumption that dividends and capital gains will be valued differently. But apart from these a priori arguments, our empirical results can be interpreted as providing another argument against the yield-tilted index fund.

If the traditional beta calculation (β_M) does not provide a full description of systematic risk, the yield-tilted index fund may well fail to mirror the market index. Specifically, during periods when inflation and interest rates rise, it may well be the case that high-dividend stocks are particularly vulnerable; that is, they have high δ_P and δ_r coefficients. Public-utility common stocks are a good example. While they are known as "low-beta" stocks, they are likely to have high systematic risk with respect to interest rates and inflation. This is so not only because they are good substitutes for fixed-income securities, but also because public utilities are vulnerable to a profits squeeze during periods of rising inflation because of regulatory lags and increased borrowing costs. Hence the yield-tilted index fund with $\beta_M = 1$ may not mirror the market index when inflation accelerates.

The actual experience of yield-tilted index funds during the 1979–80 period shows that these funds did not live up to expectations and their performance was significantly worse than the market. Of course, we should not reject a model simply because of its failure over any specific short-term period. Nevertheless, we believe that an understanding of the wider aspects of systematic risk, such as those analyzed here, would have

---

12. For corporate investors, 85 percent of dividend income is excluded from taxable income while capital gains are taxed at normal gains rates.

helped prevent what turned out to be (at least over the short term) some serious investment errors.

Our findings on systematic risk still leave some major and intriguing perplexities. We found in both versions of the valuation model that the most important aspect of risk for valuation was that represented by the extent to which forecasters were not in agreement about the future growth of the company. Exactly what is the basis for this finding is not clear.

It might be quite reasonable to interpret s_g^2 as representing specific risk. In that case, the findings go against most recent models of valuation including both the CAPM and the APT. On the other hand, it may indirectly measure sensitivity to underlying common factors and thus serve as a very effective proxy for a variety of systematic risks. Finally, it may arise from technical difficulties having to do with undetected biases in our data. It seems unlikely that this would fully account for the strength we found for this variable, but it cannot be ruled out. Further investigation probably requires a data set less beset by problems of missing observations and an adequately specified model of earnings. Overall, our results do suggest that risk undoubtedly has dimensions not fully captured by the covariances with market indexes or other variables that have dominated recent work on valuation. They also suggest that the variance of analysts' forecasts may represent the most effective risk proxy available.

4.6.3 Efficient Markets

We find it encouraging that we were unable to use the expectations data to select securities with subsequent above- or below-average performance characteristics. We would not expect that analysts' forecasts would be sounder than those apparently used by the market or that they would be irrelevant to market valuations. Apparently, the expectations formed by Wall Street professionals get quickly and thoroughly impounded into the prices of securities. Implicitly, we have found that the evaluations of companies that analysts make are the sorts of ones on which market valuation is based. Thus, while our work raises questions about some currently popular valuation theories, it strongly supports the view that the market is reasonably efficient in incorporating into present prices whatever information there is about the future.

References

Anderson, T. W., and Rubin, Herman. 1956. Statistical inference in factor analysis. In Neyman, J., ed., *Proceedings of the third Berkeley symposium on mathematical statistics and probability*, vol. 5, pp. 111–50. Berkeley: University of California Press.

Blume, M., and Friend, I. 1975. The asset structure of individual portfolios and some implications for utility functions. *Journal of Finance* 30: 585–603.

Cragg, J. G. 1982. Estimation using regression coefficients as explanatory variables. UBC Econ. Discussion Paper 82–13.

Cragg, John G., and Malkiel, Burton G. 1968. The consensus and accuracy of some predictions of the growth of corporate earnings. *Journal of Finance* 23: 67–84.

Fama, Eugene F. 1970. Multiperiod consumption and investment decisions. *American Economic Review* 60: 163–74.

———. 1971. Risk, return, and equilibrium. *Journal of Political Economy* 79: 30–55.

Friedman, Benjamin. 1980. Survey evidence on the "rationality" of interest rate expectations. *Journal of Monetary Economics* 6: 453–65.

Friend, Irwin; Westerfield, Randolph; and Granito, Michael. 1978. New evidence on the capital asset pricing model. *Journal of Finance* 33: 903–20.

Gordon, Myron. 1962. *The investment, financing, and valuation of the corporation.* Homewood, Illinois: Irwin.

Graham, B.; Dodd, D. L.; Cottle, Sidney; and Tatham, Charles. 1962. *Security analysis*, 4th ed. New York: McGraw-Hill.

Holt, C. C. 1962. The influence of growth duration on share prices. *Journal of Finance* 17: 464–75.

Jarrow, Robert. 1980. Heterogeneous expectations, restrictions on short sales, and equilibrium asset prices. *Journal of Finance* 35: 1105–13.

Keynes, John Maynard. 1936. *The general theory of employment, interest, and money.* New York: Harcourt.

King, Benjamin F. 1966. Market and industry factors in stock price behavior. *Journal of Business* 39, no. 1, pt. 2: 139–90.

Levy, Haim. 1978. Equilibrium in an imperfect market: A constraint on the number of securities in the portfolio. *American Economic Review* 68: 643–58.

Lintner, John. 1965. The valuation of risk assets and the selection of risky investments in stock portfolios and capital budgets. *Review of Economics and Statistics* 47: 13–37.

Lintner, John, and Glauber, Robert. 1972. Higgledy piggledy growth in America. In James Lorie and Richard Brealey, eds., *Modern developments investment management.* New York: Praeger.

Little, I. M. D. 1962. Higgledy piggledy growth. *Oxford Institute of Statistics Bulletin* 24: 387–412.

Malkiel, Burton G. 1963. Equity yields, growth, and the structure of share prices. *American Economic Review* 53: 1004–31.

Malkiel, Burton G., and Cragg, John G. 1970. Expectations and the structure of share prices. *American Economic Review* 60: 601–17.

Markowitz, Harry. 1959. *Portfolio selection: Efficient diversification of investments.* New York: John Wiley & Sons.

Mayers, David. 1972. Nonmarketable assets and capital market equilibrium under uncertainty. In Michael C. Jensen, ed., *Studies in the theory of capital markets*, pp. 223–48. New York: Praeger.

Merton, Robert C. 1971. Optimum consumption and portfolio risks in a continuous-time model. *Journal of Economic Theory* 3: 373–413.

Miller, Edward M. 1977. Risk, uncertainty, and divergence of opinion. *Journal of Finance* 32: 1151–68.

Miller, Merton H., and Modigliani, Franco. 1961. Dividend policy, growth, and the valuation of shares. *Journal of Business* 34: 411–33.

Mincer, Jacob, ed. 1969. Economic forecasts and expectations: Analysis of forecasting behavior and performance. New York: National Bureau of Economic Research.

Mossin, Jan. 1966. Equilibrium in a capital asset market. *Econometrica* 34: 768–83.

Muth, John F. 1961. Rational expectations and the theory of price movements. *Econometrica* 29: 315–35.

Myers, Stewart C. 1968. A time-state-preference model of security valuation. *Journal of Financial and Quantitative Analysis* 3: 1–33.

Nerlove, Marc. 1968. Factors affecting differences among rates of return on investments in individual common stocks. *Review of Economics and Statistics* 50: 312–31.

Ohlson, James A., and Garman, Mark B. 1980. A dynamic equilibrium for the Ross arbitrage model. *Journal of Finance* 35: 675–84.

Pearce, Douglas K. 1978. Comparing survey and national measures of expected inflation: Forecast performance and interest rate effects. University of Houston, Mimeograph.

Pesando, James E. 1975. A note on the rationality of the Livingston price expectations. *Journal of Political Economy* 83: 849–58.

Roll, Richard. 1977. A critique of the asset pricing theory's tests; pt. 1, On past and potential testability of the theory. *Journal of Financial Economics* 4: 129–76.

Roll, Richard, and Ross, Stephen A. 1980. An empirical investigation of the arbitrage pricing theory. *Journal of Finance* 35: 1073–1103.

Rosenberg, Barr, and Guy, James. 1976. Prediction of beta from investment fundamentals. *Financial Analysts Journal*, May/June, pp. 60–72; July/August, pp. 62–70.

Ross, Stephen A. 1976. The arbitrage theory of capital asset pricing. *Journal of Economic Theory* 13: 341–60.

————. 1977. Risk, return, and arbitrage. In Irwin Friend and James L. Bicksler, eds. *Risk and return in finance*, vol. 1, pp. 189–222. Cambridge, Massachusetts: Ballinger.

Sharpe, William F. 1964. Capital asset prices: A theory of market equilibrium under conditions of risk. *Journal of Finance* 19: 425–42.

Siegel, Sydney. 1965. *Nonparametric statistics for the behavioral sciences*. New York: McGraw-Hill.

Stapleton, R. C., and Subrahmanyam, M. G. 1978. A multiperiod equilibrium asset pricing model. *Econometrica* 46: 1077–96.

Theil, Henri. 1966. *Applied economic forecasting*. Amsterdam: North-Holland.

Tobin, James. 1958. Liquidity preference as behavior towards risk. *Review of Economic Studies* 25: 65–85.

White, Halbert. 1980. A heteroskedasticity-consistent covariance matrix estimator and a direct test for heteroskedasticity. *Econometrica* 48: 817–38.

Williams, J. B. 1938. *The theory of investment value*. Cambridge, Massachusetts: Harvard University Press.

Wonnacott, Thomas H., and Wonnacott, Ronald T. 1972. *Introductory statistics for business and economic*. New York: John Wiley & Sons.

Zarnowitz, Victor. 1967. An appraisal of short-term economic forecasts. New York: National Bureau of Economic Research.

Zellner, A. 1962. An efficient method of estimating seemingly unrelated regressions and tests for aggregation bias. *Journal of the American Statistical Association* 57: 348–68.

Index